# LINGUISTICS
## for
# WRITERS

# Linguistics
## for
## Writers

### COLLEEN
### DONNELLY

STATE UNIVERSITY OF NEW YORK PRESS

Published by
State University of New York Press, Albany

© 1994 State University of New York

For information, address the State University of New York Press,
State University Plaza, Albany, NY 12246

Production by Bernadine Dawes
Marketing by Dana Yanulavich

**Library of Congress Cataloging-in-Publication Data**

Donnelly, Colleen Elaine.
Linguistics for writers / Colleen Donnelly.
p.   cm.
Includes bibliographical references and index.
ISBN 0-7914-1571-6 (hard) — ISBN 0-7914-1572-4 (pbk.)
1. Linguistics.   2. Discourse analysis.   I. Title.
P123.D65   1993                           92-36122
410—dc20                                   CIP


1 2 3 4 5 6 7 8 9 10

*For my sprite,*

*Katriana*

# Brief Contents

# *Expanded Contents*

# *Preface*

Until recently, linguistics has been a discipline that has unfortunately remained inaccessible to the layman. In part, this is because linguistics is a descriptive science which is primarily devoted to identifying and describing the rules that govern spoken discourse. Conversely, rhetoric and composition studies have concentrated on methods by which people can use their language more effectively. Linguistics offers many insights into written discourse, even though it has been primarily concerned with the description of spoken discourse. Much of what linguists have had to say about speaking can be modified and developed into heuristics and methods that will help writers compose and edit texts, if we take care to note the differences between speaking and writing (as discussed in chapter 1). This book is designed for student writers who will become practitioners in all fields of professional writing, such as technical and scientific writing, editing, journalism, and public relations. It is also intended for present and future rhetoric and composition teachers who wish to expand their knowledge of language by looking at it from the perspective of another discipline and who would like to explore the insights offered by linguistics for improving student writing. While I am dealing with a rather diverse audience, you all share one trait: there is a writer inside of each of you. It is that writer whom I have chosen to address. I hope that each of you will adapt the methods you will find here for your own present and future needs.

This book has two main purposes. The first is to demystify some of the most worthwhile and powerful linguistic theories which illuminate spoken and written discourse. My intent is to familiarize the reader with basic principles and theories in linguistics. In many cases, the theories have been simplified and the technical vocabulary kept to a minimum to make the material accessible to the nonlinguist; consult the extensive bibliography provided if you wish to pursue a more technical and rigorous study of the material presented here. The second and primary purpose of this book is to present ways in which these theories can be turned into practical tools for dealing with writing and editing texts. Most of the heuristics and methods discussed are based on theories originally designed to explain spoken discourse which I have modified to make useful for writers. Moreover, since this book is oriented toward users—people who are seeking methods to improve texts—rather than for linguists interested in describing language, I have included numerous examples as well as exercises complete with answers. Although, at first it may seem that some of these theories and methods do not apply to your work, please read the application section at the end of each chapter before coming to this conclusion; the theories are quite easily adapted to deal with texts. Finally, think of the book as a smorgasbord of linguistic tools: sample those approaches and methods that look appealing and explore further those which seem to pertain to your own work. I encourage all readers to modify and adapt the methods to fit their own texts.

I hope that this book will contribute to the advancement of an interdisciplinary approach to language by making it possible for writers to begin to incorporate the insights of linguistics into their study of language, communication, and writing. Nils Enkvist has already set the stage for such an approach by calling for a new direction in language studies called "applied discourse linguistics"—an interdisciplinary field that combines the insights of linguistics, rhetoric, cognitive science, communication, and stylistics.[1] Students of these disciplines will find that some of the issues of inquiry that arise in areas such as rhetoric and communication also arise in linguistics, where they are examined from a different perspective. Bringing together the insights offered by these various fields presents exciting new avenues for language studies. While this text is dedicated to exploring a linguistic approach to communication, a good deal of the material presented here is influenced by rhetoric, cognitive psychology, philosophy of language, and sociology, and throughout this book, when appropriate, relevant work in these other fields is mentioned.

The first chapter of this book is a basic introduction to linguistic studies. It explains the linguistic approach to language and provides some information on what makes the English language unique. Before jumping into a detailed linguistic study of written texts, Chapter 2 examines some fundamental issues pertaining to how the mind processes information. The insights provided by studies in psycholinguistics and cognitive psychology discussed in this chapter can help us design texts to better exploit the mind's abilities to process information. After Chapter 2, the book is organized based on an expanding view of text. We initially look at text from the narrowest perspective, concentrating on the words on the page (chapters 3–7).

Chapters 3 and 4 introduce nontraditional grammars by examining two alternative forms—transformational and case grammar—that may be of use to writers. These grammars also offer new insights into how texts are constructed and provide tools for dealing with common writing problems. Chapters 5 and 6 deal with textual coherence and cohesion. The chapter on coherence (chapter 5) focuses on how ideas are connected and offers methods that a writer can use to check for and improve textual coherence. Chapter 6 examines the devices writers use to link statements together. Chapter 7 deals with the global issues of how texts are constructed and organized and provides methods for creating abstracts and summaries, diagnosing lack of textual development, and revising texts.

Chapters 8 and 9 examine the text in the world, as an object which communicates information. Chapter 8 considers the writer's intent and the reader's response and concludes with a discussion of the role of the writer and reader in a socially defined communication situation. Chapter 9 examines how people are defined by their social situation and how social circumstances affect communication.

I would like to thank both the University of Colorado at Denver for a Faculty Development Award that helped support this project and my graduate students in Applied Linguistics whose work and enthusiasm have stimulated and encouraged my own work in this field. Warmest thanks to my graduate assistant Katy Wegner, whose help in revising the text was invaluable, and to Elizabeth Lenell and Robin Calland for their help in the final preparation of the manuscript.

# 1

## Language and Linguistics

Before pursuing the study of language and discourse from a linguistic perspective, let us examine our preconceptions about language. If you ask people to define language, most will tell you that it is our means of communication; some may add that it is the ability to produce and understand words, rather than simple cries and yells, that separate humans from animals. While these observations are correct, a more exacting linguistic definition of language will provide us with an invaluable foundation for our inquiry into how to improve the quality of our written texts.

## THE COMMUNICATION CIRCUIT

What is necessary for communication to take place? Communication occurs when a sender deliberately and intentionally sends information to a receiver via a signaling system. The communication circuit consists of three primary elements: sender, receiver, and text.[1] The sender's intent is to convey some kind of meaningful information to the receiver. He

1

does this by selecting the appropriate medium, such as speaking, writing, dancing, or drumming, and the appropriate form, such as conversation, personal letter, tribal ritual, journal article, or picture. Thus communication is not limited to written and spoken discourse; it also includes sign language, codes (such as Morse code and FORTRAN), pictures (including international road signs, graphs, and drawings), and animal cries. The text is the specific message sent, and if the sender is successful, the receiver will understand the sender's intended meaning.

Sender   ⟶   Text   ⟶   Receiver
(sent via selected media)

In rhetoric, these three elements correspond to the corners of the rhetorical triangle. Whereas communication participants have received substantial attention in rhetoric, in linguistics it was not until the recent development of the fields of pragmatics and sociolinguistics that the roles of the sender and receiver really received systematic attention. Traditionally, linguistics focused on the text and treated the people communicating as ideal and stereotypical, as abstract entities. Consequently, linguists could not account for individual and group differences in how people speak and use language. For example, a Southern speaker may say "ya'll come with," while a Northern speaker would say "you all will come with me." Both convey the identical message; however, the difference in pronunciation ("ya" for "you"), the dropping of the modal verb (e.g., "can," "may," "will") and the personal pronoun referring to the speaker are entirely acceptable in the South. Such differences are inconsequential; they do not affect the message. In addition, linguistics had concentrated on describing how we produce and comprehend literal utterances. It could not accommodate for the fact that a speaker might be lying, speaking figuratively, or joking. The personal and societal factors of communication—attitudes toward what is being said and who is saying it, knowledge of forms of communication (e.g., conventions for stories, journal articles, and procedures for initiating and maintaining conversations), and recognition of the impact of the social setting—were beyond the scope of linguistics. During the 1960s, interest in how language was actually being used by speakers spurred research in the field of pragmatics, which investigates how a message is used by participants to accomplish an end or goal. More recently, sociolinguistics has gone further in accounting for the role of the participants by investigating how the communication setting, as well as cultural knowledge passed down in societies, directs and provides cues to the reader about how to interpret a message.

The medium chosen also defines certain parameters of communication; speaking and writing are significantly different mediums. Spoken conversation has an immediacy that written discourse lacks. Since both participants are present, they can constantly monitor communication to ensure that all messages are successfully conveyed and correctly understood. Consider the fact that when engaged in a conversation, if you do not understand what the other person has said, you can stop and ask questions. If the speaker senses confusion by your facial expressions, she can repeat what she has said. Written discourse is different. The sender is absent. Because the reader cannot ask the writer to clarify confusing material, the writer must be especially careful in choosing how to present the text in order to ensure the intended meaning is understood.

While this description makes it sound as if spoken discourse is always preferable to written, written discourse has definite advantages. The grammar of a written text is more precise and grammatically correct than that of speech. In spoken language we find more incomplete sentences and more unnecessary filler words and phrases like "a lot of," "well," and "you know." Thoughts in spoken discourse are strung together primarily with "and" and "but" (coordinating) constructions, whereas "that," "which," "while," and "besides" (subordinating) constructions predominate in written discourse. Written texts are more polished. Speakers refine and qualify expressions as they go along by phrases, such as "I meant" and "it was really." In writing, readers expect that the writer has finished refining the text before disseminating it. In addition, the writer can take more time choosing words and arranging the text and can revise the text before it is ever read by the intended audience. The receiver can also read the text more than once, extracting more information, and perhaps correcting initial false impressions about the writer's intended message by continually referring back to the text. The choice of medium will be dictated by the needs of the sender and receiver. As specialists in the field of communication, we must be aware of the fact that the rules and strategies for creating successful written prose are not the same as those for spoken discourse.

## HUMAN LANGUAGE

Apes, chimpanzees, and dolphins seem capable of communicating with one another; however, their communication systems are very simple. They cannot communicate about abstract concepts and ideas or "talk" about objects that are not in their immediate vicinity. Their communication apparatus is limited to simple gestures and a very limited range of vocal utterances that vary primarily in pitch and volume. On the other hand, human speech is made up of discrete units which, loosely speaking, correspond to vowel and consonant sounds.

While animal communication systems are genetically inherited, this is not true of human language. At birth, humans are predisposed to learn language: the ability to learn is genetically inherited, but language itself is learned from interaction with individuals in society. If a child were raised in an environment where language was never used, that child would never learn a language. Fortunately, children are nurtured in a language-rich environment, and they quickly acquire language skills.

Social interaction is fundamental to human language. More precisely, our language is socially dependent and conventional. This means that our language is defined and controlled by the community in which we live; all speakers within our language community agree to abide by a system of rules, called grammar, which governs our language.

## THE ELEMENTS OF HUMAN LANGUAGE

Language is like a game of chess. In chess, there is a set of rules we must learn in order to play the game. Each piece can only move in certain directions: the bishop can only move on the diagonal. Some pieces can move only a certain number of squares: the king only moves one square at a time. How a player captures an opponent's pieces is determined by the rules of the game: pawns capture on the diagonal. And the game can only be won by checkmating the king. But there is an infinite combination of moves that may ensue during the course of each individual game, and a player freely selects each individual move. Language works the same way as chess. Grammar is our set of language rules. It governs our language and assures us that we will be understood. While the meaningful units of each individual utterance are freely selected by the speaker from an infinitely large number of morphemes, the grammar imposes structure on the way those selections are combined and actually uttered or written.

Look at the following group of words. Can you decipher the sentence?

> that of is rules all speakers to by agree
> grammar called abide system the

As this jumble of words proves, without grammar we could not understand one another. (The sentence is, "All speakers agree to abide by the system of rules that is called grammar.") Without this system of rules we all agree upon, our grammar, any jumble or sequence of words would be allowed. If all combinations of words were permissible, language users would not be able to produce, decipher, or understand any combinations. We would have no clues about how to extract the meaning from a sentence or utterance.[2]

Grammar consists of two elements: syntax and morphology. Syntax is the order of words in a sentence. Morphology concerns the units of meaning into which words can be divided, both what the word denotes and the prefixes and suffixes which indicate such information as the tense of a verb and the number—singular or plural—of a noun. Morphemes, units of meaning, are divided into two types: free radicals are the base words and bound radicals are the prefixes and suffixes appended to words. For example, "anti-," "re-," "un-," "-ed," "es," and "-tion" have no meaning when they stand alone. "Un-discipline-d" has three morphemes, as does "re-use-able": "discipline" and "use" are free radicals; "un-," "-ed," "re-," and "-able" are bound radicals. Though the grammars of all languages consist of rules for both syntax and morphology, many languages are more dependent on one of these two components for the basic information about the function of words in the sentence. Consider how different languages signal whether a noun is being used as a subject or object. English and other Germanic languages have a fairly fixed sentence order; we know how the word is being used by its position (relative to other words) in the sentence. Romance languages, such as Latin and Spanish, depend more on inflections to indicate the function of words in a sentence; it is the suffix of the word rather than its position that signals its function.

In addition to the grammatical elements of a language, there are phonological elements. Every language has a grammar and a phonological system. Phonemes are the smallest discrete sound units of language, and the study of phonemes is called phonology. Phonemes correspond to sound elements, not to the letters of the alphabet. There is not a direct one-to-one correspondence between the vowels and consonants of the alphabet and the phonemes in English. Consonant clusters such as "ch," "th," and "sh" are phonemes. Some phonemes can be represented by more than one letter, as in "cease," where both "s" and "c" correspond to the same phoneme. Some letters can also be used to represent more than one phoneme such as "c," which is hard in "cat" (also represented in English by the letter "k") and soft in "niece" (also represented in English by the letter "s"). Recognized phonemes vary from one language to another: English recognizes the phoneme represented by "sh," while some other languages do not; Greek recognizes "kh" as a phoneme and English does not; some African languages recognize guttural sounds and clicks as phonemes, although they are not recognized in any European or Asian language. Taken together, the grammar and phonological system make each language unique.

## THE FUNDAMENTAL QUALITIES OF LANGUAGE

Surprisingly, we can utter phrases and sentences that we have never heard before. This means that our language is not imitative; what we have heard and read before does not limit what we may say or write in the future. Our ability to produce utterances we have not heard before is known as language productivity or creativity. A native speaker can speak an infinitely large number of utterances he has never heard before, and he can also understand a speaker or a text containing combinations he has not encountered before. Remember, without grammar this would be impossible. The finite number of rules and conventions of grammar restrict the infinite number of combinations of language elements, thereby ensuring that we understand others and they understand us. Creativity, or productivity, is one of the defining features of language identified by Hockett.[3] He proposed a set of design features of language that would serve to characterize how language differs from other forms of (animal and human) communication. In addition to creativity, arbitrariness, discreteness, and duality are the fundamental qualities of all human languages.

Arbitrariness refers to the fact that there is nothing intrinsic in an object such as a table that demands we call it "table" in English or "mesa" in Spanish. The word chosen to represent the thing is arbitrary and is accepted by society. The society must share the same "words" for objects and ideas for communication to be possible.

Discreteness is a feature of the phonological system. In animal communication, the pitch of a cry may have different meanings: a shrill cry may signal danger; a lower pitched cry may express pleasure. In human language, there is no gradation of units of sound. Each phoneme is absolute. In music, fortissimo signals loudness, a note drawn on the third space of the staff signals high C versus middle C, and the whole notes, half notes, and quarter notes signal different durations. In language there is no loud "b," high "b," or half "b." There is only the phoneme, represented by the letter "b." The sounds of each language are absolute, and in each language only certain phonemes may follow one another. For instance, English does not recognize the sequence "bh" or "dl."

The last of the fundamental qualities is duality. Language duality simply refers to the fact that each language has two essential components—a grammar and a phonetic system.

Hockett lists twelve additional design qualities of language, and two worth noting here. The first is prevarication, the ability to deceive, misinform, or lie to a receiver. Linguistics had until recently only dealt with situations where the speaker genuinely wants her message to be understood. We will see how this quality remains one of the most difficult for linguists to account for in communication theories. The last quality worth noting is language reflexiveness. Reflexiveness refers to the ability of people to create a language which comments on language itself. This language about language is often referred to as "metalanguage." Linguistics, rhetoric, philosophy of language, and critical theory are all types of metalanguage; these types of discourse allow us to examine and evaluate the language that we use.

## THE EVOLUTION OF ENGLISH

English is descended from the Germanic family of languages that also includes German and Dutch. This group differs from the Romance language family which includes Spanish, French, and Italian. All Germanic languages have a two-tense verb system. Germanic languages recognize only the past and present tense, and commonly use the "d" or "t" suffix to indicate past tense. Future, progressive (ongoing), perfective (completed), and punctual (occurring at a single point in time) action in these languages are expressed through the use of modal and auxiliary verbs, not by simply modifying the form of the main verb itself, as in Romance languages.

Both Germanic and Romance languages, as well as many other languages spoken in Europe and Asia, descend from the original parent language, Indo-European, which was spoken approximately 5,000 years ago. We do not know what this language was like, since we have no written records, but efforts are being made to reconstruct some of its elements based on the evolution of the more modern languages. All languages descending from Indo-European began as inflectional languages, including English. The conjugation of verbs was much more complicated than it is today: a verb had a different form depending on whether the subject was "I," "you" (singular), "he/she/it," "we," "you" (plural), or "they." Inflections were used to signify a noun's case, gender, and number—information conveyed in Modern English by word order and prepositions. For instance, the word "stone" in Old English (English before the Normal Conquest of 1066), was declined as follows:

| Case | Singular | Plural |
|---|---|---|
| nominative (subject) | stan | stanas |
| genitive (possessive) | stanes | stana |
| accusative (direct object) | stan | stanas |
| dative (indirect object) | stane | stanum |
| instrumental (object used to accomplish an action) | stane | stanum |

During the Middle English period (1066–1500) the declension was reduced to one we recognize:

| Case | Singular | Plural |
|---|---|---|
| common case (includes nominative, accusative, dative) | stone | stones |
| genitive | stone's | stones' |

(We no longer use the instrumental case; we signify it in other ways as with the prepositions "by" and "with.")

Though Old English may look very complicated, even foreign, Modern English shares many qualities with its predecessor.[4] Sixty to seventy percent of the words we use in every sentence descend directly from Old English. Many of the words that have descended to contemporary English are function words (as well as many monosyllabic nouns for common items and simple action verbs). Function words include articles, prepositions, and conjunctions. They are a small and stable set of words that allow us to make sense of utterances, giving such information as the function (or case) of the noun that follows. Their primary role is to indicate how other words in the sentence relate. Note the number of function words that occur in the following sentence (the function words are italicized):

> *They are a* small *and* stable set *of* words *that* allow
> us *to* make sense *of* our language.

The rest of the words in the sentence are content words which name objects, concepts, qualities, processes, and actions. ("Small," "set," "word," and "make" are content words that also descend from Old English.) The function words, like grammar, are tools that render our language comprehensible.

Today, we are able to make sense of utterances because syntax allows for only certain word combinations in certain sequences. Instead of depending primarily on inflection, Modern English depends primarily on function words and word order. The most common sentence type, a simple declarative sentence, has subject-verb-direct object word order. In Old English, the direct object could precede the verb, and listeners and readers would have no problem comprehending the language, since the inflectional ending signaled that the first word was the object. In contemporary English, a shift in order signifies a sentence type other than declarative, such as a command or question, or marks a dialect, such as Hawaiian Pidgin.

Together, function words and syntactic restrictions are essential for generating coherent phrases and sentences that all language users can understand.

## A BRIEF HISTORY OF LINGUISTICS

### Linguistics and Philology

Before the turn of the century, linguistics was synonymous with philology. Philology, meaning "love of the word," was primarily a study of literature and other written records. The first philologists concentrated on written texts (particularly literary texts), comparing various periods and styles of writing. By the end of the eighteenth century, philology diverged into two schools: the old interest in the styles of literary works continued, along with a newer and more narrowly defined field that concentrated on "the interpretation of the language of written records." This more narrowly defined philological study delved into phonology (the way the language was spoken, as deduced from written records) and morphology of the texts under scrutiny. In the nineteenth century, philological studies were predominantly of this latter type.

The early part of the nineteenth century was dominated by the work of Rasmus Rask of Denmark, Jacob Grimm, Franz Bopp, and other Germans, men devoted to the comparative study of Indo-European languages, particularly the comparison of phonetic and morphological features. Because of the pioneering work of these men, comparative philology—the comparison of related languages—gained recognition as an independent science. While scholars of this time were interested in comparing records of various languages, their studies were ahistorical. That is, they did not recognize that certain languages or dialects predated others. Therefore, many errors about the relations of various languages were made due to the fact that a language currently in use may have been compared to the records of another language that had been in use 500 years earlier. Once philologists took history into account, great strides in comparative philology were quickly made, and philologists became better able to identify and compare features of languages that revealed their actual historical relationships.

Influenced in part by Darwin's biological work (1850–80), philologists soon became interested in constructing genealogical trees of language families, illustrating how modern languages evolved from ancient ones. By comparing languages with respect to the period in which they were actually in use, a true picture of the development of languages could be achieved. Attempts were also made to reconstruct a prototype of the first language, Indo-European, which gave rise to the languages of most of the Eurasian continent. By the 1870s, historical comparative philology was well established through the contributions of such men as Hermann Paul, Eduard Sievers, and William Whitney. Until the work of the structural linguists, beginning with Ferdinand Saussure, linguistics remained primarily a historical study.

## Saussure and the Dawn of Structural Linguistics

Ferdinand Saussure is the father of modern linguistics. In the early part of this century (ca. 1915), he succeeded in pioneering a formal system of linguistic study called structural linguistics.[5] Saussure introduced many important principles for a systematic study of language, among the most important: the distinction between diachronic and synchronic language study, the distinction between langue and parole, and the description of the nature of the linguistic sign.

Diachronic linguistics is the historical study of language, whereas synchronic linguistics is the geographic study of language. Diachronic linguistics refers to the study of how a language evolves over a period of time. Tracing the development of English from the Old English period to the twentieth century is a diachronic study. A synchronic study of language is a comparison of languages or dialects—various spoken differences of the same language—used within some defined spatial region and during the same period of time. Determining the regions of the United States in which people currently say "pop" rather than "soda" and "idea" rather than "idear" are examples of the types of inquiries pertinent to a synchronic study.

While vocabulary and pronunciation vary across geographic region, Saussure also recognized that there is a difference between how a given society or language community defines language and how any one individual uses it. Socially defined language, which Saussure terms "langue," corresponds to what was earlier described as the conventional aspect of language. It is the shared system of rules, the knowledge of what others will accept and understand, that we all share. "Parole" is the individual's use of, and facility with, the language. To study parole, the linguist looks at individual's actual utterances.

Saussure was also the first to define the symbolic nature of human language. Symbols, icons, and indices are all types of signs, but a symbol differs from the other two types which have some intrinsic connection to, or share some inherent quality with, the objects they represent. Icons communicate their meaning by their physical similarity to the item represented: imagine the now popular international road signs—silhouettes of pedestrians crossing a road or of rocks falling. Indices point to the item signified by their physical proximity to the object referred to: a black cloud is an index of rain, the scent of chocolate chips is an index of fresh-baked Toll House cookies. Thus, there is some logical connection underlying the relationship between an icon or index and what it refers to, its referent. But language is a symbolic system. Symbols share no inherent quality with their referents. No logical connection exists between the word and the concept, object, or action to which it refers. The relationship is conventional. There is no reason "t-a-b-l-e" rather than "s-t-e-p" should refer to that four-legged flat surface on which small items are set, other than the fact that English speakers agree to accept that "table" is a symbol for that object.

Saussure describes, in detail, the symbolic nature of language by delineating the nature of the linguistic sign. Remember that the sign used in language, the linguistic sign, is always a symbol. It is composed of two parts: the signified and the signifier.

### The Linguistic Sign

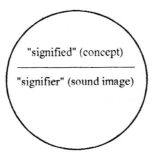

The signified corresponds to the concept referred to. But this is not a physical object set in the real world; it is a concept formed in each individual's mind. This is important since if I say "tree," some people may think of deciduous maples, while others think of coniferous pine trees. Some may imagine a tree ornamented with the red and gold leaves of fall. Some may imagine the bare branches of a winter tree. Some may imagine a tree in bloom. But no matter the image, each is still a "tree." The signifier is the sound image of the word, which is in part defined by the language of the speaker: "t-r-e-e" in English or "a-r-b-o-r" in Latin. Together the signified and signifier form a mental construct: they do not represent the thing we see and the word we utter, but instead, a concept and a sound image. Saussure emphasizes this distinction. Traditionally, sign referred simply to the "word," but the sign for Saussure consisted of the two intimately united elements—signified and signifier. The signifier is arbitrarily chosen to represent the signified; the language community then agrees to accept the association. The linguistic sign is totally arbitrary.

The acceptance of the theory of the arbitrariness of the linguistic sign quelled all theories that language originally developed by onomatopoeia. Onomatopoeia refers to words which resemble the sounds associated with the things to which they refer, such as "choo-choo" for train. Saussure and his disciples successfully argued that the few onomatopoeic words could not account for the development of the vocabulary of a language.[6]

## Chomsky's Transformational Grammar

In the late 1950s and early 1960s, Noam Chomsky's work created a revolution in linguistic theory. Chomsky introduced the theory of transformational grammar, a system by which he proposed to explain all potential sentences uttered and understood by all people. Transformational grammar consists of a set of rules and options for transforming the ideas or content of an utterance into syntactically ordered, grammatically acceptable sentences.[7]

Chomsky's primary goal was to explain language productivity and creativity. Building on Saussure's concepts of langue and parole, he distinguished between language competence (our ability to produce and perceive language that we have not heard before, obviously owing to our knowledge of grammar) and language performance (the individual's utterances). His grammar is a dynamic and innovative explanation of how various individual utterances can be derived, and is one of the first attempts to explain how the mind actually uses langue—grammatical rules and information—to come up with proper sentence structures, and individual's parole. His grammar, along with other alternatives to traditional grammar that we will look at, may be more powerful systems for analyzing language than the eight parts of speech grammar we learned in elementary school, because these alternative grammars more accurately represent the way we use and understand language.

Chomsky's theory works on the assumption that everyone who speaks a given language uses the same grammatical constructions as everyone else; all speakers belong to a "homogeneous" language community. This means that everyone who speaks a particular dialect of English, such as Midwestern or Southern, speaks it without any (significant) variation in pronunciation or grammatical constructions, and does not borrow forms from other dialects. Thus, you speak a dialect of American English such as Southern, or you speak a dialect of British English such as Cockney. Once your language community has been identified, it is assumed that all speakers of that community will use the same grammatical constructions; individual variations are marginal and insignificant. This has been found to be incorrect. While most people do only speak a limited number of languages or dialects, all people use a range of styles when they speak. Each of us belongs to many language communities, and the styles we speak to our children, to our loved ones, and to our co-workers all have different characteristics. We use different degrees of formality, various intonations, different types of idioms, jargon, and technical terms, all of which constitute our discourse in different settings with various people.

Basically, Chomsky's system dealt with language and grammar isolated from the circumstances in which it was uttered or written. The concerns, attitudes, and inclinations of speaker and hearer were not considered. Language was abstracted from its interpersonal context. Yet, Chomsky's work is fundamental to all subsequent developments in linguistic theory and artificial intelligence, spurring linguists to explore language in new ways.

### Pragmatics and Sociolinguistics

Through the 1950s, linguists treated language as if its primary function was transactional: language was the means for the efficient communication of information. But during the 1960s, this stance began to be challenged. Some theorists, in the emerging fields of pragmatics and sociolinguistics, recognized that the acceptance of the transactional model meant excluding many other functions of language from study.

For instance, language can be used to enlist someone's help in achieving a goal, to elicit an emotional response, to entertain, or to deceive. Pragmatists and sociolinguists are better equipped to examine such uses of language, because in these fields the participants and the communication setting are considered essential elements that must be studied in order to understand how language is used in any given situation. No longer is the text of a conversation or of a written communication studied in isolation. Pragmatics focuses on what the participants intend to accomplish through language. Sociolinguistics stresses the fact that the participants, as well as the setting in which they are communicating, shape the ensuing discourse.

Pragmatics was the first of the two fields to emerge. John Austin[8] and John Searle[9] laid the foundation for this still vital field of linguistic research. Pragmatics is the study of language in use. Pragmatists assert that language is always used to achieve a goal—to inform, to motivate someone to do something, to make a promise or request. Pragmatics aims to identify the conditions placed on the speaker, the listener, the text, and the setting in order to ensure that the goal is accomplished.

People's expectations, attitudes, desires, and goals will all impact the success or failure of any communication. Sociolinguistics examines the interpersonal and social factors that influence communication.[10] To understand the interpersonal dimensions of communication, we must know more about the participants, including their age, education, and ethnicity. We must know what relationship exists between the participants. Are they peers? Are they intimate? Are they from different rungs of the social ladder? Is one a superior and the other a subordinate in the workplace? Such relationships determine the formality of the language we use, the amount of slang and technical jargon we use, and how much we feel we can intimate and still assume we will be understood. The setting is also a factor determining how we speak: the speech in a men's locker room will be different than that of a college classroom. The place itself imposes certain restrictions on what is acceptable.

Pragmatics is considered to be a more systematic and analytical study than sociolinguistics. In pragmatics, the goal is to identify, delineate, and categorize the rules and conditions that determine whether communication will succeed or fail. Sociolinguistics tends to deal with the less tangible aspects of communication, dealing more with how human behavior influences what we say and understand.

## MODERN LINGUISTICS AND THE WRITTEN TEXT

Modern linguistics has always strongly asserted the primacy of the spoken word over the written. Thus, linguists of this century have been far more interested in studying oral discourse than in explaining how written texts are constructed. Written discourse, which has only existed in the past 5,000 years, has always been treated as a derivative of speech—subordinate to it—since social interaction can be achieved by spoken discourse alone. Yet, from anthropologist Claude Lévi-Strauss to philosopher Jacques Derrida, a compelling argument has been made that written discourse is central to the establishment and preservation of the institutions of knowledge and learning that constitute history and culture.[11] Written texts provide a historical record that can be disseminated throughout a society and passed on to later generations. But such a record is not necessary to ensure the survival of a community; speech suffices for societal communication needs such as the tasks of food gathering and bartering. Illiteracy is the norm in Third World countries, and people there go about their daily business without the advantage of knowing how to read and write.

Written texts, in and of themselves, did not become a subject of linguistic study until the late 1960s, due to the emergence of the field of text linguistics. Text linguistics, often building on the work of earlier linguistic theories, attempts to explain how texts are produced and comprehended. "Text" refers to both spoken and written communication that extends beyond a sentence. As a larger unit of communication, a text must be coherent—make logical sense—and the ideas must be connected and presented in a grammatically acceptable form. Text linguistics differs from other fields of linguistics in making written discourse one of its central objects of investigation.

Text linguistics has actually become an interdisciplinary pursuit. To understand how texts make sense, linguists have had to enlist the aid of cognitive psychologists in an effort to understand how the mind actually processes language. Text comprehension depends on our ability to relate new ideas to knowledge we have already stored in memory. Thus, some familiarity with how we cognitively process information is a prerequisite for discussing texts. How cognitive psychology illuminates the study of written discourse is the subject of chapter 2, and psychology also provides a foundation for the discussion of coherence and cohesion that follows in chapters 4 and 5. One of the most recent areas of investigation in text linguistics has been in the area of macrostructures. Macrostructures, which are the subject of chapter 6, help to explain how large-scale concepts, themes, and topics are organized and delimit text development.

This book covers theories fundamental to research in text linguistics. But, while text linguistics is devoted to describing how texts are created and understood, my intent is also to demonstrate how practical applications of linguistic theories can enhance the writing, editing, and analysis of nonliterary texts. For this reason, I return to many areas of modern linguistics which have been concerned solely, or primarily, with spoken discourse. Much of this material, with some slight revision, also sheds light on written communication. You will find that throughout the chapters, I will discuss "the speaker" and "listener" (or "audience") when discussing theories that were originally intended to examine spoken utterances, in an effort to remain true to the theorists' work, but the application sections will show how, with care, principles used to study spoken discourse can be adapted to illuminate aspects of written discourse as well.

# 2

## *Processing Information*

Before we can discuss how to design texts so that they are easier to comprehend, we need to understand how the human brain processes language and text.

## MEMORY

Psychologists talk of human memory as a three-part system, consisting of short-term memory (STM), working memory, and long-term memory (LTM).[1] A picture or a text appears to you, and in your mind you simultaneously construct a complete sensory image—a replica of what you saw. Once the picture or text is removed, you momentarily keep the sensory image in mind. This image decays rapidly: you quickly forget what type of shoes the person you were intently watching was wearing, and just as quickly you forget many of the words on a page you just read. We say that the image is held in STM and that it is subject to forgetting. If we are to remember any part of the image it must be stored in LTM. For the storage process to occur, the image has to be processed. If it is not processed, it will be forgotten.

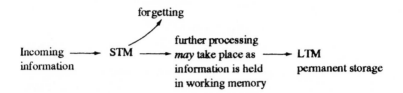

STM actually holds very little material; it facilitates holding a phone number in mind until you've dialed it or repeating a list of words you've been asked to study until someone asks you to recite the list a few minutes later. The process of rehearsing material until asked to deliver it is called maintenance rehearsal. Once called upon to spew the material you usually forget it; it is not incorporated into LTM.

But what about material you wish to remember, that you would like to retrieve and use at a much later time? This material must reach LTM. In order for material to pass from STM to LTM, further processing, called elaborative rehearsal, must occur. While elaborative rehearsal takes place the information is said to be held in working memory. Material selected as significant is held here while it is processed further and incorporated into LTM.[2] In order for elaborative rehearsal to take place, the new material must be evaluated in terms of its relation to material previously stored in LTM. Associations between the new and old material are made, and then the new material is processed. For instance, bats may be recognized as being animals that fly like birds. But they are not birds; they are mammals like mice. Thus, "bats" may be stored in LTM in relation to birds, mammals, and rodents. This example points out an important feature of storing new material. Material is not simply stored in isolation, but is actually stored in relation to numerous bits of old information. If a number of relationships between new material and old are not made, we can only access the newly stored material in a limited number of ways. However, using the network of relations that are made between stored bits of information, we can retrieve necessary bits in various situations. For instance, because you have burned a steak and found out it tastes terrible, you will know not to eat the pork chop you just burned. Proceeding to eat a burned pork chop is a new experience, but you can access information that is analogous,

retrieving from LTM the fact that burned food tastes terrible. You thereby save yourself from "relearning" how burnt food tastes.

How much and how long the information will be retained, as well
as how easy it will be to retrieve, depends on the depth of processing. If
the processing is "shallow," then it is easily forgotten. Maintenance
rehearsal is a type of shallow processing as well as a form of temporary
storage that alleviates some of the burden on LTM, since there are some
things that we just don't need to remember. When you rehearse a
telephone number until you dial it, you are engaging in shallow processing. You have not processed the material in any meaningful way, for
example, by relating the phone number to an important date already
stored in LTM or by creating a mnemonic. If the phone number is
subject to a greater depth of processing by one of these methods, it will
not be forgotten as easily.[3] For information to be processed to any
depth, it must be recognized and broken down into meaningful units—
concepts, themes, tasks, or images that we recognize. Information that
we are conscious of learning passes through many processing stages
before it is permanently stored. At first, new information is matched
against stored material in LTM. In later stages, processing involves
pattern recognition and systematic storage, as items are matched and
processed in terms of how they compare to already learned information.
Information that enters memory is like a radioactive isotope: it has a
half-life, and it decays. In other words, the information becomes less
and less distinct and memorable over time. Rehearsal impedes the decay
process, but once it stops, decay will proceed. That is why elaborative
rehearsal is so important; it allows the data to be integrated into LTM.
The more processing a piece of information receives, the easier the
material will be to retrieve at a later time.

The concept of rehearsal types may explain why programmed
learning texts do not work. Programmed learning texts consist of pages
with short paragraphs of information, followed by a question that is
usually a restatement of what was just said. After answering the question, you flip to the next page; there you find the answer in the margin,
followed by another paragraph and another question. You continue to
flip through the text, following this procedure. Educators soon discov-

ered that such texts were poor teaching tools; students retained very little of the material. The texts only encouraged maintenance rehearsal; once you'd answered the question you moved on to something else. And since the questions were so often a restatement of the text, there was no real impetus to perform elaborative rehearsal. Texts facilitate elaborative rehearsal if they require readers to synthesize the material they have learned by posing problems to be solved or by providing the reader with tasks to perform. Engaging material in a meaningful way through elaborative rehearsal is crucial, if the material is to be learned and incorporated into LTM.

Once, I was asked to evaluate a study guide designed for a class on the computer language Pascal. The course was taught in a large manufacturing company to people who had no previous computer experience; this course was their chance to advance, to move from assembly work into computer programming. The study guide thoroughly repeated all the essential material covered in the lectures. In fact, you could say it was redundant. The instructors were distressed to learn that, despite such repetition, 75 percent of the people flunked the exams. One of the instructors asked me if I had any idea what they were doing wrong. First of all they had incorrectly assumed that their students knew how to study. Most of these people only had a high school education and had been out of school for years. Simply memorizing pages of material, even repetitious material, was very difficult for them. Because of their poor study habits and the fact that the text did not stimulate them to engage in elaborative rehearsal, all they could do was fall back on maintenance rehearsal. This did not help them to assimilate the material, nor were they able to memorize enough to perform well on the exams. However, the situation could be remedied, not by teaching the students how to study, but by redesigning the study guide as a workbook. A workbook could provide, for example, outlines of flowcharts and diagrams that students could fill out during, or immediately following, the lectures. This would serve two purposes: 1) the diagrams and flowcharts would enhance conceptual processing by making the relations between elements clearer, and 2) the students would be engaged, through filling out the workbook, in elaborative rehearsal.

The best way to facilitate the permanent storage (learning) of new information is to have the reader use the material in a meaningful way. However, flowcharts and diagrams may be inappropriate for some types of text. Informative or persuasive texts offer several options: ask questions of the readers and include analogies and metaphors that will encourage them to compare objects, concepts, and issues with which they are already familiar to the newly presented information. These methods facilitate depth processing and will help readers to remember your text.

## PROCESSING INFORMATION

To make sense of material we hear or read, we must begin with the linear surface of the text—the words in the order they are presented. Because there is a limit to how much material we can absorb when listening or reading, we do not process every word to any great depth. Rather than processing sentences word for word, we take in clauses; we "lag behind" until we read or hear a meaningful unit. Called shadowing, this process is an essential component of our ability to understand language, and fortunately for us it is a fairly automated process.[4] Try an experiment on yourself. Quickly read the first few sentences of this paragraph again. Then close your eyes and recall as much as you can. You will not be able to reproduce the sentences word by word, but you will be able to recall some of the concepts and key phrases. This is the result of shadowing; you have processed the material based on the meaningful units you have recognized.

If the brain were to match each word it hears or sees with already stored information, it would quickly be overloaded by more information than it could handle. In actuality, we screen out many function words such as articles ("a," "an," and "the"), prepositions (such as "in," "to," "near," and "of"), and conjunctions and adverbs (such as "and," "but," "yet," and "however"), since these words do not carry meaningful information necessary to expand or delimit a concept. Such function words simply clue us how to evaluate the concepts being presented and clarify the relationships established between the ideas in the text.[5] Without these elements we could not make sense of a text, but we do not need them to store information in LTM.[6] Once the essential concepts have been identified and broken down into manageable units, the processing of these concepts begins.

Two different types of processes are used to handle new information: conceptually driven and data-driven.[7] Most information that we receive requires both types of processing, but one type often dominates, depending on the type of information. Conceptually driven processing involves elaborative rehearsal. Our ability to recall or use new information is improved by elaborative rehearsal, since we process the material to a greater depth and make meaningful connections with material already stored in LTM. This type of processing is important if we want to learn information and be able to use it later. In addition, our power to recall or utilize material can be limited by our ability to take in a certain amount of data. Data-driven processing is limited by the amount of information the mind can process over a given period of time. We use data-driven processing when reading or listening to information that we will only use once or only need for a short period of time.

Reading is a task that engages both conceptually driven and data-driven processing. Reading a book calls upon our knowledge of grammar, vocabulary, language conventions, and related ideas and concepts already stored in LTM; therefore, we engage in conceptually driven processing. But reading is also a data-limited task; a reader can process only so many words per minute. The maximum amount of "data" that a reader can absorb is her "data limitation."

The term "top-down" is used to describe texts that invite conceptually driven processing, while the term "bottom-up" describes texts that invite data-driven processing. Texts can be adapted to facilitate one type of processing (or both types at the same time).[8] Most well-written texts will be of a mixed design, but often a text is written so that readers are invited to prefer one type of processing over the other. Texts that invite data-driven processing are dominated by a bottom-up design. Instruction manuals for assembling children's toys and workout equipment or for hooking up VCRs and stereos are examples of bottom-up designed texts. The writer assumes that you will only be performing the task once (or no more than a few times); therefore, he will assume that talking you through the procedure step-by-step is the best approach. Usually it is, but if you get stuck, if the instructions don't make sense, or if you perform a step incorrectly, later you may find that the pieces you have left don't fit together or the equipment doesn't work. Then you might wish that the writer had also divided the process into stages of five to seven steps that described how one part of the whole object was assembled. By dividing the work into stages, the writer helps the reader to conceptualize the task. The parts, each assembled during a single stage, would then be assembled to produce the whole. Having completed a single stage, you would be able to determine whether a part was assembled correctly. If it were not, you would just have to repeat that one stage, rather than having to disassemble the whole object. The instruction manual writer who groups the steps of building a home gym by frame, weights, and pulley systems, with a way to check that each assembled part has been put together correctly (perhaps by providing illustrations) saves the consumer from discovering that the last two-and-a-half-inch bolt that she used to attach a pulley was supposed to be used in the frame. Good instruction manuals break down long tasks into stages, thereby introducing some top-down design into the text.

Top-down designed texts facilitate conceptually driven processing, by providing schemas, concepts, or groupings of pieces of data thereby allowing us to recognize the relationship between new and old pieces of information, understand the significance of the new information, or recognize outcomes and goals incumbent on learning that new information.[9] Most textbooks are top-down designed. For example, let's consider a language textbook. First, you are taught to recognize the cases of the nouns and the tenses and aspects of verbs; then you are shown how to inflect nouns and verbs to arrive at the proper forms. In English, you were taught that weak verbs take "-ed" to form the past tense. You learned the general rule and applied it to specific words.[10] As you memorize more words, you can then use the rules to construct the correct forms for each statement you speak, read, or write. Many crash courses in language for travelers work in the opposite way. The traveler is bombarded with many phrases and sentences that she memorizes in order to move about freely in a foreign country; this is a bottom-up or data-driven approach. Since the traveler has not learned any general rules or a system by which to relate all these pieces of information, she will forget what she has learned much faster than the student who learned the language by the rules.

One further example may help to clarify the differences between top-down and bottom-up design. Look at the list of R-groups of amino acids below. You do not need to know organic chemistry to see some of the structural similarities and differences. Note that the R-groups are listed in alphabetical order. If you tried to memorize the material in this order, you would be performing data-driven processing. The text, organized as it is, invites this kind of processing, because it is dominated by a bottom-up design.

Look at the chart again. Did you notice the rings in some of the R-groups? Did you notice that some groups are nonlinear, instead containing branches. Some contain "S" (sulfur). What if the chart were reorganized so that these individual R-groups were organized into groups based on such similarities? The material would be easier to learn. In this case, the text designer would have facilitated conceptual processing by using a top-down designed chart. Indeed, those differences we have observed do account for the similarities in chemical reactions among certain R-groups. Reorganization (to promote conceptual processing) actually reflects the way chemistry students eventually learn this information and store it in LTM.

If you want to learn something and be able to utilize the material later, conceptually driven processing is imperative. As a writer you can facilitate such processing by properly organizing the text. Group like pieces of information. Do not simply organize your text based on chronology, an organizing principle that works best in narratives and stories. When you are writing informative, evaluative, or persuasive prose make sure that related ideas and concepts follow one another. By properly organizing a text, you can increase the amount of information that your readers will remember.

# R-groups of Amino Acids

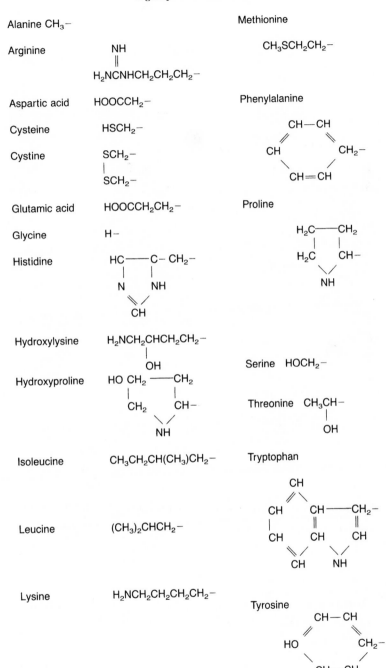

Alanine $CH_3-$

Arginine
$$\underset{H_2NCNHCH_2CH_2CH_2-}{\overset{\overset{\displaystyle NH}{\|}}{}}$$

Aspartic acid $HOOCCH_2-$

Cysteine $HSCH_2-$

Cystine
$$\underset{SCH_2-}{\overset{SCH_2-}{|}}$$

Glutamic acid $HOOCCH_2CH_2-$

Glycine $H-$

Histidine

Hydroxylysine $H_2NCH_2CHCH_2CH_2-$ OH

Hydroxyproline

Isoleucine $CH_3CH_2CH(CH_3)CH_2-$

Leucine $(CH_3)_2CHCH_2-$

Lysine $H_2NCH_2CH_2CH_2CH_2-$

Methionine

$CH_3SCH_2CH_2-$

Phenylalanine

Proline

Serine $HOCH_2-$

Threonine $CH_3CH-$ OH

Tryptophan

Tyrosine

Valine $(CH_3)_2CH-$

## CHUNKING

We have talked about how the mind processes information, but we have yet to deal with the fact that we are continually bombarded with more information than we are capable of processing. Research has shown that human recall tends to be limited to approximately seven units, plus or minus two.[11] We call this the "magic number seven"; we are able to hold five to nine items at a given instant in STM, either for recall or for further processing into LTM. But obviously, almost hourly, when we are involved in a task as simple as listening to the TV or reading a book, we are exposed to more than five to nine pieces of new data at a time. How do we process an amount of material that seems to be beyond our capacity? Chunking is the strategy the mind exploits to overcome data limitations.

Chunking is a process by which small units of material are recoded into larger bits of material, thereby allowing us to remember more material. For instance, learning a list of fifteen single-digit numbers is very difficult (3, 8, 5, 4, 7, 1, 8, 9, 2, 6, 4, 7, 3, 0, 5), but if you recode them into five three-digit number sequences (385, 471, 892, 647, 305) you have increased the amount of information you can assimilate. By associating and grouping new information we need to process, we can decrease the actual number of pieces of information we need to learn. We continue to recode information until there are few enough chunks that we can process and retain all of the original information.[12] Chunking is essential to learning. If you return to the list of amino acids, you will see how grouping the individual R-groups by like characteristics would make learning easier. By providing some necessary preliminary conceptualization, chunking the information—into rings, branches, sulfur-containing groups, etc.—the text designer helps the reader to learn the information.

## FACTORS IN RETENTION AND RECALL OF INFORMATION

Besides the limitation on our ability to take in only so much new data at a time, a few other factors also determine how much material we can process, retain, and recall at a later time. Recency, superordination, primacy, and proactive interference have a great impact on retention and recall:[13]

1. The Recency Effect: We best recall the most recent or last material in a text. Since no more material comes in for processing after the last piece of data, the reader can dwell on it and will retain it best. By recapping important points and putting summaries and conclusions at the end of an essay, you help the reader to remember what is important.

2. Superordination: We best recall concepts and ideas that are highlighted as being of greatest significance. Repetition highlights concepts, as does referring directly to the concept in headings and titles.

3. Primacy: As we begin to attend to any new material we immediately direct our full attention to the first new item. The first item (or items) requires our complete attention because at this time we activate conceptually driven processes that will facilitate the processing of subsequent information. Often subsequent items do not receive the same attention as the first item, since we try to complete processing of the former items before we can move on (and we also have to deal with data limitations). Thus, there is a greater potential for forgetting subsequent information.[14] By including an overview or introduction, you provide the reader with a framework by which to interpret the information that follows and help him to engage in conceptual processing.

4. Proactive Interference: If asked to process a number of similar pieces of information, the reader's attention may wane as he continues to read familiar material; therefore, his ability to retain all the information decreases. The information in the middle is most easily forgotten. As suggested by the recency and primacy effects, items processed first and last will be remembered best. To combat proactive interference, you may introduce important points in the introduction, recap them at the end, and use repetition to reinforce those ideas that are at the heart—and middle—of your essay.

A skilled writer can design a text at every level—sentence, paragraph, and complete composition—to exploit recency, superordination, and primacy, and to avoid proactive interference. At the sentence level, place important material at the opening and closing of the sentence. Do not waste these two positions by using empty introductory clauses such as "it is," "it was," "there are," and "there was," which do not provide initial information or a context that will help the reader process subsequent information. Do not end the first and last sentences of your paragraphs vaguely with a pronoun such as "it" or an indefinite reference such as "something," and avoid ending a sentence with a preposition (place it next to the verb it naturally follows). Try to end those most important sentences—the first and last in the paragraph—with nouns, verbs, or significant phrases.

The same advice holds true for paragraphs and whole compositions. Put your most important information in the beginning and/or closing sentences of a paragraph. In terms of the whole composition, especially those designed to inform or educate the reader, use an introduction or overview that will activate conceptually driven processing and a summary or conclusion that confirms and recaps the important information and insights offered in the text. A reader will best remember the last words of a paragraph or essay, and as a writer you want the last words your reader processes to be important. By following this advice you can actually avoid the negative consequences of interference and thereby help your reader to retain the most important concepts.

## EXPECTATIONS, PRIOR KNOWLEDGE, AND EXPERT KNOWLEDGE

When we approach any text, our expectations, prior knowledge, and individual expertise all affect our ability to process that text.

What factors influence our expectations about texts? We form some expectations based on the genre in which the text is written. The genre is the class to which the text belongs—newspaper article, editorial, instructional manual, proposal, scientific paper, novel, poem, etc.—and each genre has a range of acceptable contextual material and an expected form. For example, a journalist's personal opinion is not appropriate in reporting a presidential press conference for a front-page feature story, but is appropriate material for the editorial page. We also have expectations based on facts we have learned throughout our lives. If we read a story about the launch of a space shuttle, we expect to hear that the shuttle was launched into the vacuum of space, not that it is floating around the earth in a liquid ether, as was believed true until the early part of the twentieth century.

The expectations we form and hold about what is to come in a text are shaped by prior knowledge.[15] As an extreme example, the Bushmen in Africa would not understand a comment about launching the space shuttle because they have no concept of space flight. Frequently, we, too, must deal with the limitations of our own prior knowledge. If you are not a mechanic, trying to read your car's maintenance manual in order to perform a simple tune-up may prove impossible. If you have no legal training and are buying your first house, the contracts necessary to close on the house can be nearly impenetrable, and you may be at the mercy of the real estate agent, lawyer, or banker who offers to explain them to you in what he believes are "simple terms." And how many people have been baffled by the explanations doctors have given of their ailments? In each case a text has been constructed by speakers or writers with particular expertise—made possible by their prior knowledge of the field—and written or spoken as if the reader or listener shares the expert's knowledge.

Experts and novices differ not only in the quality of knowledge they have on a given subject; they also differ in how they organize that knowledge. Much expert knowledge is stored in memory in the form of heuristics (techniques/aids for solving problems and dealing with complex information), rules, strategies, spatial arrays (such as matrixes, charts, and graphs), and schemas that allow experts to process information.[16] Schemas provide templates by which experts process new information. When experts encounter texts, they automatically call to mind schemas that will allow them to recognize and extract the pertinent material, quickly chunk it into meaningful units, and relate it to other already known information. Typically, the schema provides information about the nature of material that should be contained within the type of text presented (for example, an editorial will present an opinion on a controversial topic) and information about the purpose of the text (such as instructing the reader how to use a new software program). Thus, schemas provide a controlling framework or a set of parameters that the reader uses to begin to comprehend the significance of the incoming new information.

To make texts communicate more effectively, we need to learn to exploit experts' methods: chunk material into sections to help readers to better process new information, and utilize plans and heuristics to organize texts effectively. This will help not only the novice, speeding up learning by providing guidance to perform conceptually driven processing; it will also help the expert, who will appreciate a streamlined text which allows her to quickly extract the essential information.

Speakers and writers always assume that they share a certain amount of knowledge with their audience. However, the number of times writers actually create texts for an audience that share their same prior knowledge is probably much smaller than we think. Writers depend heavily not only on shared conceptual prior knowledge, but also on shared schemas. As communicators, the further we move from common everyday experience toward material that requires specialized learning, the more we must be aware of the potential shrinking pool of knowledge we may share with our audience. Therefore, we must consciously help our lay audience to construct schemas and conceptualize the information, by including overviews, headings, and summaries, and by highlighting or repeating key concepts.

Many texts must, in fact, be read by nonexperts or by mixed audiences that include experts, relatively informed lay people, and even uninformed lay people. For example, a proposal for a new city airport will be read by city planners, architects, government officials, engineers, and city and rural residents. Some groups will be interested in the costs associated with the project, others in the economic impact on the city, and some will be interested in the environmental impact. Very few will have the expertise to understand every aspect of the plan, but the proposal can be written so that it is accessible to all: by dividing the proposal into sections, and by using headings to signal which sections are appropriate for the expert and which are appropriate for the lay person. Overviews and summaries of the most important aspects of the project can be written in lay people's terms so that the nonexpert can get the gist of the ideas. (The expert will simply skim or skip this information and turn to the more specific charts and tables.) All readers benefit from this type of textual design: the lay person obtains at least a minimal understanding of the project in general—as well as an understanding of how his particular concerns are being addressed—and the various experts also find the information they require to consider and complete the project.

## ORGANIZATIONAL STRATEGIES

Two different organizational strategies can be used to facilitate different learning processes: object organization and aspect organization.[17] If the writer uses object organization, he focuses on each item, going through all of its aspects or qualities and then proceeding to the next item. When the writer uses aspect organization, he focuses on the aspects of items that can be compared or contrasted. The writer examines the same aspect for all objects being compared, and then proceeds to the next aspect and repeats the process.

This may remind you of two different approaches to writing persuasive essays. For a given issue you can state the proponent's side in total and then state the opponent's. To organize by object you could first give the Democrats' platform and then the Republicans'. To organize by aspect take each factor (aspect) of the issue and examine each side's position, for example, compare the Democrats' and Republicans' views on the budget deficit, foreign aid, and women's rights. Many kinds of texts, reports, and proposals can be organized by choosing one of these options; the choice will often depend on what you perceive to be your audience's needs. What if you have to write a report on two or more companies bidding for a job? Employing object organization, you could divide the report into sections on each bidding company, giving their charges, ability to stay on schedule, service record, etc. Employing aspect organization, you could divide the report into sections based on costs, ability to meet deadlines, service record, etc., and compare companies in each of these sections. In fact, the most useful way to organize the report may be to use aspect organization in the body of the report (each aspect could be a section) and then use object organization (an overall comparison of the two companies) in the conclusion.

When choosing how to organize a text, consider your audience and how you want them to approach the information. Object organization requires little prior knowledge of the material, and it is more accessible to the inexperienced reader. Aspect organization facilitates conceptually driven processing, engaging the reader in elaborative rehearsal. A reader (usually only a well-informed or expert reader) may perform elaborative rehearsal on an object-organized text, but the writer cannot count on such rehearsal happening, since the text does not invite that kind of processing. Aspect-organized texts, in general, require more reading and processing time, but a text organized in this fashion is often more useful to readers with some prior knowledge of the subject.

## DESIGNING TEXTS TO FACILITATE COMPREHENSION

In practical terms, what can we do to produce texts that are easier to comprehend? Consider using the following elements of textual design to facilitate processing and learning.[18]

*Organize:* Clear organization is fundamental to creating accessible texts. Simply stringing a sequence of ideas together using rhetorical connectors such as "first," "second," and "third" does not create logical coherence. Organization needs to be based on logical connections that exist between the concepts under discussion. Good organization facilitates conceptually driven processing, chunking, and the activation of schemas in LTM that aid in learning. Organization can be improved and made more explicit by:

    1) *Overviews or introductions:* These tell the reader the purpose of the text and provide information about the nature of the informa-

tion to follow. The writer conveys her intentions and the expectations that she believes the reader should have about what the text will accomplish.

2) *Advanced organizers:* Tables of contents and menus facilitate learning by telling the audience where they are, what step they are on, and where they will be going.

3) *Hierarchical ordering:* Items should be ranked in order of importance. Items that are superordinate—presented as most important—will be remembered best. Put the most important item first and work down to the least important, or start with the least significant item and build up to the most significant. In either case make sure you have a logical strategy in mind for developing your text; logical organization will make the text easier to comprehend.

*Create Goals or Provide Meaningful Tasks:* If the audience knows they are working toward a goal, such as completing a project (like running a computer program correctly or assembling a bicycle), they will work harder to understand the text. Therefore, make sure your objectives are clearly presented to the reader. You may want to encourage the reader by breaking the task down into smaller stages and pointing out the achievement of minor goals. The accomplishment of small tasks culminates in the completion of the project. A reader will then find satisfaction in meeting short-term expectations while working toward the completion of long-term goals.

If there is not a task or goal around which you can design the text, you may still be able to engage the reader in conceptual processing. When asked to answer a question, fill out a chart, summarize what has been read, or solve a problem using the new information, a reader will engage in elaborative rehearsal and learn the information more effectively.

*Highlight Critical Items:* You can highlight important points for your reader with titles and headings, as well as by placing the essential ideas in first and last sentences of paragraphs and in the subject position in the sentence. Headings should not be empty, generic headings like "introduction," "major factors," and "conclusion" (unless required by the genre), since these do not facilitate conceptualization. Use headings that highlight key terms and concepts or that orient the reader in terms of the task you wish her to perform (e.g., "starting the computer," "installing the program"). Topic sentences and grammatical subjects of sentences can also be used to highlight important information and thereby facilitate conceptually driven processing. Information presented first, as suggested by the primacy effect, is among that remembered best.

*Create Manageable Units:* For a complex task or concept, it is best to group data into clusters of about five elements (chunking), under a heading that provides a conceptual framework by which to interpret the elements. By limiting the number of elements in each grouping, you make sure that you do not overload the reader's data-driven processing capacity.

*Concretizations and Analogies:* Concretizations make concepts and abstract ideas easier to imagine and identify. Concretizations can be created through examples, well-labeled diagrams, charts, pictures, and spatial representations. (Remember experts often prefer diagrams, charts, and other spatial and visual representations rather than a lengthy written explanation. They rely on spatial arrays and schemas already stored in LTM to process new data. As writers we can help our audience conceptually process information if we carefully introduce some of the techniques used by the experts.)

Analogies are mental images invoked by comparing a new, unfamiliar object to a common object. For example, "the word processor is a typewriter that doesn't require a carriage return at the end of the line and that enhances a writer's ability to edit as he writes." The unfamiliar object or concept is demystified by comparison to the common object. (Usually an analogy first shows how the two objects are similar and then points out how the unfamiliar object differs from the more common one.)

Conceptualization and analogy are particularly useful when you have an audience who does not share your prior knowledge. Both techniques facilitate processing unfamiliar material by providing the audience with a point of reference from their own prior experience.

These design elements can be used to construct informative, evaluative, and persuasive texts that are intended to be conceptually processed, as well as to construct data-driven texts such as instruction manuals and reference guides. (Advanced organizers are a great aid to the frequent user of such manuals and guides, since they allow readers to find quickly the particular section they need rather than demanding that they read through the whole text.) Different design elements take precedence in different types of texts. For example, analogies and examples are appropriate for textbooks where the writer intends that the reader learn the concepts. But analogies and examples are not useful in texts written to describe a task that will only be performed once, such as a set of instructions for assembling a child's toy. As a writer, you select the design elements appropriate for your text and for your particular audience.

## APPLICATION

I will end this chapter by posing a problem for you that will illustrate how an understanding of the concepts presented in this chapter can help a writer to design a text. It invites you to engage in elaborative rehearsal of the material presented in this chapter.

### *Problem*

The benefits clerk took the following notes at a meeting on the company's new insurance plan. The clerk has been asked to prepare a brochure for the company. Chunk the following material so it is easier to comprehend (so that a company employee can easily access and refer to the material) and prepare the text for the brochure.

M- —No coverage of preexisting conditions on Major Medical
—Automatic $12,000 term life, paid by employer

D  — —75 percent of orthodontics costs covered
—All full-time employees are covered—no contribution required

D — —Dental benefits = preventive treatment, 100 percent; other major charges, 80 percent

M— —Major Medical—fifty dollar deductible for each hospital admission
—Optional term life—200 percent of your annual salary. Employee pays fifty cents per $1,000

F- —Part-time employees, spouses, and children each pay forty dollars a month for coverage

D — —Annual deductible—dental—fifty dollars on major dental care

M- —Major Medical exclusions—acupuncture, chiropractic services

F- —Children must be added into coverage within thirty days of birth

D- —Dental exclusions = preexisting conditions and occlusions

M- —Eligible expenses of Major Medical—hospital stays, diagnostics, hospice, and home health

L- —Life insurance may be purchased for spouse and children at additional cost

# 3

## *Alternative Grammars (Part I)—Transformational Grammar*

Do you know what a gerund is? Are you baffled by progressives and perfectives? Did you know that adverbs can modify adjectives? More than likely, you are a member of the vast majority of people who are either unfamiliar with, or who have a less than perfect knowledge of, the traditional "parts of speech" grammar. For many, it has been years since they studied grammar and they have forgotten much of the information; others simply were not taught grammar adequately during their formative years. Educators find that most adults have a sense of what a subject is, what a verb is, and what a noun is. Beyond that we are often treading on thin ice when we discuss sentence structure in the workplace or classroom.

The development of alternative grammars was not prompted by a need for a simplified grammar, but rather by a desire to find a grammar that better described the way the mind actually processes language.[1] What you will find, as we discuss two of the most influential and powerful alternative grammars, is that they enable us to discuss language with writers without having to completely reteach traditional grammar in the process. Chomsky's generative transformational grammar works with only a few basic units: noun phrases, verb phrases, prepositional phrases, and the units that constitute each of those phrase types. Case grammar, first developed by Charles Fillmore, and also known as role relation grammar, defines and categorizes nouns based on their function in relation to the verb; it is a commonsense approach to grammar based on the type of information that words convey in a sentence.

## GENERATIVE TRANSFORMATIONAL GRAMMAR

Generative transformational grammar is a dynamic grammar system created by Noam Chomsky to explain how we can be confident that the utterances we create are acceptable and will be understood. Chomsky's goal was to explain language creativity: how we are able to utter and interpret sentences we have not heard before. Creativity is made possible by the generative nature of transformational grammar. In order to create and understand newly generated sentences, we must depend on our language competence. Our competence derives from our knowledge of grammar: grammar shapes each of our utterances, setting the boundaries for what is acceptable and ensuring that we will be understood. We compose and structure each of our utterances based on our knowledge of what is acceptable according to the grammatical system.[2]

Chomsky's model is composed of the elements shown in the diagram on p. 41.

## WORD CONCEPTS

Word concepts exist in the mind prior to the formation of any sentence. The words are in no particular order and are unmarked. Unmarked refers to the fact that there are no inflections added to the words to indicate such information as whether the word is plural, possessive, or past tense. You can think of an unmarked form as corresponding to the lexical entry for a word that you would look up in the dictionary. You look up "break" instead of "broken" or "breaking." The dictionary often

**Producing Sentences by Transformational Grammar**

*[handwritten marginalia: traditional grammar gives account of things as you find them in place]*

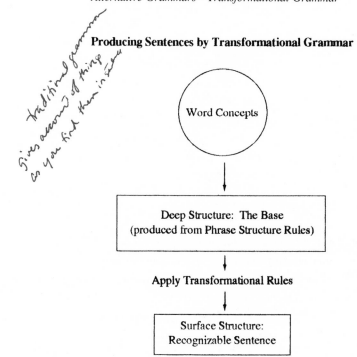

Word Concepts

↓

Deep Structure: The Base
(produced from **Phrase Structure Rules**)

↓

**Apply Transformational Rules**

↓

Surface Structure:
Recognizable Sentence

cites more than one possible meaning and/or part of speech for the word ("break" can be used as a verb or a noun). The particular meaning of the word is indicated by how the word is used and its position relative to the other elements of the sentence. To compose or interpret a sentence we must determine if the word is to be used as a verb or noun. If it is to be used as a noun, will it be a subject or an object? If it is to be used as a verb, does it require an object or a prepositional phrase? In addition, will the verb require an auxiliary or a modal? And in what order can these words occur, if they are to be properly understood?

Answering these questions, determining how we add inflections and choose an acceptable word order—to create a correct syntactic structure—is at the core of Chomsky's grammar. Chomsky is not interested in words and their meanings, but rather in accounting for how word concepts are modified, through inflections, and then ordered to create understandable sentences. This multistepped process of ordering

*[handwritten: what happens in our brain when we chunk things together]*

and modification constitutes the syntactic description at the heart of transformational grammar. Word concepts are combined using phrase structures (rules that provide information about the skeletal structure of a sentence) to form a base. The base is a deep structure representation. It is an utterance that contains words, information on how to put the words into an acceptable order, and information on inflections, modals, and auxiliaries that need to be added. However, this information does not yet provide a recognizable sentence (a surface structure) that we would speak, write, or understand; that requires further transformations.

Why did Chomsky develop such a complex notion? The components and steps of this process are intended to represent how people actually utilize language units and language rules that they have learned in order to speak and understand their language.

## THE BASE—PHRASE STRUCTURE RULES

The phrase structure rules provide some of the basic information about how to order and combine word concepts. The word concepts are treated as a given or prerequisite that undergoes syntactic transformation.[3] Therefore, in all practicality, the model begins with a description of the base, particularly with how the phrase structure rules account for the skeletal structure of the sentence.

The phrase structure rules explain how the basic units of a sentence are assembled. Chomsky explains that they are basically "rewriting" rules. For instance: a sentence can be rewritten as a noun phrase plus a verb phrase. In the notation of transformational grammar, this rule is written as: $S \rightarrow NP + VP$. Such derivations, as the process of rewriting sentences in terms of their constituents is called, always proceed from a single unit to a string of constituent units (or from a smaller string of units to a string with a greater number of units). A noun phrase can simply be a noun such as "he" in the sentence "he walks." And a verb phrase can have only a single element, as the verb "walks" in the same sentence. But the noun phrase can also contain many other elements such as articles, adjectives, and adverbs that modify the noun. And the verb phrase may contain an auxiliary verb such as "is" and/or a modal verb such as "will." Sentences may also contain more than one noun or verb phrase, as well as a number of prepositional phrases. In all cases, English sentences must have at least one noun phrase and one verb phrase.

Word concepts and the phrase structure rules provide all the material we need to create a well-formed sentence that is simple, active, and declarative. All sentences in deep structure are simple, active, and declarative, and are called kernel sentences. Transformations performed on the base—in deep structure—before it becomes a recognizable utterance—a surface structure—create complex and compound sentences, passives, and other sentence types such as interrogatives (questions), imperatives (commands), and negatives.[4]

Let us now look at the phrase structure rules that yield the base. The following table first lists the phrase structure rule in the notation of transformational grammar, followed by an explanation. We work backwards from the complete sentence to a description of its smallest component parts. Here you will notice a departure from the traditional parts of speech grammar. We do not speak of direct objects, indirect objects, or complements, but only of three phrase types: noun, verb, and prepositional phrases. Obviously, when children learn language they have no concept of the categories of objects and complements, but transformational grammarians believe that they do learn to distinguish between these three phrase types.

### Phrase Structure Rules[5]

Note: Parentheses signal optional elements.
1. S → NP + VP. A sentence can be rewritten as a noun phrase plus a verb phrase.
2. NP → (DET) N. A noun phrase *must have* a noun and *may have* a determiner. A determiner can be an article and/or an adjective. For example, in the phrase "the intercontinental missile" there

are two determiners, the article "the" and the adjective "intercontinental."

3. VP → V (NP) (PP). A verb phrase, also known as a predicate, *must* have a verb and *may have* a noun phrase and/or a prepositional phrase. For example, consider the sentence, "He sang a song to his sister." In the verb phrase "sang a song to his sister" "a song" is a noun phrase, and "to his sister" is a prepositional phrase. "Sang," the verb alone, as in "He sang," could also be used as a complete verb phrase. "Sang a song," a verb followed by a noun phrase, V(NP), could also be used as a verb phrase. Finally, "sang to his sister" could also be used; here, we have the verb followed by a prepositional phrase, V(PP).

4. V → aux + verb. The verb consists of the verb plus its auxiliary.

5. Aux → Tense (+ M). The auxiliary must have tense, either past or present. (Past tense is generally marked with "ed" as in "walked" or a change in the stem vowel of the verb, as in "ran.") The auxiliary may also take an optional modal verb: "have" and "be" create progressives and perfectives.[6] The other modals are: "will," "would," "can," "could," "shall," "should," "may," "might," and "must."

6. PP → prep + NP. A prepositional phrase has a preposition plus a noun phrase, such as "to the woods." (This noun phrase can then be further broken down employing rule 2).

## TRANSFORMATIONAL RULES

Transformational rules change the active declarative sentences into other sentence types. Some of these rules are obligatory, meaning they are required to produce other basic sentence types such as questions (interrogatives), commands (imperatives), and negatives. Others are optional and produce stylistic variations, most significantly the passive structure. Interrogatives, imperatives, and negative sentences can all be explained by one transformational rule:

7. Sentence → (NEG) (Q or Imp) NP + VP.

A sentence *must have* a NP and VP. It *can be* a question or command. In addition, a declarative, imperative, or interrogative sentence *can be* made negative.

Chomsky's descriptions of sentences are called derivations, and they are expressed as tree diagrams. Let us now look at a transformational description of a sentence. Since we are interested in describing how real sentences arise, we start with the recognizable sentence and work back to a description of how it was put together.

The distributor has sent the computer to the office.

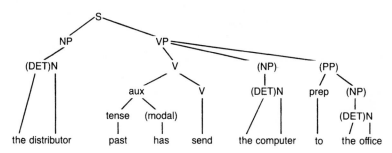

You will notice that the base elements are no longer in the same order as the surface structure elements. Transformational grammar also includes a set of rules for assembling elements in the right order, which we will not pursue here.

The second example illustrates how a basic sentence type, other than the declarative sentence, is described.[7]

Must you go home?

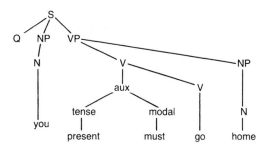

Now, let's look at one optional, stylistic transformation—the one used to generate passive sentences. The rules for passive transformations are included here because most writers, at one time or another, are faced with the task of eliminating passive sentences from their texts. By understanding how passive sentences arise from active ones, we can more easily change our passive discourse into active discourse.

Passive sentences are derived from active sentences. For example, the passive sentence "The boxes are carried by the movers" is derived from the active sentence, "The movers carried the boxes." We will start with the passive sentence, since we are usually trying to revise to create a more active prose style (and because in transformational grammar we work back to the active kernel sentence). The above sentence can be described as follows:

$$\text{The boxes} \quad \text{were} \quad \text{carried} \quad \text{by} \quad \text{the movers.}$$
$$NP_1 \;+\; \text{"be"} \;+\; V + by \;+\; NP_2$$

In every passive sentence there are two noun phrases that are labeled $NP_1$ and $NP_2$. To create an active sentence:

1. Cross out "by."
2. Cross out the "to be" auxiliary which is usually "is," "are," "was," or "were." (Sometimes you will also have to change the inflection of the verb form.)
3. Reverse the order of the noun phrases.

The sentence then becomes:

$$\text{The movers carried the boxes.}$$

Passive sentences always contain two noun phrases, even if they are not both evident in the surface structure. For instance, "he was tricked" still implies that he was tricked *by someone*. Thus sometimes, when analyzing passive sentences, we need to look for an $NP_1$ + be + V where the $NP_2$ is deleted. The rewrite to an active sentence first requires identifying the deleted second NP.[8]

You can also make your prose more active by deleting structures consisting of a pronoun + a form of the "to be" verb, such as "it was," "it were," "they were," "that was," "that is," and "that were." While not directly described by the passive transformation rule under discussion, these structures also quite commonly generate unnecessary passive constructions. Cross out the pronoun + "to be" verb and restructure the sentence around the true subject and verb.

> It was then that I discovered the true solution to the problem.
> ~~It was~~ then ~~that~~ I discovered the true solution to the problem.
> Then I discovered the true solution to the problem.

Sometimes you will have to identify the action verb that has been buried or deleted by this weak verb construction. Simply restructure the sentence around the true active verb.

> There were five regional representatives at the meeting.
> ~~There were~~ five regional representatives (attended) the meeting.
> Five regional representatives attended the meeting.

Rewriting passive sentences as active sentences creates more vivid prose that conveys the writer's intended meaning more precisely.[9]

## GENERATING AND ANALYZING COMPOUND AND COMPLEX SENTENCES

All the sentences we have examined so far have been simple sentences. Transformational grammar also accounts for compound and complex sentences by demonstrating how they arise from the combination of two or more simple sentences; this process is called recursiveness. In turn, compound and complex sentences can be analyzed by breaking them down into their component simple sentences.

Compound sentences are created by combining two or more independent clauses (simple sentences) with a coordinating conjunction such as "and," "but," or "or." For example, "he took his last test yesterday and then he celebrated the end of the term" would be described as:

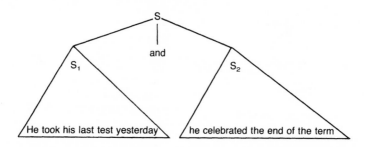

Subordination is the result of embedding one clause within another, which gives rise to complex sentences. One of the most common ways to generate a sentence containing a subordinate clause is by employing a relative pronoun such as "which," "who," or "that." For example, the sentence "The lawyer, who is a good judge of character, does not believe his client is telling the truth" can be broken into the two component simple sentences: 1) The lawyer is a good judge of character; 2) The lawyer does not believe his client. In this sentence, the relative pronoun "who" is used to avoid repetition of "the lawyer." The transformational grammar representation of this sentence would be:

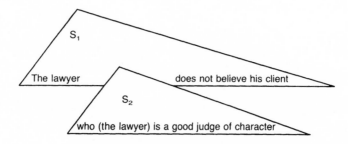

The component simple sentences can then be further broken down by applying the transformation and phrase structure rules.

## USING TRANSFORMATIONAL GRAMMAR

Powerful applications of transformational grammar can be made without having to learn all the intricacies of the system. As we have seen, recognizing how the (stylistic) optional transformations work allows us to develop a simple process for identifying and correcting passive sentences. Transformational grammar also offers an alternative to the eight parts of speech grammar that is complicated to teach and to learn because some parts can occur in numerous relations with other grammatical elements found in the sentence (for instance, an adverb can modify an adjective, verb, or another adverb, as well as introduce—and thus modify—an entire clause or sentence). In transformational grammar, we only deal with three phrase types (noun phrases, verb phrases, and prepositional phrases). A description of a sentence based on the interaction of these three phrase types is often sufficient to explain the most common syntactic errors. More importantly, reducing our discussion of grammar to a few powerful components that people readily recognize can make it easier to revise turgid prose.[10]

# 4   

## *Alternative Grammars (Part II)—Case Grammar*

As we saw, to discuss the skeletal structure of a sentence, transformational grammar still utilizes a terminology derived from traditional grammar (dividing the sentence into "parts of speech" components— such as noun, verb, and preposition—believing that these components probably represent how we process verbal and written information). However, other linguists believe that these elements do not provide a natural means by which to understand how components of a sentence are related and communicate a message. Yet, in another proposed alternative grammar, case grammar, the base elements of the utterance provide not only syntactic information (on the functional relationships between the elements in the sentence), but also semantic information (about meaning).[1] Challenging the purely syntactic model of transformational grammar, case grammar is a model in which syntax and semantics (meaning) interact. By developing a model in which sentence structure and meaning are related, Charles Fillmore intended to provide a grammar that could account for how we perceive objects and ideas interacting in our world, as well as a grammar that could better illuminate how we express those perceptions through language.

## THE CASE GRAMMAR MODEL

In case grammar, the sentence is first divided into two primary parts: the verb—the action of the sentence—and its arguments. The "arguments" are the various noun phrases found in the sentence. Each noun phrase has a function, or role, defined in terms of its relation to the verb. Verbs often do, in fact, determine which noun phrases will be found in a sentence and in what role. Consider the verb "strike." "Striking" is an action which only a person or animate being can perform. The role of the person or being is "agent." Though we have determined that the verb "strike" requires an agent, as "the man strikes" illustrates, that information alone is not enough to create a complete grammatical sentence. The verb "strike" also requires an object or being acted upon. The being acted upon is called the "patient." In "the man strikes the dog," "dog" is the patient. In traditional grammar we would say the verb is transitive (requires a direct object). But case grammar provides more information about the nature of the object, addressing how the elements of the sentence are related semantically, and how they function in relation to one another.

Writers intimidated by, or unfamiliar with, traditional grammar may find that the analysis of noun phrases according to their roles in a sentence is an effective method for dealing with some of the grammatical issues in texts. It is fairly easy to identify the function of each noun phrase in a sentence. Below is a list of common roles that noun phrases can occupy.[2] To aid in your understanding of role types, I have also included how these roles sometimes relate to traditional parts of speech, as well as how certain roles may require specific phrase or sentence structures and/or particular prepositions.

### Common Roles for Animate Beings

Agent: Animate being who instigates an action. The agent is generally found in the subject position. Agent can also follow the prepositions "by" or "with," particularly in passive sentences.

> *The principal* ordered the students to end the demonstration.
> Plato was taught by *Socrates*.

Patient: Animate being affected by the action. Patients are passive—beings acted upon. The patient is often found in the direct object position. And the direct object position in English does not require a preposition.

> The babysitter fed *the toddler.*

Experiencer: Animate being emotionally or cognitively affected by an event or characterized by an emotional ("distress," "elation") or cognitive state ("consider," "believe"). The experiencer can appear as the subject of a cognitive or emotive verb. (These verbs will not take the progressive—"is being" or "was being," as in "Catherine is being unhappy.")

> *Modern people* know that the world is not flat.
> *Jews* do not believe Jesus is the Messiah.
> *She* is saddened by the loss.

Often experiencers are expressed spatially. The "heart" or other organs afflicted by emotions, as well as cognitive structures such as the "brain," "mind," and "consciousness" are represented as the location in which the experience takes place or to which it comes. Thus, these organs and structures appear as autonomous entities. While we cannot say "my legs took me for a walk," we sometimes do tolerate speaking—especially in creative or metaphoric prose—of our organs as detached from our body when we speak of emotive or cognitive experiences.

> Envy seized his *soul.*
> The sensuality of the statue of the Madonna struck his *eye.*
> *My mind* was the victim of conflicting thoughts. (Rather than, I was the victim of conflicting thoughts.)

Experiencers can appear as the objects of the preposition "to."

> The music was pleasing to *me.*

Experiencers can also appear as the direct objects of verbs with an in-/en- prefix.

The water *in*vigorated *me*.

Opponent (Malefactor): Animate being who deters one from acts and goals. Opponent can be found in the subject position or following the preposition "by." Opponent is used with a verb signifying deterrence.

The groupie was prevented from entering by *the security guard*.

Adjuvant (Benefactor): Animate being who aids one in accomplishing his acts and goals. Adjuvant can be found in the subject position or following the preposition "by." Adjuvant is used with a verb signifying help or aid.

*Cinderella's Fairy Godmother* gave her a dress and a coach to go to the ball.

Possessor: Animate being defined by the fact that it has an object. Many grammarians view the possessor as a location in which an object is found. Possessor may be the subject of verbs such as "have," "hold," "keep," and "belongs to."

*The President* has more political clout than anyone in America.

The possessor can also be used as a modifier, identified by " 's" or following the preposition "of."

The CPA does the *shopkeeper's* taxes.
She is the third daughter of *the king of England*.

### Common Roles for Inanimate Objects

Force: Inanimate force that has NO VOLITION and that is the cause or perpetrator of the resulting action.

*The tornado* destroyed five houses.

Instrument: Inanimate object employed to elicit the ensuing action. (These are objects that must be wielded by an agent/animate being.) Instrument often follows the preposition "with."

Professor Plum did it, with *the rope,* in the dining room.

An instrument can also occur in the subject position with certain verbs. In this case the agent is implicit.

*The car* struck the telephone pole.

Object: Inanimate object affected by the action of the verb. The object may occur in the direct object position and does not require a preposition in that position.

The fly ball broke *the window.*

Possessions are a particular type of object, defined by their relation to a noun phrase in the possessor role.

The CPA does the shopkeeper's *taxes.*

*Places and Movement*

Location: Place in which action occurs. The being or object found at a location is static. Location can follow certain prepositions such as "at," "in," "on," and "under." (Note, in English, that some confusion can occur since "on" and "in" can be used to indicate movement and direction. These prepositions are then associated with the role "path.")

Professor Plum did it, with the rope, in *the dining room.*

Location can also be the subject of a sentence.

> At sunset, *the dock* is romantic.

Source: Place of origin or direction from which something or someone comes. Source can be a place or an animate being (sender) and often follows a preposition.

> The present came from *his grandmother.*

Goal: Place or direction in which something or someone goes. Goal can be a place or an animate being (receiver). Goal often follows the preposition "to" and is often found in the indirect object position if the goal is an animate object.

> The waiter gave the bill to *him.* OR
> The waiter gave *him* the bill.[3]

Path: Route taken by a being or object. The path may be implied rather than directly stated. It is extremely rare that path will be used as the subject of a sentence. Path is found with many common prepositions including: "around," "by," "across," "over," "through," "along," and "on."

> The thief doubled back through *the alley* to escape the police.

A noun phrase can have more than one role in a sentence. For instance, in the sentence "The boss gave the secretary a raise," the boss is the secretary's benefactor, as well as the agent responsible for the action. In the sentence "Czar Nicholas' body was riddled with bullets," Czar Nicholas' body could be called either patient or location. (The army would probably prefer to call it a location, dehumanizing Nicholas.) In the sentence "Grandmother gave him a gift," grandmother is both the agent and the source of the gift.

To begin with, you may find it easier to deal with a more limited list of roles. The following roles will suffice to analyze many common writing problems that need attention: agent, patient, instrument, object, and location. Keep in mind these simple definitions:

—agent is responsible for the action

—patient is the one affected by the action

—instrument is an object used to accomplish the action

—object is a thing acted on

—location is the place where the action occurs

As you become accustomed to this terminology, which will happen very quickly, you can add more roles and nuances of the roles to the list you are already using. As a writer, you may find that looking at the elements of the sentence in terms of their function is simpler and more appealing than trying to deal with traditional grammar, since roles are easy to define and identify.

## ROLES IN ACTIVE AND PASSIVE SENTENCES

Using case grammar, some useful generalizations can be made about the relation of the active declarative sentence, which has subject-verb-object word order, to passive sentences. If the agent appears in an active sentence, it will be the subject. For example:

*Sigma Chemical* polluted the neighborhood lake.

In a passive sentence the agent is moved to a less prominent position, and the patient or object becomes the subject.

The lake was polluted by Sigma Chemical.

Oftentimes, the writer will then delete the "by agent" phrase; then, the agent is cloaked.

The lake was polluted.

Experienced writers often deliberately use passive structures to obscure agency, to mask the identity of the party performing the action. These structures are also used when the writer wants the object or patient in the prominent subject position and when the agent is obvious or irrelevant. As responsible writers, we must be sure to include the agent when it is essential, and delete the agent—and create passive prose—only under the appropriate circumstances.

Other roles may be deliberately deleted if they can be easily inferred from the context of the text. Transitive action verbs require an agent, a patient or object, and may take an instrument. In the sentence "She hit the baseball," the instrument is deleted. We assume that the instrument is a bat, unless another, less likely instrument is specified.

## CASE GRAMMAR AS AN EDITING AID

Case grammar can be used to identify a variety of sentence problems. Here, we shall examine how it can be used to identify and correctly assign agency, as well as how it can help to remedy the problem of obscurity resulting from assigning multiple roles to a single noun phrase.

### The Agency Problem

Clarifying agency is a major issue in many areas of writing today. Why is agency sometimes obscure? Writers may deliberately mask agency to avoid the issue of responsibility; this is popular in propaganda and advertising. For many years, there was a move to suppress agency in scientific prose. Scientists believed that if the prose concentrated on the object of inquiry rather than on the agent, the prose would be more objective. Today this position is being challenged, and the problems that arise from displacing agency in scientific prose will be addressed here. Finally, we look at how the agent is often absent in the prose of insecure writers, particularly if the agent is "I." Afraid to assert their own authority, these writers deny agency and end up with prose heavily laden with passive sentences. If writers reintroduce agency into their prose, the problem of passive prose often disappears. Let us now examine various cases where agency has been deleted and discuss how case grammar can be used to analyze and edit such prose.

## Deliberately Masked Agency

First, let's look at how agency is treated in two different passages. In the first passage from "Three Mile Island," what is the role of "instruments" in the first and last sentence?

> But their instruments still show that the water in the pressurizer is off the high end of the scale. The pressure in the reactor may be dangerously low, but there is no way of telling, because the instruments are lying. (Michael Gray, "Three Mile Island")[4]

We would expect "instruments" to be in the role of instrument. But in this passage the instruments are, in fact, agents. However, this is an ironic usage, since instruments can't lie, only people can. Instruments will only be observed to be "lying" if they are malfunctioning or mis-read. Taken within the context of the whole article, this passage suggests that any malfunctions or misreadings are the result of human errors in calibrating the instruments or carelessness in servicing and reading them. Nevertheless, the party responsible for the catastrophe has been deliberately masked by the author. No person seems responsible. Since objects are named and people are absent, blame cannot be placed on anyone present during the catastrophe. Using carefully constructed sentences to excuse the technicians, Gray proceeds to demonstrate how they were pawns of truly responsible agents: the nuclear industry and the designers who did not disclose certain dangers, and the government, whose concern about negative publicity prevented them from promptly responding to the crisis.

In the second passage from "The Atomic Bombing of Nagasaki as Told by a Flight Member,"[5] what roles can be assigned to "destiny" and to "winds"?

> But at this moment no one yet knows which one of the several cities chosen as targets is to be annihilated. The final choice lies with destiny. The winds over Japan will make the decision. If they carry heavy clouds over our primary target, that city will be saved, at least for the time being. . . . The winds of destiny seemed to favor certain Japanese cities that must re-

main nameless. We circled about them again and again and
found no opening in the thick umbrella of clouds that covered
them. Destiny chose Nagasaki as the ultimate target.

The sentence, "The final choice lies with destiny" could be restated as
"destiny makes the choice." "Destiny" functions as an agent. Agency is
obscured by the fact that the agent has been displaced to the end of the
sentence following "with." Destiny is also the agent in the last sentence,
"Destiny chose Nagasaki." We expect "destiny" to occupy the role of
force. However, destiny is not assigned the role of a nonvolitional force,
since it is the subject of the verb "chose" that requires a subject that is an
animate being. Destiny is not an animate being, but is represented by
the author as an agent. The same thing is true of "winds." "Winds"
should also occur in the role of force. Even though the predicates linked
to winds—"make the decision" and "favor"—define actions that require animate beings as agents, "winds" rather than people are presented as agents. Responsibility is again obscured to protect the agent
immediately responsible for the bombing—the bombers themselves.

The narrator of this account was a member of the crew that bombed
Nagasaki. By assigning winds and destiny the roles of agents (whether
consciously or not), he is able to deny his culpability, claiming it was
not men, but greater forces that determined which Japanese citizens
would die. Such displacement of responsibility is a useful tool for such
institutions as the military: if agency is displaced, then those who carry
out orders are unlikely to question commands or feel remorse about
their actions. If people realize they are responsible for their actions,
then perhaps they would not be able to carry out their orders or live with
the consequences. Obscuring agency is a powerful way to deceive the
public about who is responsible for a particular affair; therefore, it is
often a common component of propaganda and brainwashing.

### The Objectivity of Scientific Discourse

In scientific and technical writing, the agent is often deleted, and the
subject of the study is used as the subject of the discourse in order to
create the illusion of objectivity. Frequently, the writer employs passive

voice, and the text sounds stilted and becomes hard to follow. Simple syntactic manipulation does not create objectivity. Instead, rather than making the discourse clearer and seemingly more factual, deleting agency commonly creates more dense and convoluted prose.

In such discourse, objects are often inappropriately assigned to verbs requiring personal agents. For instance:

> The data conclude that more research is necessary.
> The process judges and selects the elements necessary.

Sentences such as these are quite common in scientific and technical prose. Case grammar indicates that the verbs which appear in these sentences—"conclude" and "determine"—require personal agents. But here, inanimate objects replace agents, and the result is ungrammatical, dense prose. The writer needs to identify verbs that require personal agents and to rewrite the sentences using the appropriate agents. (Another option is to replace the verb requiring a personal agent with a verb that can accommodate an inanimate subject. The verb "indicate" can be used properly with "data.")

When a writer makes an effort to emphasize the object of the action rather than the agent, confusion often arises concerning who's doing what. This is a direct consequence of the profusion of pronominal forms, such as "it" and "one," inevitably employed in passively written scientific discourse. When a passage is heavily laden with pronominals, it may be hard to determine what each individual occurrence of the pronominal refers to, as in "one analysis logically precedes the other, though one may also apply them alternately." (The first "one" refers to the analysis, and the second "one" refers to a person.) Obviously, such switching between agents and objects, common when pronominals are used extensively throughout a passage, creates unnecessary confusion. In methodology and instruction sections of technical papers, pronominals are often overused:

> (1) Benzene solution was poured into the beaker. (2) It was then placed in a distillation apparatus. (3) Then alcohol was added to it.

(4) One then shook it. (5) The mixture separated. (6) The bottom layer
was then extracted. (7) That one was placed aside.

In this passage, "it" is an unclear referent. In sentence two "it" refers to
the "benzene solution," but since "beaker" is the closest (antecedent)
noun, the reader might expect that the "it" refers back to beaker. The
reader must then take extra time to unravel the sentences in order to
arrive at the correct referent, benzene solution. In sentence three, "it"
could refer to either "apparatus" or way back to the benzene solution;
the pronominal refers to a referent which is hard to find. In sentence four,
"it" refers to the yet unnamed "mixture," first referred to in sentence
five. To avoid confusion, pronomials should not be used to refer to an
object not already named. When "it" is used to refer to more than one
object and/or is used inconsistently throughout any passage, the prose
becomes dense and confusing. More importantly, because of the unclear
references that result from using "it" in many roles, a procedure may be
reproduced incorrectly, thus calling the researcher's conclusions into
question.

In trying to emphasize the process rather than the agent, the writer
of the passage above has written in the passive voice, using verbs such
as "was poured" and "was placed." Instead of naming the agent, she has
used the elusive and nameless "one" that results in stilted prose. In this
passage, the pronominal "one" is used to refer to an agent in sentence
four and to an inanimate object (extracted layer or beaker) in sentence
seven. Reintroducing the agent into the prose will help: it will help to
eliminate the passive constructions; the agent performing the procedure
will become clear; and the objects will be found in the more natural
object and instrument roles and positions in the sentences.

> The student poured benzene solution into the beaker. She then placed
> the solution in a distillation apparatus. She added alcohol. She shook
> the mixture. The mixture separated into two layers. She extracted the
> bottom layer. She placed the beaker containing the extracted layer
> aside.

The passage still sounds rather stilted because it is written in basic,
primer style sentences; yet the passage is easier to follow, since the

passive voice has been eliminated and unclear objects are identified. Sentence combining will eliminate the primer style and reduce the repetition of the pronoun "she." Another option, more commonly employed to write procedures, is to rewrite the passage in terms of directives or imperatives. This can be done after the agents have been identified and all referents of all pronomials have been made clear. To write directives, the writer must recognize that all directives begin "you + verb." Each sentence will have a clearly implied underlying agent, "you." This underlying construction must be recognized, if the writer wants to ensure that the objects of the actions are in the correct position and that all sentences follow the same sentence pattern. This way, the "you" can be deleted from each sentence without creating obscurity. To correct the previous passage two steps are necessary. The agent performing the procedure must be identified; if the procedure is to be repeated by a reader, the implied, imperative "you" is an appropriate choice. Then, the pronomials must be sorted so clear assignment of actions and roles can be made.

> Fill the beaker with benzene solution.
> Put the solution in a distillation apparatus.
> Add alcohol.
> Shake the mixture.
> Watch the mixture separate into two layers.
> Extract the bottom layer.
> Place the beaker containing the extracted layer aside.

One more problem that commonly creeps into discourse when the writer tries to create the illusion of objectivity deserves mention: passive sentences containing nominalizations. Nominalizations are formed by the addition of suffixes such as "-ment," "-tion," and "-ance" to the verb (e.g., "creation" from "create," "displacement" from "displace"). The verb then becomes the subject, followed by a form of the "to be" verb. This results in tentative, weak prose. Such prose can be dangerous if it is intended to convey important information like a warning. A sign in a lab that states "avoidance of fumes is suggested" is much less powerful and more likely to be ignored than "avoid breathing fumes." The use of the nominalization "avoidance" obscures the message. Once writers recognize sentences containing nominalizations, they can correct these sentences by deleting the "to be" verb and rebuilding the sentence around the active verb that was the base for the nominalization.

## The Insecure Writer

If agents are absent or obscured, as a writer you will sound unassertive, as if you fear to claim credit for what you have written. You should never be afraid to be authoritative; you are always the authority for your own text. Often in trying to sound more professional and objective, a writer obscures agency by using passive sentence constructions and confuses passive constructions with past tense constructions. Frequently, the author who writes one or two passive sentences will continue in that same manner, instinctively maintaining the stylistic pattern already established. The results are disastrous; the prose will be riddled with passive sentence constructions, as in this hypothetical example of a student paper:

> After reviewing the available articles, it appears that there had been misreporting of the facts. The facts given out by the press were controlled by the government. Any statements were first looked over by government channels. And even after the statements were looked at, programming was still watched by agents.

Problems immediately arise as a result of the omission of the agent "I" from the first sentence and from the subsequent displacement of the agent throughout the passage. A pattern of passive construction has been established in which objects occupy the subject position. To create less stilted prose, the possible agents (often following the preposition "by") must be identified, and the sentences restructured around the real agents: "I" in sentence one, "press" or "government" in sentence two, "government channels" in three, and "agent" in sentence four.[6] (Press is really a patient controlled by the government, and the passage can be reconstructed to reflect that.) Passive prose sounds less vivid than active prose, because the sentences are often constructed around weak, imprecise verbs like "give," "make," "do," "go," and "take." Once writers turn their passive sentences into active ones, they find it easier to come up with more vivid and precise verbs. Since active sentence structures are easier to manipulate, subsequent revisions will create more forceful and precise prose. The earlier example can be revised to read:

> After reviewing the available articles, I concluded that the press had misreported the facts. The government controlled the facts disseminated by the press. First, government channels censored any statements. And even after censoring was completed, agents still monitored the programming.

The passage now sounds more assertive and forceful, and sentences are constructed around more precise and vivid verbs.

Dangling modifiers are another common problem, as in the sentence: "Having adjourned the meeting, we stood up and left." Most cases of obscurity result from the fact that the agent of the dependent clause is not the same as the agent of the main clause. (Participial clauses beginning with the "-ing" form of the verb seem to create the most problems.) The writer simply needs to identify who or what is performing the action in the dependent clause and to add that agent back into the dependent clause, or to rewrite the sentence so the agent is the same in both clauses.

A series of questions can be devised to help writers identify agents and recognize and develop appropriate sentence structures. The writer should ask himself:

1. Who or what is performing the action? This question identifies the agent.
2. What object or person is acted upon? This identifies the patient or object.
3. With what object was the action performed? This identifies the instrument.

Such questions may also be useful for analyzing how to construct proper passive constructions, when they are indeed called for. To identify the subject of a passive sentence ask "who or what has had something done to him/her/it?" The "who" or "what" of this question identifies the patient, the subject of the passive sentence. Agent is identified by the question "by whom was the action done?" The writer must then decide if the agent must be explicitly stated, or if the agent is an optional element that can be deleted. Writers may want to develop more questions to help them to identify what other roles noun phrases occupy in their sentences. Once roles are properly identified, the writer may find it easier to revise the text. Editing and stylistic revision are much easier if the roles of the fundamental elements are explicit—or unambiguously implied—in the early drafts of a text. Continually and consciously applying this approach during the writing process will make it easier to construct clear, lucid prose. With practice, this process will eventually become intuitive.

### Multiple Roles

Dense, complicated prose also arises when a single noun phrase takes on more than one functional role. Though a noun phrase can take on more than one function, all functions must be clear. And, if too many functions are associated with a single noun phrase, the prose then becomes difficult to follow. If relations between noun phrases are inconsistent or shift within a short span of text (such as a paragraph) then the reader may become confused.[7]

Let's take, for example, a piece of philosophical prose, an excerpt from Hazel Barnes' explanation of Sartre's concepts of ego and consciousness in her introduction to *Being and Nothingness*. Philosophical prose is inherently dense because of the use of metaphysical language that is incomprehensible to most lay people. Barnes' introduction is designed to explain key concepts to the uninitiated; yet, her language is at least as dense as Sartre's.[8] In philosophic and academic texts such as this, it is often difficult to determine the roles and functional relationships of noun phrases, because the nouns are used more abstractly than in more concrete prose that is concerned with identifiable real world objects and issues. Still, case grammar may give some insights into how the passage is constructed, revealing that it is not only the unfamiliar terms that make it dense, but the syntactic structure—the relations between sentence elements—as well.

According to Sartre, the Ego is not in consciousness, which is utterly translucent, but in the world; and like the world it is the object of consciousness. This is not, of course, to say that the Ego is material but only that it is not a subject which in some sense manipulates or directs consciousness. Strictly speaking, we should never say "my consciousness" but rather "consciousness of me." This startling view is less extreme than it at first appears. It does not mean that consciousness is general, a universal pan-psyche. A consciousness is even at the start particular, for the objects of which it is conscious are particular objects and not the whole universe. Thus the consciousnesses of two persons are always individual and always self-consciousness, but to be individual and to be self-conscious does not mean to be personal. Another way of putting it is to say Ego is "on the side of psyche."[9]

Let's examine the roles of "Ego" and "consciousness" in the first three sentences, as well as the relationships of these terms to one another.[10]

*Sentence 1*: The Ego is not in consciousness, which is utterly translucent, but in the world; and like the world it is the object of consciousness.

Ego and world are objects of consciousness, patients receiving the attention of consciousness (as well as possessions of consciousness).[11] Consciousness is location, a place where Ego is not, as well as an experiencer—that is an "utterly translucent" part of the animate being—experiencing a cognitive state, spatially expressed. It can also be considered an agent working on Ego (and the possessor of Ego).

*Sentence 2*: This is not, of course, to say that the Ego is material but only that it is not a subject which in some sense manipulates or directs consciousness.

Ego is placed in the agent role, as one that does not manipulate or direct; thus its role is negated—a not-agent. By the same construction, consciousness is placed in the role of patient, but the agent manipulating consciousness is undefined and obscure. In the previous sentence, consciousness was agent and Ego was patient. Roles now appear to be reversed, though this is not the author's intent. In addition, the negation of roles—with no clear statement as to the new role of each term—makes the prose confusing. Such sentence structures beg the questions: Who (or what) is agent and who (or what) is patient? If the passage is intended to be comprehensible the reader expects the answer to follow immediately.

> *Sentence 3*: We should never say "my consciousness" but rather "consciousness of me."

Consciousness is defined as not-possession and as experiencer, cognitively experiencing the self. (This conclusion is further supported by sentence five in which consciousness is conscious of objects.) Implicitly, consciousness may still occupy the patient role since "the consciousness of me" must be perceived; consciousness is acted upon or perceived by an agent or experiencer. Ego then drops out and the agent of the next sentence is "we," though we is not the agent for the patient, consciousness.

We can already draw a few conclusions as to why this passage is dense and obtuse. There are too many roles introduced in the first few sentences, and the writer quickly shifts a noun phrase from one role to another without making the relationship between the old and new role clear. Consciousness is location, experiencer, agent, patient, and possessor, all within three sentences. It is particularly confusing to have an agent become a patient without a clear statement of how that change occurs. The definition of Ego is also hard to grasp for many reasons. First, Ego drops out of the paragraph after sentence two and does not reenter until sentence eight, where its relation to consciousness is difficult to ascertain. Its sudden absence makes the passage difficult to comprehend. In addition, the writer defines Ego by what it is not. Mentally, we proceed by identifying Ego as agent in sentence two, and then "erase" it in this role. Such negation is a standard technique in definition; but to use negation among the myriad of confusing relations expressed here, without clearly stating what Ego is (if it is not an agent), impedes comprehension. Further complicating matters is the introduction of "we" as an agent in sentence three, and "pan-psyche" as agent and experiencer in sentence four. Both we and pan-psyche appear only once in this paragraph, and due to their abrupt appearances, neither is clearly defined in relation to the main elements—consciousness and Ego.[12] If they introduce material peripheral to the main argument, their appearance here only serves to make already dense prose more obtuse. Such complexity makes the prose virtually impossible to follow.

Before revising the first few sentences, let me emphasize the main points the author intends to communicate. Consciousness is directive. Consciousness creates Ego when it analyzes the world. Consciousness acts upon Ego; Ego cannot act upon consciousness. Keeping these basic definitions and relationships in mind, the first few sentences of the paragraph can be revised so that roles are presented clearly, and so that the number and type of role relations established between various noun phrases do not overwhelm and confuse the reader:

> 1) Both the world and the Ego are objects of consciousness. 2) Ego exists in the world. 3) But Ego is not material as is the tangible world. 4) Ego does not direct consciousness; rather consciousness creates Ego. 5) Consciousness is not something we possess; rather it is an essential element of the self. 6) Therefore we should never say "my consciousness," but "consciousness of me."

*Roles:*

1. Ego and World are presented as patients (or objects) of the agent, consciousness.

2. Ego is object. World is location.

3. Ego is not tangible like the world. (Simple sentences such as two and three could be combined into one complex sentence: "While Ego exists in the world, it is not material as is the tangible world." And in turn, complex sentences can be broken down into simple sentences for analysis according to case grammar.)

4. Ego is still a patient/object of consciousness and the intangibility of Ego is reinforced.

5. Consciousness is experiencer (and as not-possession, clearly defined as not belonging to "we," the not-possessor).

6. The role of consciousness, as in sentence four, is reinforced.

In the passage above, case grammar helped to elucidate how the passage should be revised and illuminates why the revision is more intelligible. The passage is easier to follow, since the number of different role relationships has been reduced. Note how much easier it is to deduce the relationships between noun phrases. For the most part, each element is assigned one role per sentence, and the relationships between noun phrases are clearly expressed. Ego is presented consistently as an (intangible) object or patient acted upon by the agent consciousness. Consciousness is experiencer and agent. The elements of the argument are clearly presented, and the passage is more lucidly developed. (To continue with the rewrite would require changes that would continue to explore the relationship between Ego and consciousness central to the argument; therefore, Ego could not abruptly drop out and suddenly reappear later in the paragraph as it does in the original text. In addition, a concrete analogy might also help the reader to comprehend these highly abstract terms and relationships.) The revision is longer than the rewrite, so that the functions of noun phrases and relationships between them are presented unambiguously. While the expert's philosophical knowledge is still needed to ensure that the material is presented correctly, case grammar helps to ensure that the contextual material is presented in the clearest manner possible and even helps the lay reader to understand what the passage says.

One useful rule for the writer to follow, suggested by this grammar, is to limit the role of each main noun phrase to one per sentence (two at most if you are expressing a change in the element or comparing it to something else).[13] The number of relations between elements in a paragraph, such as agent-patient, possessor-possessed, should also be limited; the greater the number of relationships, the greater the potential for obscurity and miscommunication.

### More Advanced Analysis, Adding Roles
### for Specific Prose Types

As writers become comfortable with role analysis, they can add roles that are appropriate and useful for dealing with the particular types of prose they most often produce. (In all, there are probably not more than twenty-five roles that noun phrases can occupy.[14]) Remember, the strength of case grammar is the fact that it is a commonsense approach: words and phrases are analyzed according to their function and relation to one another. Therefore, the system should be kept simple and economical, yet flexible enough to accommodate the needs of writers. A few suggestions for roles to add when analyzing scientific prose include:

Result: State or object that is the result of the action. Result is found in sentences with change-of-state verbs such as "dissolve," "transform," "grow," and "become."

> The Word became *flesh*.

Cause: A specific type of agency that can be a force, animate being, inanimate object, or state. The cause is determined to be necessary if the action is to occur. This role is often found with change-of-state verbs.

> *Snow* forced the closure of the mountain passes.

Quality: State, facet, or element of an object or being. Quality is commonly found with state of being verbs such as "has" and "is."

> The exam is *difficult*.

## LIMITATION OF CASE GRAMMAR

Case grammar forms the basis of coherence studies today. Many psychologists and linguists believe that it is the model which best depicts the way the mind actually processes texts.[15] A case grammar analysis is best done during the revision process; at that time, the writer can identify and correct any sentences that are obtuse or difficult to follow.

The greatest obstacle to applying case grammar is that it requires a writer to have a good working knowledge of the topic at hand. Obviously, this is a greater problem for beginning writers. In discourse on abstract or conceptual ideas, the roles become much harder to identify, and here expertise on the topic is often necessary in order to assign the proper roles to the noun phrases. But if writers keep the need for lucid prose and clearly defined roles and role relations in mind, they will produce prose that is more intelligible. Even experts reading a text in their field appreciate more lucid prose, as it requires less of their time and effort to read and comprehend.

Certain components of sentence structure are not illuminated by case grammar. It does not address all the components of the predicate, such as tense and aspect. Nor does it help to distinguish between elements that give rise to different sentence types, such as commands and questions, though it can help to illuminate the difference between related sentence structures—active and passive. But the choice of which structure to use is still the writer's; case grammar will not dictate which structure is better. This depends on the author's intent. Indeed, there are times when the agent is implicit and need not appear in the surface structure; then the writer may choose a passive sentence structure that focuses on the object of the action. No grammar can deal with the author's intent. Intent must be discussed in terms of the pragmatics, as well as the social and interpersonal aspects of the communication situation.

While case grammar may help the writer to clarify and control the relationships between elements, it will not specify the order in which these elements should be presented. Case grammar cannot aid us in decisions about how to develop and organize texts. But, by using role analysis in conjunction with techniques presented in the next chapter that facilitate coherence, we can create superior quality prose.

## APPLICATIONS

1. Assume that the following passage is part of a report submitted to you by a junior member of your firm. Outline how you would direct

the writer to improve the passage, making use of Chomsky's transformational grammar. What pattern problem would you teach him to recognize, and how could you teach him to correct it?

> The manual was written by the company's technical writer. The editing that now needs to be done should be supervised by a technical writer. Approval of the final document must then be given by the marketing team.

2. Assign roles to the italicized words in this passage. What does this assignment of roles tell you about how the author treats his contextual material?

> Now that I know about the situation, I can find all kinds of things to worry about. Viruses, for example. If my *organelles* are really symbiotic bacteria, colonizing *me,* what's to prevent *them* from catching a *virus,* or if *they* have such a thing as lysogeny, from conveying a phage to other *organelles*? (From Lewis Thomas' "Organelles as Organisms")[16]

3. Here is an example of ineffective prose. Discuss how you could use case grammar to advise the writer to revise her resume cover letter.

> To Whom It May Concern:
>
> This letter is responding to your advertisement for a the Paralegal position. The advertisement stated that the entry-level position sought a paralegal to review and organize documents.
>
> Four years of experience as a paralegal makes me qualified for this position. I have researched for various employers and organizations many legal issues. My experience demonstrates an ability to research and organize complex data.
>
> Thank you for your consideration. I hope the position can be discussed by us in the near future.

# 5

## *Analyzing and Improving Coherence*

When we are confronted with writing or reading a text, we are concerned with both textual coherence and textual cohesion. A text that is coherent is easier to comprehend and is processed more effectively. If the text is also highly cohesive, it will be processed even more efficiently. Coherence refers to establishing logical connections between the ideas and concepts presented. Cohesion is created by using structural features of sentences (such as repetition and ellipses) and cohesive devices (such as conjunctions and coordinating and subordinating adverbs) to increase the speed at which we can read and process text. Cohesive devices highlight the connections between sentences, rather than between ideas. Coherence takes precedence; if ideas are not coherent, there is no text. This chapter is devoted to an exploration of methods for analyzing and improving textual coherence.

## METHODS FOR IMPROVING COHERENCE

Any method for examining and improving textual coherence must take into account what is explicitly stated, as well as the underlying assump-

75

tions and implications that hold ideas together; there are no simple techniques that can be mechanically applied—no software programs which check style—that can actually analyze whether ideas and concepts connect. And herein lies the difficulty in analyzing textual coherence; often the writer will see implicit connections between the ideas being presented, while the readers feel that the text lacks coherence and that more explicit connections need to be made. How do we determine what needs to be explicitly stated in a text? No hard and fast rules that we can learn as communicators will dictate what needs to be explicitly stated in a text. A good amount of the decision making we do when we write and read coherent texts is intuitive or unconscious. We do not have to stop and consciously consider if what we have just said or read is connected to the preceding idea. Yet, while there is still much to learn about how we actually process texts, if improving coherence is our goal, we can limit our discussion to methods for determining where a break in coherence occurs and for repairing such disjunctions. In particular, we shall explore the efficacy of the given-new contract and Christensen's rhetoric.

I do not advocate using the methods that we will be discussing to write texts. They are methods to be used during revising and editing. While working on a first draft, a writer should allow ideas to flow freely. Concentrating on coherence—making sure that each sentence logically connects to the preceding one—can cause a writer to forget essential points and stifle ideas and connections which would naturally occur. Conscious attention to coherence should be an issue of revision. Having sufficiently developed a topic during the revision process, the writer can then reorganize, tighten, and further develop the prose so that the ideas are presented in a coherent manner. While we tend to think in logical and coherent patterns, sometimes what we actually write on a page may reflect our own idiosyncratic way of envisioning an idea. The text may include material that we would consider obtuse, irrelevant, or digressive, if we looked at the text dispassionately and objectively. In addition, the pen, which moves slower than the mind, sometimes fails to record a fleeting thought that may be worth including. Thus, we may have to expand, reorganize, tighten, and/or develop ideas more fully, in order to make a text that may seem coherent to us, coherent to the reader.

## THE GIVEN-NEW CONTRACT

The given-new contract has become a popular tool used by writers to check for and to improve the coherence of their texts. Of the methods we are about to discuss, it is the one with which you may already be familiar. The given-new approach assures *linear, not global,* coherence. In other words, it guarantees that each sentence connects to the next, but it cannot guarantee that the overall paragraph or essay makes sense. Given-new cannot tell us if the topic or main idea of one paragraph connects logically to the next, or if all the ideas developed independently in paragraphs actually make sense as a whole essay. (The issue of global coherence will be dealt with in chapter 7.)

The given-new formula works on the premise that every sentence contains some material that will be familiar to the reader, "given," and some material that is unfamiliar, "new." Most often the given is found at the beginning of the sentence, followed by the new. The new information of a sentence often becomes the given of the subsequent sentence; thus, new information is incrementally added with each ensuing sentence.[1] The given part of the sentence is said to be speaker oriented; the speaker announces what he is concerned with. Subsequent references to given material (including new material that will become given in subsequent sentences) can be made by simple repetition, using pronouns (such as "this," "it," "they") or synonyms. This creates variety while still recalling some given information, thereby making it easier to acquire and process more new information as we continue to read.

| This memo is written | to invite you to a conference on management systems. | The conference |
|---|---|---|
| given | new | given |

| will be held at the Sumpton Ranch, on July 28th, from 9:00 to 5:00. | You | will be introduced to |
|---|---|---|
| new | given | new |

| how | these systems | can be used to store and organize client data. |
|---|---|---|
| new | given | new |

Given information is information that is recoverable because it has been referred to explicitly in the preceding discourse or that is easily inferred from the context and situation of the text. Such inferable material is called the "implicit given." The new part of the sentence is hearer or reader oriented and conveys the focus of information. It is material that the speaker or writer believes should be of interest to listeners or readers and which they cannot infer from the preceding discourse or context.[2] If writers plan to observe the given-new contract to maintain coherence in a text, then they should: 1) repeat the word (once new, when mentioned a second time it is given); 2) use pronouns; and 3) use words related in meanings—synonyms or other words associated with the previously mentioned words and concepts (i.e., attire for clothes). This is good advice, but easily misunderstood by inexperienced writers who believe repetition and substitution (i.e., pronoun for noun) are all you need to adhere to the given-new contract.[3] This reduces the given-new contract to a mechanical formula, and the results are often disastrous.

> Example: The river is full of pollutants. The pollutants include sewage and industrial wastes. The industrial wastes come from Gopher Chemical. Gopher Chemical makes paper products. The paper products come from the forests of Oregon. The Oregon forests are suffering from drought. The drought may be the result of global warming. Global warming changes seasonal weather patterns.

This paragraph strictly adheres to the given-new formula. As you can see, however, while each sentence is connected to the previous one, the text as a whole makes no sense. The theme or gist of the paragraph could be any of the following: 1) the problem of pollutants in a local river, 2) chemical waters dumped by Gopher Chemical, 3) how drought affects tree harvesting, or 4) global warming. Linear coherence (sentence-to-sentence connection) does not necessarily create a coherent text. This may seem to be an extreme example of lack of global coherence, but everyone occasionally runs into texts that do shift topic or emphasis once or twice, thereby creating substantial problems for the reader who is trying to comprehend the writer's meaning. Unfortunately, since the given-new contract is often the only tool writers have been taught for creating coherent texts, such texts may be much more common than you would think.[4]

Highly coherent and well-written texts are more sophisticated in their use of the given-new contract; such works depend much more

upon words related in meaning and information inferred by context—
implicit givens—to create coherence. Take, for example, the first paragraph of the essay "Autonomy," by Lewis Thomas. Thomas is known as
a lucid and entertaining writer, and his prose is highly coherent:

| Working a typewriter by touch, like riding a bicycle or strolling on a path, | is best done by not |
|---|---|
| given: writer oriented, introduced as tasks we share | new |

| giving it a glancing thought. | Once you do, | your fingers fumble and hit the wrong keys. |
|---|---|---|
| new | given | new |

| To do things involving practiced skills, you | need to turn loose the systems of muscles and nerves |
|---|---|
| given: actually referring to first sentence and other implied tasks, same semantic field | new |

| responsible for each maneuver, place them on their own and stay out of it. |
|---|
| new |

| There is not real loss of authority in this, since you get to decide whether to do the thing or not, |
|---|
| given: authority is linked to "responsible" in same semantic field, and "decide to do" refers to previously mentioned actions "turn loose," "place them on their own and stay out of it" and the resulting actions.[5] |

| and you can intervene and embellish the technique any time you like; | if you want to ride a |
|---|---|
| new | given |

| bicycle | backward | or walk | with an eccentric loping gait giving a little skip every fourth step, |
|---|---|---|---|
| given | new | given | new |

| whistling at the same time, | you can do that. But if you concentrate your attention on the details, |
|---|---|
| new | given: "details" summarizes earlier examples, same semantic field |

| keeping in touch with each muscle, thrusting yourself into a free fall with each step and catching |
|---|
| new |

| yourself at the last moment by sticking out the other foot in time to break the fall, you will end up |
|---|
| new |

| immobilized, vibrating with fatigue.[6] |
|---|
| new |

Note that the given of a sentence may refer to ideas and concepts further
back in the passage than the directly preceding sentence. Given material
can also be a new word that groups together a number of specific
elements given in earlier sentences ("things" or "details") or a way of

naming previously given material in a new way ("do" referring to a previous action); these are all instances of using words of related meaning. Thomas also makes use of implicit givens. He expects the reader to recognize and process clauses such as "no real loss of authority in this, since you get to decide whether to do the thing" as implied by previous context, as previously given.

There are many cases in which an implicit given is at work. Take for example the preparation instructions on the back of a can of soup. "Preparation: Empty can into pan. Add 1 cup water. Heat at medium temperature until warm." Though there are no explicit givens here, the instructions are comprehensible for two reasons. Implicit in the instructions are the subject or agent "you" and the object "soup" which connect all the sentences. If there were a need to be more explicit, the instructions could be restated: "You empty the can of soup into a pan. Then you add 1 cup of water to the soup. Then you heat the soup at a medium temperature until warm." But such explicitness is unnecessary. In addition, because when we see the instructions on the label we read them as instructions for cooking—"preparation" or "recipe." A first word or title, such as preparation or recipe, establishes a coherent focus for the information that follows. Titles and headings often work to establish overall textual coherence or a framework that helps to establish a (global) given or focus that then connects the subsequent discourse.

Used responsibly, the given-new formula can be helpful in identifying sentences in texts that create problems for coherence, especially if we take into account implied given material as well as overtly stated given material. As we have discussed, one of the biggest problems in using the given-new contract is dealing with implicit information. Texts inherently have discontinuities that are filled in through inferencing. When we actually employ the given-new formula, we should take into account implied givens by considering whether the audience will be able to correctly infer the implied given. In any case, the given-new contract should never be used alone as a check for coherence. Coherence must be maintained globally as well as locally, and managing global coherence requires other techniques (as discussed in chapter 7) in addition to local coherence checks such as the given-new contract.

## CHRISTENSEN'S RHETORIC OF THE PARAGRAPH

Francis Christensen developed a generative rhetoric of the sentence and paragraph to teach students to generate and write cumulative sentences and tighter paragraphs.[7] Christensen intended this method to be used during the initial stages of writing, but rather than having people write paragraphs as prescribed by any methodology, I encourage writers to use his method in the editing stage, to check paragraphs they have written and may need to revise, and to look for weaknesses in coherence. We will, therefore, adapt the rhetoric of the paragraph so that it can be used to edit, check, and improve cohesion within paragraphs.

Christensen's rhetoric resembles the given-new contract in that both focus attention on local coherence, by analyzing the relationships between sentences that are next to one another; neither deals with the overall, global structure of the essay or text. Christensen refines the notion of a paragraph as moving from general to specific, instead defining the movement of the paragraph as toward more concrete, specific, qualifying statements. In general, each additional sentence is added at a lower level of generality. There are some exceptions. An additional sentence may be at higher level than the previous one (called *super*ordinate), especially if it is the last sentence of a paragraph that summarizes or concludes the paragraph, or if it is a transition sentence that prepares the reader for the subject of the next paragraph. Still, in general, the development of a paragraph is from general, abstract statements about an idea to specific qualification of that idea. The more sentences a writer adds to a paragraph, the more the idea is developed and the greater the "texture" or "depth" of thought exhibited in the paragraph.

In most cases, the paragraph begins with the topic sentence. There are two notable exceptions: 1) The topic sentence can appear in the directly preceding paragraph, and at times, the entire preceding paragraph may act as a topic "sentence" for the paragraph that follows it; and 2) a topic sentence can also be implied rather than explicit. In addition to topic sentences, paragraphs are composed of two types of sentences, coordinating sentences and subordinating sentences. Coordinating sentences emphasize the "sameness" of ideas; the ideas are treated as if they are at the same level of generality. These sentences restate, contradict, contrast, or conjoin a successive statement to a preceding one at the same level. The best clue that sentences are coordinate is the presence of a partially repeated sentence structure, particularly at the beginning of the sentence. Look for repeated structures such as "it is" in a series of sentences. Perhaps one of the most famous examples of the use of repeated coordinating structure is the introduction to *A Tale of Two Cities:*

> It was the best of times, it was the worst of times, it was the age of wisdom, it was the age of foolishness, it was the epoch of belief, it was the epoch of incredulity, it was the season of Light, it was the season of Darkness, it was the spring of hope, it was the winter of despair, we had nothing before us, we were all going direct to Heaven, we were all going direct the other way—in short, the period was so far like the present period, that some of its noisiest authorities insisted on its being received, for good or for evil, in the superlative degree of comparison only.[8]

Included in the category of coordinating sentences are those that restate previously stated ideas in a new way. Subordinating sentences expand or examine the idea at what is considered a lower level; the concept is reexamined in more detail, in more specific and less abstract language. Such sentences explain, define, or give examples of the ideas already mentioned at a higher level and treated in a more general manner.

Let's look at how a paragraph would actually be described. Each sentence is assigned a number defining its level of generality. If you sketch the paragraph on the page, each lower level is indented. By identifying the levels and sketching the paragraph you can visualize the development of the paragraph. For example:

1 But it is also true that the fashions we are speaking about have changed several times since 1911;

1 we know that during the 1920s, women were binding their breasts and bobbing their hair and hoping to look like boys;

1 and we remember that in 1960 Marilyn Monroe, when she made the film *Some Like It Hot,* was still permitted to be as large as a woman in a drawing by Modersohn-Becker.

> 2 We who fell in love with her then and yearned as growing girls to look like her, seeing this film now, and the size of the woman who was our heroine, must marvel at what has happened to our very perception of beauty.
>
> > (Subordinate—more specific about Monroe and dependent upon the introduction of Monroe as a topic)
>
> > 3 For Monroe, if she were alive now, and still as grand and voluptuous as she was then, would today no doubt be considered fat.
> >
> > > (Subordinate—specifying how perception of beauty has changed)
>
> 2 It is unlikely that today someone seeing her for the first time would be taken with jealousy because of the abundance in her body, the way Susan Strasberg was, the first time she saw her.
>
> > (Parallel to level of 2 above: a generic group watching Monroe)
>
> > 3 "We are talking after the scene," says Strasberg, "when suddenly a stream of energy vitalized the stage.
> >
> > > (Subordinate—more specific action and defined speaker)
> >
> > > 4 Heads began to turn and people stared as Marilyn Monroe undulated across the room in a dress so fitted she could barely move.
> > >
> > > > (Subordinate—specifies action on stage)
> > >
> > > > 5 I was instantly jealous of her, her 'zaftig' body, her blondeness, the ease with which she commanded attention."
> > > >
> > > > > (Subordinate—more specific description of action; "we" narrows to "I")

from "The Boutique," Kim Chernin[9]

This paragraph, like most, is made up of both coordinating and subordinating sentences. Notice the repetition of structure in the first three independent clauses ("we" + verb—"we are speaking," "we know," "we remember") that creates coordination. (For a more accurate description of paragraph development, the independent clauses on each side of a semicolon should be treated as independent sentences. Semicolons and coordinating conjunctions connect coordinate clauses and sentences.) In the example, in the subordinating sequences, the subject—the changing perception of beauty—and the object being observed—Marilyn Monroe—are more developed, using more specific and visual language (at the lower levels).

This method can be used to describe the development of coherent paragraphs, and you may enjoy practicing this method by analyzing a paragraph of your favorite writer's work. More importantly, after familiarizing yourself with Christensen's rhetoric, you can use it to identify sentences in paragraphs that upset the coherent, logical pattern of development. Let's take a look at a pamphlet on geysers published by the U.S. Geological Survey.

### What is a Geyser?[10]

A geyser is a special kind of hot spring that from time to time spurts water above ground. It differs from most hot springs in having periodic eruptions separated by intervals without flow of water. The temperature of the erupting water is generally near the boiling point for pure water (212°F or 100°C at sea level). Some geysers erupt less than a foot and a few erupt to more than 150 feet. Some small geysers erupt every minute or so, but others are inactive for months or even years between eruptions. Contrary to popular opinion, most geysers are very irregular in their behaviour, and each is different in some respects from all others. Among the major geysers, only a few, such as Old Faithful in Yellowstone National Park, are predictable enough to satisfy an impatient tourist. But even for Old Faithful the interval between eruptions varies from about 30 to 90 minutes, with an average of about 65 minutes.

1 A geyser is a special kind of hot spring that from time to time spurts water above ground.

   2 It differs from most hot springs in having periodic eruptions separated by intervals without flow of water.

     ? The temperature of the erupting water is generally near the boiling point for pure water (212°F or 100°C at sea level).

      3 Some geysers erupt less than a foot and a few erupt to more than 150 feet.

      3 Some small geysers erupt every minute or so, but others are inactive for months or even years between eruptions.

      3 Contrary to popular opinion, most geysers are very irregular in their behaviour, and each is different in some respects from all others.

        ? Among the major geysers, only a few, such as Old Faithful in Yellowstone National Park, are predictable enough to satisfy an impatient tourist.

        (subordinate to preceding sentence) But even for Old Faithful the interval between eruptions varies from about 30 to 90 minutes, with an average of about 65 minutes.

This paragraph, too, is made up of both coordinating and subordinating sentences. Sentences four and five—which are both level three—are obviously coordinating because of the repetition of sentence structure; in addition, I would include sentence six at the same level because it is another sentence that talks about the behavior of some geysers. All three sentences are subordinate to sentence two—which is level two. Sentence two distinguishes between geysers and hot springs, and sentence four further defines periodic eruptions; thus we have identified a subordinating structure here based on qualifying statements. But what of sentence three? As it is written, it discusses the temperature of erupting water and does not develop further any of the concepts in sentence one or two. This tells us that sentence three—the level of which is unassignable as it is written and placed in the paragraph—disturbs the coherence of the paragraph. The reader must infer that the writer is talking about geyser water; still, the material is too specific at this point in the paragraph, since the following sentence returns to a discussion of how geysers behave. Talking about the temperature of geyser water transports the reader to a much lower level of generality than the rest of the paragraph. The last two sentences also create a problem. Since the writer has been discussing what geysers are and how they behave, at what level does reference to a tourist attraction fit? It does not fit directly above or below the level of the preceding sentence. Rather than a smooth transition from one level of generality to the next, levels of generality have been skipped, signaling a break in coherent development. The last sentence is subordinate to the one directly before it, but these two sentences disturb the coherence of the paragraph and belong in another, separate paragraph.

In doing a Christensen analysis, it is less important that you assign levels correctly, than that you notice when a sentence is not at the same level or the next level of generality, since this signals a coherence problem. A leap in levels of generality provides evidence that the paragraph is not coherently structured. Such a leap creates a large gap or discontinuity that the reader must fill in through inferencing; if the gap is great enough that one or more levels of generality are skipped, then the inferencing required may overtax the reader.

Development problems also occur if a paragraph is exclusively composed of either subordinating or coordinating sentences. If a paragraph contains only subordinating sentences, the primary focus may be unclear because no special emphasis has been used to identify the theme. (Such emphasis can be achieved by rephrasing the main idea, or by using coordinate sentences to highlight the theme of the paragraph.) For example:

Rapid growth and development are becoming the rule rather than the exception in Wyoming as resource extractive industries become more important to the state's *economy. Rap-*

*id economic* and social changes often require decision-makers to handle increased work loads in shortened periods of time.

More often than not, the most difficult *decisions are made by persons* serving on planning boards, county commissions, and city councils. Although few of *these persons* are trained economists, they often are required to decipher *complex economic data. One such piece of data is the economic* multiplier. Because multipliers yield quick results, they are used more frequently than any other measure in determining impacts of economic change. For this reason, it is imperative for decision-makers to know whether a multiplier will provide useful information or whether it will render misinformation. This article will explain multipliers, examine how they are used in making calculations, and provide some criteria for determining whether a given multiplier can be used in a specific situation. ("Some Uses and Abuses of Economic Multipliers" by Eugene Lewis)[11]

Since the first paragraph provides an opening, I will treat both paragraphs together as one unit. While this text rigidly adheres to the given-new contract, it is not easy to process. (The italicized words show how each new concept is picked up as a given in the subsequent sentence.) The sequence of the passage is 1-1-2-3-4-5-6-4. The first two sentences of the first paragraph are not well related at all; therefore, they are both assigned level one. However, I make these assignments with some reservations, since no apparent connection is explicitly stated. The second sentence does in fact serve as a transition into the second paragraph, and the second paragraph descends down the ladder of generality, until, in the last sentence, we skip back up to level four. (Actually, the second to last sentence presents a problem: it reintroduces the "decision-makers" of the level three sentence, and since it is subordinate to that level three sentence, it could be considered a level four, rather than a level six. Still, the skip back up in level, or difficulty in assigning level, indicates a problem.) In any case, the passage is designed primarily as a subordinating structure. The passage is difficult to comprehend because each sentence simply elaborates on the preceding one, and the reader is burdened with too much specific material that is not organized or developed around a main idea or topic. (The main idea should be restated in a coordinating sentence.) On first reading the text, it is unclear whether the text is about the decision makers and how they carry out their responsibilities or about the methodology for making decisions. We discover the true focus of the essay quite late, and the writer's statement of focus is less effective than it otherwise would be because of the confusion already created by the preceding text.

A few simple changes could drastically improve the coherence of the passage. Coherence could be created by deleting the first sentence and simply revising the second sentence to read "Rapid economic changes in Wyoming due to new resource extractive industries often require. . . . " Then the new sentence could be combined with the following two sentences in an introductory paragraph. The second paragraph would now begin with "one such piece of data . . . ," a general statement on multipliers; the theme of the essay would be highlighted by coordinating the first and last sentence of the second paragraph:

> Rapid economic changes in Wyoming due to new resource extractive industries often require decision-makers to handle increased work loads in shortened periods of time. More often than not, the most difficult decisions are made by persons serving on planning boards, county commissions, and city councils. Although few of these persons are trained economists, they often are required to decipher complex economic data.
>
> One such piece of data is the economic multiplier. Because multipliers yield quick results, they are used more frequently than any other measure in determining impacts of economic change. For this reason, it is imperative for decision-makers to know whether a multiplier will provide useful information or whether it will render misinformation. This article will explain multipliers, examine how they are used in making calculations, and provide some criteria for determining whether a given multiplier can be used in a specific situation.

Further improvements could be made by adding more coordinate structure to the paragraphs and moving or rewriting the second-to-last sentence.

We may also find that paragraphs that are primarily coordinating, that maintain the same level of generality for too long a stretch, also impede processing, since the topic is not really being developed. For example:

> With the new, revolutionary Jack Sprat fat-burning diet pill you will lose more weight, faster, than you ever have on any other diet. It is a revolutionary diet aid, because with the Jack Sprat diet pill you actually burn fat. The Jack Sprat diet pill gives fast results. Your weight loss will be greater than any other you have ever experienced using any other diet aid.

This paragraph is totally coordinating. Each sentence, after the first, simply restates the information in the first sentence, either by changing word order or by using synonyms. After the first sentence, the paragraph basically says nothing. This kind of writing is often called double-talk, particularly when all the material is presented in vague generalities. The ad is a form of written gymnastics that simply restates the first general statement. This type of writing is common both in advertising and in the political arena; it is, in fact, a form of propaganda.

The best rule of thumb for developing a good coherent paragraph that we can derive from the preceding methods is: main ideas need to be supported by both coordinating and subordinating sentences. Coordinating sentences will highlight and draw attention to the main point, while subordinating sentences will develop, elaborate, or qualify the idea. If a paragraph depends solely on one structure or another or the pattern continues over three or four sentences (i.e., 1-2-2-2-2 or 1-2-3-4-5) communication may be impeded; the reader will either get lost because there is no development of the concept or because there is so much elaboration that major points being made do not stand out from the details.

## EXPANDING UNDERDEVELOPED PARAGRAPHS

Once you understand the rhetoric of the paragraph and understand the difference between subordinating and coordinating sentences (which is best done by first analyzing well-written paragraphs), you can use this technique to edit your own texts.[12]

At one time or another, most of us have been told to expand upon our ideas or to develop our paragraphs, but our critics usually fail to provide practical advice on how to do so. If you know how to use coordinating and subordinating sentences, you can easily rework and expand a vague paragraph. You might consider how you could use coordinating and subordinating sentences to develop your paragraph further:

Add coordinating sentences:

1. *Compare* the idea presented to a similar notion.
2. *Contrast* your idea with an idea you feel may bear some resemblance to yours, but which is really different.
3. *Restate* your idea in another way to emphasize what you said.

Add subordinate sentences:

1. *Give an example.*
2. *State more specifically* what you meant, using more vivid, precise nouns and verbs. (For example, specifically name who is involved and what he is doing.)
3. *Give a reason* for what you have just said.
4. *Tell the results* of the action just described.
5. *Discuss what caused* the action to occur.
6. *Discuss the conditions* surrounding the action taking place.[13]

These concrete suggestions should help you to expand vague paragraphs.

## LIMITATIONS OF CHRISTENSEN'S RHETORIC
## OF THE PARAGRAPH

Remember that this method, like the given-new contract, still tends to focus on linear coherence—the connections made between adjacent sentences. Neither Christensen's rhetoric nor the given-new contract should be used alone, but should be accompanied by some method which attends to the issue of global textual coherence.[14]

## APPLICATIONS

1. Here is the second section of the Geyser pamphlet referred to earlier in this chapter:

### Why Do Geysers Erupt?

Water from rain and snow can seep thousands of feet underground. In some volcanic areas it is then heated by contact with deeply buried hot rocks. Temperatures of this water can attain 400°F (204°C) or higher—much above the temperature of boiling water at the surface. Such "superheating" is possible because of the high underground water pressure. When the water becomes heated, it expands and rises toward the surface.

Near the surface where pressures become sufficiently low, some of the water boils to steam, producing hot springs. In most hot springs, the steam and the heat energy of the hot water are lost by steady, quiet escape to the surface. A few springs, however, deliver so much energy to the surface that it cannot all be lost by steady escape. From time to time, steam bubbles become too abundant to escape quietly through the water; instead the steam lifts the water, sweeping it upward and out of the vent. As this occurs the pressure at deeper levels is lowered, boiling action increases, and a chain reaction is started that leads to an eruption. These hot springs that erupt and intermittently deliver large amounts of energy to the surface are called geysers.

Using Christensen's rhetoric of the paragraph analyze this section. After using Christensen rhetoric to illuminate problems in the text, discuss how the coherence can be improved. Look at the unity of one paragraph at a time. (Note: It is more important to identify where coherence breaks down than to make the same level assignments I do.)

2. Read the business letter below.


Dear Jean:

You are invited to attend a conference on March 19, 1987, at the Marriott.

The information you will learn will give you a tool to return to your existing and future customer base showing them how to decrease their cost of operation overall with increased efficiency in security, safety, environmental control, communication and all forms of data handling.

Reuters will be our host. Twelve years ago the engineers at Reuters developed a system which has been used and proven exclusively worldwide. This technology transfers data worldwide in 2 seconds.

Reuters, an English company, is the European International Press Association. Their public image is less than 5% of the company. 95% is financial information reporting. They are 140 years old, doing business in 160 countries. Their reputation is built on ethics. Their charter is to deliver unbiased, fair, equitable and untempered news. NOTE: Their policy has been to pay their engineers for 8 hours a day— 4 hours to do today's business and 4 hours to create anything they want. Needless to say, they defy convention. All the patented technology is priced cost effectively. Reuters is the largest single communication service in the world. Security has to be key, due to the fact that the price of gold bullion is traded between two countries that are literally at war; and no one using this Reuters system knows who did what, when, and to whom for how many Oreos! Need I say more?

I look forward to seeing you.

(Note: Reuters is like the Associated Press; it offers a teletype service that transmits information to your company.)


a. Do a given-new analysis of the fourth paragraph. Discuss the usefulness of employing this approach to this text.

b. Can Christensen's rhetoric be applied to paragraphs three and four? Why or why not? And what does that tell you?

c. What is the biggest oversight or limitation of these two approaches in terms of dealing with this particular text?

# 6

## *Achieving Cohesion*

Cohesion and coherence are the two elements necessary for producing a communicable text. Cohesion refers to the surface text devices that signal connections in a text. These devices, such as conjunctions, subordinating adverbs, and pronouns, do not necessarily have to be used to produce a text that makes sense, nor does their appearance guarantee that a text will be coherent. Take, for example, the following memo:

> The important messages are very simple, but most of us don't even start figuring them out until we're past 40. For example . . . pain and time are great teachers; there is more to life than increasing its speed; sometimes we move so fast after quantity, that we forget about quality. Another, if at first you don't succeed, you are running about average. Often, we set up so many expectations for ourselves that we declare ourselves failures before even starting. Next, your growth and wisdom can be directly gauged by the drop in your ill temper. There are a lot of grouches out there who are impatient and critical and pessimistic.
>
> —Anonymous

Every sentence after the first begins with a transitional, cohesive device; yet, the ideas are unconnected. However, when used in conjunction with coherent ideas, these devices will help to make text comprehension proceed more efficiently. Cohesive devices facilitate text processing by rhetorically signaling the relationships between concepts in the text, highlighting the connections for the reader and making the connections more verbally explicit.

Cohesion is the linking, not of ideas, but of sentences. What this means is that cohesion makes textual connections explicit to a listener or reader. Ideas can be coherent without being cohesive.[1] But if we wish to communicate our ideas to someone else, we must consider how best to make the text comprehensible; we must consider cohesion.

The elements that establish cohesion are recognized by their contribution to the structure of sentences rather than to the meaning of the sentences. For example, conjunctions and adverbials such as "but," "rather," and "instead" indicate that the two statements presented are to be contrasted, but the conjunctions do not tell us anything about the ideas presented in the statements. Pro-forms are also cohesive devices; pronouns such as "he," "she," and "it" substitute for nouns and can refer back to the antecedent (the noun that came earlier and that has been replaced). Therefore, they function as abbreviated references to antecedents, streamlining the text. Take, for example, "The czar was told to step down. The czar was told the Party would assume power." These statements can be streamlined using a pronoun: "The czar was told to step down. He was told the Party would assume power." Additional cohesive devices, such as ellipsis, can be used to highlight the relationship between the ideas and further streamline the text: "The czar was told to step down, so that the Party could assume power." Using ellipsis eliminates the redundant phrase, and the adverbial "so that" highlights the causal relationship. Note the original two sentences say the same thing, but the single compound sentence is more efficient and sounds more pleasing to the ear.

Textual continuity is improved by using cohesive words and phrases to make the relationships between the ideas being presented more explicit. A study of cohesion emphasizes the syntax of sentences and indicates how cohesive devices can be used to make a text more compact, so that the text is easier to comprehend. We will discuss five major cohesion devices: lexical cohesion, reference, substitution, ellipsis, and junction.[2]

## LEXICAL COHESION

Lexical cohesion is cohesion resulting from the selective use of vocabulary. Repeating a term is one way of creating cohesion. Rather than repeating the same term over and over, so that the text begins to sound redundant, we can create lexical cohesion by using another word to refer to that same item. There are three primary techniques of achieving lexical cohesion: repetition, synonymity, and generalization. These techniques account for much of the resulting lexical variety of a text.

### Repetition

The first technique for achieving lexical cohesion, repetition, is simply the repeated use of the same word or phrase. For example, I have already used the phrase "lexical cohesion" four times in this section; that is simple repetition. Repetition helps to cognitively reinforce key ideas and new terms. The danger of overusing repetition is that it often results in a text which drones on in a monotone. For example,

> *Critics* are often called the artists' parasites. *Critics* make their living telling other people what they should like. *Critics* do not judge art by some objective criteria. *Critics* consider what appeals to them to be good art. *Critics* call what doesn't appeal to them bad art.

By shifting the position of the repeated item in the sentence, you can avoid this problem. Avoid always using the same term at the beginning of the sentence or as the subject. Instead, place it near the end of the sentence, or after an introductory clause. This allows you to refer to the same item without creating a dull sounding text. Using these techniques, the monotonous text above can be rewritten:

In artistic circles, *critics* are often called the artists' parasites. *Critics* make their living telling other people what they should like. However, do not make the mistake of thinking that *critics* judge art by some objective criteria. Good art is simply that which appeals to the *critic*. Bad art is that which does not appeal to the *critic*.

To avoid monotony, you can also vary the modifiers (adjectives) associated with the key term. For example, an artist who has just been trashed by the critics might call them "parasitic critics," "tasteless critics," or "insensitive critics." If the item you need to repeat is a phrase, partial repetition will allow you to create variety. This means that once the reader has become familiar with the phrase, instead of repeating the whole phrase, you abbreviate the subsequent reference to the key phrase. For example, you are writing about Einstein's theory of relativity. After using the whole title, you could subsequently refer to it as "Einstein's theory," or "the theory of relativity," or even "the (or this) theory":

> *Einstein's theory of relativity* was one of the most important scientific advancements of the twentieth century. *The theory of relativity* has dramatically changed the way we view our universe. Because of *this theory,* we can no longer think of time and distance as absolutes.

You can also alter the function of the word in the sentence. You can change a noun to a verb (sometimes by adding or deleting a suffix) or a verb to a noun by creating a nominalization (again, often by adding a suffix); for example, "The *pollutants* are ruining the lake. The chemicals *pollute* not only the water but the surrounding beaches." You can also switch to adjectival and adverbial forms to repeat the same idea in a slightly different form. You can say "to avoid *monotony,*" and "to avoid creating a *monotonous* text," and you can say "don't *repeat* the same word," and "don't use the same word *repeatedly.*"

### Synonymity

A second technique for achieving lexical cohesion employs synonyms. The writer simply uses a different word that has the same meaning in the given context. I cannot stress how important "in the given context" is. If you go to the thesaurus to find more impressive-sounding synonyms to plug into your a text, the text may be returned to you with those very words that you selected from the thesaurus circled and/or marked "wrong word" or "error in usage," because you have used the synonyms incorrectly. What you may not realize is that meaning is context-dependent; words are synonyms only in certain situations. For example, "She *answered* the question" and "She *rebutted* the question" do not mean the same thing, even though "rebut" is listed as a synonym for "answer" in a thesaurus. In addition, a synonym may require a different sentence structure than the original word. In "The senator *urged* Congress to pass the bill" and "The senator *called for* Congress to pass the bill," the second sentence requires the addition of the preposition "for." ("For" would actually be called a particle in this instance.) "The package *arrived*" contains an intransitive verb; "the package *reached* us" contains a transitive verb that requires a direct object.

## Generalization

The last technique for achieving lexical cohesion involves climbing the ladder of generalization. Take, for example, the word "aspirin." If we consider the terms that could refer to aspirin from the most specific to the least, we might construct a progression like this:

aspirin—pain reliever—drug—stuff or thing

We can refer to an item by a class or group to which it belongs (such as pain reliever or drug in the case of aspirin). We can also refer to an item by abstract generic terms which simply distinguish between people, animals, objects, facts, and the like, such as:

people, human (being), person
animal, creature, (non-human) animate being
thing, object, stuff
idea, concept, fact

The further up the ladder of generalization the writer goes for a substitute name or word, the less specific the language of the text will be, resulting in a greater chance that the reader will misread or misinterpret the text. Abstract words, high up the ladder, can refer to numerous items. They do not evoke specific visual or concrete images and are harder for a reader to comprehend. Consequently, these generic terms create weak, lifeless prose and should be used sparingly. To avoid confusion when such terms are used, the referent (the specific word which is being referred to) must be clear. In literary prose, writers may exploit the ladder of generalization, starting high up with a vague term and then working toward the more specific naming of the item to create a dramatic effect such as suspense. (See the example of cataphora in the following section.)

## REFERENCE

The primary device of reference cohesion is the pro-form. Most commonly, pro-forms are used to refer back to a previously mentioned item. Pro-forms keep the meaning of the previously referred to object active, while using a shorthand form to recall the object. We are most familiar with the pronoun form of anaphora (referring back), as in the following example: "The dog got in the garbage. He got sick from eating the stale bread." In this case "he" refers back to "dog."

A pronoun can also precede the object to which it refers. Such referring ahead is called cataphora. Cataphora is used for dramatic effect. It creates suspense and keeps the reader waiting, thus slowing comprehension. Cataphora is commonly used in literary prose, as in: "It creeps slowly up the stairs, in the dead of night. It slowly pushes the door open. Do those beady eyes belong to a prowler? No, they belong to the family dog." (This example also illustrates how to exploit the ladder of generalization for effect.)

There are many kinds of pronouns: personal pronouns such as "I," "we," "you," and "she," relative pronouns such as "that" and "which," and demonstrative pronouns such as "this," "these," and "that" which point to, or indicate the proximity of, the thing being referred to. "This" and "these" refer to things that the speaker considers near in space or time, "those" and "that" to things which are further away. ("That" can actually function as either a relative or a demonstrative pronoun.) A speaker will often use "this" or "these" to refer to something just spoken about and "those" or "that" to refer to something someone else has mentioned. A speaker may also signal her psychological dislike or detachment from the object by the use of a distancing demonstrative. Take the angry mother who says to her husband, "I wish you'd have a talk with that son of yours." The choice of "that" rather than "my" or "our" reflects the mother's disdain or disapproval. Articles are also demonstratives: "the" indicates a person or object that the listener or reader has already been introduced to and will recognize, whereas "a" or "an" indicates an unspecified or unfamiliar person or object. "The hat" versus "a hat" demonstrates the difference between the definite article "the" and the indefinite article "a."

Problems with reference occur when a pronoun is used obscurely, or when it can refer back to more than one item that preceded it. Problems arise most commonly with the pronouns "it," "this," and "that." For example, "There is a cracked bell in the crumbling steeple. It can be restored." The reader may think "it" refers to bell since it is the subject of the preceding sentence. Or the reader may think it refers to steeple, since that is the closest noun to "it." The verb offers no help since "restore" could refer to either bell or steeple. Commonly, people assume "it" refers to the subject of the preceding sentence. But if the preceding sentence is very lengthy and the subject is followed by subsequent nouns (objects of the sentence) that can also serve as antecedent(s) for the pronoun in the subsequent sentence, then the reader may become confused. (Often, when a writer creates a lengthy sentence, the pronoun in the subsequent sentence is intended to refer to the last mentioned item in the preceding sentence.) Likewise, problems occur if the pronoun can refer both to an item in the preceding sentence or to a whole idea expressed in that sentence. For example, "The humanities major is a well-rounded liberal arts major including courses in literature as well as Fine Arts, which is John's favorite field of study. That is why he is majoring in humanities." "That" may refer to the predicate of the main clause which states that the major is well-rounded, or "that" may be intended to refer to the final clause which emphasizes that John became a humanities major because that major included classes in fine arts. Obviously, it is hard to determine what the writer meant because identifying the antecedent is difficult. Obscure or ambiguous reference can result in both the writer's intent and message being misunderstood. The best rule of thumb is to make sure that there is only one clear antecedent for each pronoun.

One of the most important aspects of reference and lexical cohesion (with the exception of generalization) is that both cohesive strategies restrict the subject of the discourse. Because key terms are continually repeated and referred to, the reader knows that these are the terms which are the main objects of interest within the text and knows to process these new terms, items, or concepts based on how they relate to already identified key items.

## SUBSTITUTION

Substitution is closely related to reference in that pro-forms are also used to accomplish substitution. There are pro-form substitutions for nouns, verbs, and clauses. The pro-form for nouns is "one" (plural "ones"). For example, "He lost his gloves. They were the ones his girlfriend gave him." "One" will always occur with an article when it functions as a pro-form. In substitution the pro-form must always be further defined, as with an article such as "a" or "the." This distinguishes the substitution function from the reference function where no article is required.

Confusion occurs because "one" can be used as a generic pronoun, in reference to "anyone"—a John Smith character. This "one" does not refer to someone already mentioned in the text. It is not considered to be a cohesive device, since it refers to an unspecified "who"; for example, "One must first measure out the ingredients." Used in this manner, "one" can be found as a component of compound words such as "someone," "everyone," or "anyone." In fact, seeing if one of these three words can replace "one" in the sentence is a good method for determining if "one" is functioning as a generic pronoun. The numerous functions "one" may serve in a sentence ("one" is also a cardinal number) account for its too commonly encountered obscure use, as in the sentence: "One method is better than the other, though one may employ them alternately." By recognizing the different functions of "one" and by making sure not to mix or misuse them in a short span of prose, some of the obscurity may be avoided.

"Do" is the English generic, all-purpose verb, also called a pro-verb. Just as "one" can be used to substitute for any object, "do" can be used to substitute for almost any action or event as in: "Have you washed the dishes?" "I've already *done* them"; or "He tried to start the car. He *did* it at last." Used as a pro-verb, "do" can be found in all its conjugated forms: "do," "does," "did," "doing," "done."

Sometimes, when writers are unable to think of the precise verb required to complete a sentence, they simply plug in "do"; for example, "They did the rumba" rather than "They danced the rumba." When it does not refer back to a previously used verb, "do" is not a pro-form. It is a generic verb, from the top of the ladder of generalization, and people often resort to using it simply because they are unable to come up with a more accurate verb, and "do" will suffice in most cases. Take, for example, the now popular saying, "Let's do lunch." But because of its lack of specificity, "do" often results in lifeless sentences, and therefore writers should avoid using it (except as a pro-form or auxiliary).[3] Used as a generic verb, "do" does not create textual cohesion.

## ELLIPSIS

Ellipsis is the physical deletion of elements of a sentence that the writer confidently believes the readers will insert on their own as they read. It is the reader, rather than the writer, who then supplies the missing elements to fill in the gap. If present in the text, the missing element would be the repeated word or phrase already explicitly stated. Since the pressure is on the reader to make the cohesive link, the writer can assume the gap will be filled in correctly only if: 1) the structure of the text provides the reader with the necessary clues about how to fill in the missing material, and 2) the topic and key terms of the passage remain consistent. A writer cannot shift to a different subject of discourse in the sentence that contains an ellipsis. The following pair of sentences are acceptable: "They have not finished cleaning up the accident yet. I hope they will have before rush hours starts." To interpret the second sentence the reader processes "I hope they will have finished cleaning up the accident before rush hours starts." This next ellipsis is unacceptable: "They have not finished cleaning up the accident yet. Rush hour starts soon." Here there is too much material left out to link the idea that rush hour will be worse if the accident is still there. Note that in the acceptable sentences the structure "they have" (with the added modal "will" which doesn't upset the structure) is repeated. This bit of consistent structure, properly called parallel structure, is enough to clue the reader to carry over the main idea of the first sentence; no such structural consistency is found in the second set of sentences. Parallel structure— a few significant words or phrases occupying the same positions and maintaining the same function (i.e., subject or object) or role (i.e., agent or patient) in adjoining sentences—ensures that the reader will properly infer and insert the missing word or phrase.

The ideas expressed by the two clauses or sentences (the complete clause or sentence and the one containing the ellipsis) must also be consistent. The following sentence is acceptable: "He gave his speech at the Senate meeting and at the ambassadors' dinner." "He gave his speech" is the elliptical item deleted from the second clause and can be inferred by the reader without any problem, because the second phrase is parallel to the first; "He gave his speech at the Senate meeting, and he gave his speech at the ambassadors' dinner." Commonly the verb or predicate is left out in an ellipsis and often an awkward sentence results: "He gave his speech to the Senate and at dinner." Though the phrase "he gave his speech" can precede both prepositional phrases in isolation, the two prepositional phrases cannot be joined together in one sentence. While there is no grammatical problem per se, the two clauses are not compatible. Problems in comprehension arise because "to the Senate" refers to a group of people, while "at dinner" refers to an event. To create parallelism, on which ellipsis depends, both clauses would have to have prepositional phrases referring to either people or to events.

Oftentimes function words and phrases, rather than content words, are a good clue to successful cohesion. Since function words provide the syntactic skeleton for a sentence, they are often exploited to create parallelism and ellipses. Look for parallel use of function words in two clauses or sentences in which ellipsis occurs. When the writer changes function words and thereby undermines syntactic consistency (as by shifting from the preposition "to" to "at" in a sentence containing an ellipsis), the reader will have trouble correctly identifying the elliptical item.

We all use ellipses when we write. To make sure that they are filled in correctly by our readers, we must do two things: make sure the ideas are compatible in terms of meaning and establish syntactic consistency. Reference and ellipsis are both devices for achieving compactness, but when we use these devices, we must be careful not to sacrifice clarity. If the reader cannot recover the intended meaning, compactness is not worth the cost.

## JUNCTION

Junctives, conjunctions, and coordinating and subordinating adverbs, DO NOT create coherence. They are elements that reinforce and highlight the relationship between other elements of the text. Their meaning is always constant and they have a consistent function: they signal the relationship between adjacent clauses and sentences. The relationships between ideas and sentences must already be established for the prose to be coherent; junctives, the specific connecting words used to create junction, are just an efficient way of highlighting the relationships for the reader. The choice of junctives provides the reader with clues as to how the writer perceives the statements to be related. For example, does the writer see the incidents as temporally related or believe that one incident caused the other to happen? "John resigned. Then Allen took office" highlights a temporal relationship. If instead the statement read,

"John resigned; consequently, Allen took office" the implication would be that John's resignation resulted in Allen assuming the position. Junctives ease the burden of deciphering how sentences connect. Hence, the reader processes the information more quickly, since the writer has provided explicit clues about how the reader should relate the information given in the text.

Four primary types of connective relations are expressed by junctives:[4]

> *Additive,* also known as the and-relation: The second clause or sentence adds new information that is to be linked to, and considered along with, the first clause or sentence.
>> Common Junctives: and, also, furthermore, in addition, in other words, like(wise), as (if), such that, accordingly, moreover.

> *Adversative,* also known as the contrastive relation: The two clauses or sentences contrast one another, or the information in the second calls the information of the first into question.
>> Common Junctives: but, yet, either . . . or, nor, still, however, only, even so, nevertheless, instead, rather, although, though, even though, despite, whereas, while (on the contrary), on the other hand, by contrast, otherwise, besides, anyhow.

> *Temporal,* also known as the then-relation: The two clauses or sentences are related chronologically. These junctives highlight the order of occurrence.
>> Common Junctives: next, before, after, first, second . . . finally, when, then, until, in the end, formerly, meanwhile, in conclusion, originally, while (since and as used as time references).

> *Conditional:* Clauses and sentences are linked by the fact that one is the reason, cause, condition, or consequence of the other.
>> Common Junctives: so, then, therefore, consequently, on account of, in consequence, for, because, in that case, due to, under the circumstance, in this respect, thus, hence(forth), as a result, in order to (that), so that, if, if only, since, subsequently, unless, given, as, indeed.

The misuse of junctives occurs when a writer does not understand what type of connection the junctive signals. Since junctives are function words that signal restricted relations between clauses and sentences, such misuse will confuse the reader. Adversative junctives are the most commonly misused; writers sometimes mistakenly use "but," "yet," or "however" where an additive or conditional junctive such as "and," "therefore," or "since" is required. For example, "The report must be finished, although it will be presented tomorrow." There is no explicit contrast in this sentence; the meaning of the first clause does not contrast the second. The writer has not stated any reason why presenting the report tomorrow is an action opposed to, or that calls into question, the report being finished. The sentence can be corrected in one of two ways. First, if the writer intends to convey the fact that the second clause is a condition for finishing the project, either the conditional junctive "since" or "because" is appropriate: "The report must be finished, since it will be presented tomorrow." On the other hand, if the writer intends to imply that there will be time to complete the report tomorrow, but that for some reason it must be completed today, the contrastive junctive "although" is appropriate; however, the writer needs to make the meaning of the statement clearer and easier to comprehend by adding a contrasting time reference to the first clause: "The report must be finished today, although it will be presented tomorrow." (Better phrasing would be "the report must be finished today, although it will not be presented until tomorrow.") This illustrates the fact that the ideas themselves presented in the two clauses must be coherent. The cohesive device alone does not make the ideas coherent; it just reinforces the relationship between the clauses.

When you are unsure of which junctive to choose, the following questions may help you make the right choice.

1. Is the reader to consider the second statement alongside the first? Does the second item add new information that should be linked to the first? (Then an additive junctive is needed.)
2. Does the second statement qualify the first? Does the second statement contrast the first? Or does the second statement call into question the information presented in the first? (Then a contrastive junctive is needed.)

3. Are the statements linked chronologically? (Then a temporal junctive is needed.)

4. Are the statements linked conditionally? Is the second statement the result of, the condition for, or the cause of the first? (Then a conditional junctive is required.)

Since junctives merely highlight relationships that already exist between clauses, if a junctive is inappropriate, you may have inadvertently left out information that needs to be explicitly stated to create a coherent and comprehensible text. During the editing process, add any information necessary to make the text coherent, and then be sure to choose a junctive from the correct class when you want to highlight the connection between clauses or sentences.

Sometimes writers misuse the words "by" and "with" as junctives. "By" is incorrectly used to signal a causal connection and "with" is erroneously used to signal an additive relation.

Example: The more expensive meals often differ from these less expensive ones *by* having better quality of meats and a greater variety of seasonings.

should be

The more expensive meals often differ from these less expensive ones *because* they are made with better quality meats and a greater variety of seasoning.

Sometimes, writers need to be reminded that "by" is used at the beginning of a phrase as a preposition; it cannot be used as a junctive to connect clauses. The same is true of "with"; it is a preposition and cannot introduce or connect clauses.

## HOW COHESION WORKS: AN EXAMPLE ANALYZED

Let's analyze how cohesion is achieved in a piece of well-written prose:

The center was not holding. *It was a country of* bankruptcy notices and public-auction announcements and commonplace reports of casual killing and misplaced children and abandoned homes and vandals *who* misspelled even the four-letter words *they* scrawled. *It was a country* in *which* families routinely disappeared, trailing bad checks and repossession papers. *Adolescents* drifted from city to torn city, sloughing off both the past and the future as snakes shed their skins, *children who* were never taught and could never now learn *the games that* had held the society together. People were missing. *Children were missing.* Parents *were missing. Those* left behind filed desultory missing *reports, then* moved on *themselves.* (Joan Didion, "Slouching Toward Bethlehem")[5]

The most striking aspect of the paragraph is its lyricism, created by the repetition (a form of lexical cohesion) of the phrases "it was a country" and "were missing." Didion also employs continuous repetition of the prefix "mis-" in "misplaced," "misspelled," and "missing." This repetition dramatically reinforces her point. "Children" are mentioned by the same name three times in the paragraph and by the synonym "adolescents" once. Note that Didion skillfully varies her reference to children with phrases such as "misplaced children" and "children were missing"; thus she avoids dull, monotonous-sounding prose. "Families" are broken down into more specific members, "parents" and "children," who are also members of "people" and "society." Here, Didion manipulates synonyms as well as the ladder of generalization to create lexical variety. "Reports" is another key word repeated in the paragraph, but note that it is repeated with different modifiers: "commonplace reports of casual killings" and "desultory missing-persons reports." Key terms must be repeated in a text, not only to create or maintain cohesiveness, but more importantly to create a coherent flow of ideas. Cohesion and coherence are closely tied together in a well-written, comprehensible text.

Didion uses the pronouns "they," "those," "who," "which," and "themselves" to create anaphoric reference. She uses "it" in the second sentence as a cataphoric pronoun: "it" refers to "country" which comes after the pronoun. The cataphoric reference creates more dramatic prose.

Didion also uses ellipses twice. There is an ellipsis in the clause "children who were never taught and could never learn the games." Again, Didion manipulates the language for dramatic effect. We would expect the ellipsis to follow the second verb, but this is cataphoric ellipsis; the ellipsis precedes the explicit statement of the deleted element "the games." Didion also employs ellipsis in the last clause of the last sentence: "those left behind" is deleted from that clause.

Finally, let's look at the junctives—or the lack thereof—in this passage. (The "ands" here create compound subjects or predicates and do not connect sentences or clauses; therefore, they are not used as cohesive connectors.) The only junctive that actually appears in the passage is the temporal junctive "then" which appears in the last sentence. The passage is written to achieve a cumulative effect; the reader is meant to feel overwhelmed by the list of events that imply that the country is out of control. The lack of junctives works to make the reader feel overwhelmed and adds to the atmosphere of chaos. By avoiding the use of junctives and by listing events without conditions or causes, Didion avoids explicitly stating why the events are occurring and avoids naming the responsible parties. Didion's prose is a series of pictures; she's the photographer who snaps them, but she leaves it to the viewer/reader to interpret the images. Didion depends a great deal on her reader's intuitive knowledge of how cohesion works in a text. Because she feels she can confidently take her reader's knowledge for granted, Didion feels free to skillfully manipulate language, allowing her readers to find the connections between the images and sentences for themselves.

If readers and listeners did not understand how cohesive devices work, writers would have to explicitly express every idea. We could not vary the way we refer to people or things; we could not use synonyms, pronouns, or substitution. Our prose would become cumbersome. Because we could not use reference, substitution, and ellipsis, texts would increase in length, and writers' prose styles would become ponderous and boring because of incessant repetition. Take, for example, this passage from Loren Eiseley's "The Star Thrower":

It has ever been my lot, though formally myself a teacher, to be taught by none. There are times when I have thought to read lessons in the sky, or in books, or from the behaviour of my fellows, but in the end my perceptions have frequently been inadequate or betrayed. Nevertheless, I venture to say that of what man may be I have caught a fugitive glimpse, not among multitudes of men, but along an endless wave-beaten coast at dawn. As always, there is this apparent break, this rift in nature, before the insight comes. The terrible question has to translate itself into an even more terrifying freedom.[6]

If the passage were written without cohesive devices it might look something like this:

It has ever been my lot, to be taught by none. I was myself a teacher. There are times I have thought to read lessons in the sky. There are times I have thought to read lessons in books. There are times I have thought to read lessons from the behaviour of my fellows. My perceptions of the behaviour of my fellows have frequently been inadequate or betrayed by my fellows. I venture to say that man may be something. I have caught a fugitive glimpse of what man might be. I caught a fugitive glimpse not among multitudes of men. I caught a fugitive glimpse along an endless wave-beaten coast at dawn. There is this apparent break. This apparent break is a rift in nature. The insight comes. The terrible question has to translate itself into an even more terrifying freedom.

Note the droning dullness of the prose. Without junctives, as the rewritten passage illustrates, the reader has to work hard to determine what relationship between ideas the writer intended to convey. In actuality, the compactness created by the cohesive devices in the original passage facilitates comprehension. As this example illustrates, junctives offer clues about how the writer intends his ideas to be related.

By making a text more compact and by highlighting the relationships between statements, cohesion makes a text easier to read. Cohesion is an essential quality of a well-written text.

## APPLICATIONS

1. Identify the cohesive devices in the following passage.

Yet if our agriculture-based life depends on the soil, it is equally true that soil depends on life, its very origins and the maintenance of its true nature being intimately related to living plants and animals. For soil is in part a creation of life, born of a marvelous interaction of life and nonlife long eons ago. The parent materials were gathered together as volcanoes poured them out in fiery streams, as waters running over the bare rocks of the continents wore away even the hardest granite, and as chisels of frost and ice split and shattered the rocks. Then living things began to work their creative magic and little by little these inert materials became soil. (Rachel Carson, "Realms of the Soil")[7]

2. Here is piece of prose in which cohesive devices are mishandled. Identify the misused cohesive devices and discuss how they are misused.

[*The Story of Women*] is based on the true story of a woman in Nazi occupied France during the war. Because of having an ineffectual husband and two children to care for, she starts doing abortions which were illegal in France at the time. She does the first one as a favor for a friend and then eventually starts doing them for money which vastly improves her family's living conditions. Since this is a true story, it has a tragic yet triumphant ending. (Peg Yorkin, "Reviews From a Feminist Perspective")[8]

# 7

## *Analyzing Macrostructures*

While texts are made up of linear arrays of words on a page, we retain much less than the word-by-word presentation. In our minds, we summarize and organize what we read and hear into macrostructures. These are condensed versions of text that embody the most important ideas and essential concepts. Macrostructures reduce the amount of complex information, creating a more generalized or global meaning that has been derived from the individual sentences. Such global meaning is an inherent quality of any well-written essay, since a text is not merely a string of sentences. If we look at each paragraph, each paragraph has a unifying idea or "macrostatement"; moreover, if we list the macrostatements of the paragraphs in order, we should find that these statements develop the theme or "gist" of the essay. The connectedness of the macrostatements creates the "global coherence" of the essay; without this global coherence an essay would not seem to "flow." It would not read as a coherent whole but simply as a collection of unconnected sentences.

Macrostatements taken together and unified by a single theme or purpose form macrostructures.[1] We form macrostructures in our minds to reduce and organize the barrage of incoming information that we read or hear. No text has just one macrostructure. In any given text, there are numerous levels of macrostructures that form a pyramid, with the most generalized, least specific statement (the theme or gist) at the top. As we move toward the bottom of the pyramid, more and more information gets added. The bottom of the pyramid is the linear string of sentences that comprises the unreduced text; this is called the microstructure. At this level all local meaning is still intact. As you move up the pyramid, more and more local information is deleted.

| IV | x | Most generalized statement (theme or gist) |
| III | x—x—x | More local material removed, more generalization |
| II | x—x—x—x | Some local material removed, some generalization |
| I | x—x—x—x—x | Represents the unedited, linear text |

Each level above "I" represents a macrostructure, in which more generalized macrostructures have been derived from more specific sentences or statements. The number of macrostructures that can be derived from a given text is variable, depending on how much local meaning is deleted or absorbed into more generalized statements.

An understanding of macrostructure formation facilitates writing. Often, we find ourselves faced with writing an abstract, summary, or outline. For some, this is an easy task. For others, determining what material should be included in an "abbreviated" version of a text is arduous and tedious. By utilizing the principles of macrostructure formation, we can learn how to extract the most important concepts and ideas and how to reduce the amount of information in order to summarize a text. When intuitive ability is not enough, writers can rely on this method. Identifying macrostructures also helps us to recognize points where the global coherence of an essay breaks down, and will, therefore, help us to improve the overall organization and development as we write and revise.

## THE ROLE OF GENRE

Creating abstracts and summaries, through macrostructure analysis, depends on more than just recognizing the main ideas and identifying the

theme of the text and the main idea of each
ments are actually most important is partly d(
the piece. Genre is the class to which an in(
text belongs. Telephone conversations, verb
conversations are types of verbal genres. Wr
poems (epic, lyric, etc.), scientific reports,
reports, and editorials. Genre often indicates how the ....
should be ordered and distributed throughout the text, and it may place
constraints on what is to be included.

The genre, for a large part, determines the perspective that the
writer uses to select the important material that will appear in the macrostructure. While a written narrative might include wonderful descriptions of the characters and the setting, in the summary the plot takes
precedence, and description is one of the elements that can be deleted as
irrelevant or peripheral. Abstracts of scientific papers allow for the
deletion of whole formal sections of the paper. The scientific journal
article typically includes in introduction, a review of literature, materials and methods, data, a discussion and/or a conclusion. But most
abstracts that researchers are asked to produce need to be less than 200
words. Therefore, an abstract can only include a brief statement of what
the researcher did, what results he ascertained, and the significance of
the findings. Thus, before even ferreting out the essential material in
the discussion and conclusion sections, the author can simply delete the
review of literature, materials and methods, and data sections (if the
essential data is presented in an abbreviated form in the discussion
and/or conclusion).

## AUDIENCE AND PURPOSE

In addition to genre constraints, the writer's purpose and the audience's
needs should be taken into account when creating abstracts and summaries. By including such considerations when we generate macrostatements and macrostructures, we address the pragmatic dimension of the
text.[2] Macrostructure analysis means looking at a given statement in
context, but context does not simply refer to how sentences in a text

ate to one another. Context must also include the situation in which the text is delivered; context includes the pragmatic situation—the perceived relation of writer or speaker to the audience. What material is irrelevant or peripheral and what material is to be considered most significant depends, in a large part, on what the reader expects and wants to get out of the writer's summary or abstract. Genre designation creates some expectations about what is to be included, but adding the factors of audience and purpose narrow the possibilities even further. Take for example a proposal for replacing a large manual labor work force of a company with a new technologically advanced, mechanized assembly line that might be read by three different audiences: owners and stockholders, engineers and contractors, and the current manual work force. While all may, in fact, look at the whole proposal, summaries are often presented to these different groups at various meetings (or in letters and press releases in order to disseminate information about the project) stressing the needs of each individual group. A version of the proposal (which may include a summary) for owners and stockholders would probably emphasize the potential increase in revenue and savings generated by decreasing the company's dependence on manual labor. If the audience were contractors and engineers, then questions of design, cost, and labor involved in building the assembly line would move to the forefront. The current plant workers would be most concerned with the security of their jobs, so an in-plant newsletter would delete most, if not all, of the information of interest to the engineers, contractors, and stockholders. A newsletter would need to summarize information concerning the impact on the present work force—the number of jobs that would be generated or abolished.

Audience also puts constraints on specific details to be included as well as the vocabulary that can be used. If we are discussing technological advances in a daily newspaper, intended for the average reader, high-tech jargon will impede communication. If the article is intended to communicate information about a new technological advancement to a lay audience, technical wording should be very sparse and only used when necessary to correctly identify major concepts. The introduction of a technical term should be followed by a definition (and an analogy to some familiar object is often useful). If the audience is conversant in the specific technical discourse, use the technical vocabulary, which is both a briefer and a more precise way of identifying the issues and concepts. Examples, definitions, and analogies, crucial for the lay audience, can be used much more sparingly and in many cases totally deleted when you are writing for an expert audience.

As a writer, you should always try to define your audience and what they will need to know before you begin to summarize. You should also identify the purpose of the summary or abstract before you begin writing. Try to construct a sentence or brief statement that identifies the purpose that you intend to convey to your particular audience. Consciously refer to this purpose as you construct you summary.

## ACTION-ORIENTED TEXTS

There is no hard and fast set of rules for determining what contextual material is essential, since the material you must retain will be determined by the content of the text, the genre, and the pragmatic situation. But it may be helpful to look at one common text type in order to try to make some useful generalizations. One type of text you may deal with frequently is "action-oriented," where an action or actions, a change in the course of events, or a change in the state of the subject of the text, is the major concern. Narratives, essays dealing with discoveries and advances, progress reports, and feasibility studies are all action-oriented texts. Such texts usually contain the following fundamental elements:

> A description of the initial state/the setting
> Causes of change/action
> Motives and reasons for action
> Initiating actions
> Steps taken to achieve outcome
> Outcome to action
> Consequences of action

In an attempt to summarize an action-oriented text, all material that does not fit into these categories could be deleted. If there is still too much material, the elements themselves can be prioritized, and the least important deleted. The description of the initial state and the outcome of the action will always be essential, but a detailed description of the steps taken to achieve the outcome is often one of the first elements to be eliminated.

## PROCEDURE FOR CREATING ABSTRACTS AND SUMMARIES

We all must summarize any visual, verbal, or written text in order to process it, since we cannot remember and process every detail. For most people, much of the time, the process is fairly automatic. But what happens when a writer is asked to write an abstract of a philosophical treatise or summarize a technical article for the first time? Unfamiliar, dense material presents a challenge, and often the writer feels unable to call upon those processes that only moments earlier seemed so automatic. At such a time, consciously practicing a strategy, such as the one presented here, may make the impossible task possible.

By using a macrostructure procedure to create a summary or abstract, the writer will preserve the essential meaning of the text, and the writer will not have to worry about deleting important facts and concepts, since macrostatements are derived from sentences that appear in the text. The macrostructure is based on reducing, organizing, and constructing new, broader concept statements from lower level, more specific sentences.

To create a summary or abstract, begin by identifying genre, audience, and purpose. Then employ the following steps:[3]

### Creating Abstracts and Summaries: A Macrostructure Approach

1. *Delete* all material that readily appears irrelevant.
2. *Reorganize* all associated details spread throughout the text so that they now follow one another.
   (This step also allows us to analyze how well the essay is organized.)

3. *Construct/Combine* all locally relevant details that can be joined.

Initially, the identification of the genre, audience, and purpose of the text may help the writer to delete whole sections of peripheral or irrelevant details. Once the text has undergone one round of deletion-reorganization-construction (steps 1–3), it can be repeatedly subjected to rounds of:

4. *Deletion:* Select and delete statements that now seem peripheral or irrelevant.
5. *Construction:* Same as step 3 above.
6. *Generalization:* First combine related details, then make a more general statement that subsumes the details.

   *Retain:* Statements which contain essential information that cannot and should not be deleted, combined, or generalized remain unaltered.

   To generate a higher level macrostructure, that is more general and more succinct, repeat steps 4–6 until you produce a text that suits your needs.

Subsequent rounds of deletion require that the writer make new determinations about what material now appears peripheral or irrelevant. As one moves up the pyramid of macrostructures to greater generalization, more local material will be considered irrelevant, and the writer will have to continually reassess what information is most significant.

Generalization is essential when dealing with longer essays and works. When whole paragraphs and pages of specific support, examples, and elaboration need to be summarized briefly, one effective technique for creating an abbreviated text is to copy down the first and last sentence of each paragraph, then apply the procedure above to further condense your constructed text. This procedure will usually work, since writers normally place their most important points in the first and last sentences of paragraphs; therefore, those sentences contain the material which is essential to the macrostructures.

You might question whether applying a macrostructure approach is practical when dealing with longer texts. While these techniques are most practical for dealing with article-length texts, the initial deletion of irrelevant local detail, and/or the selection of first and last sentences of paragraphs will also allow a writer to tackle much longer texts. This procedure is intended as a heuristic for people who need guidance in writing summaries and abstracts. Hopefully, after consciously practicing this procedure it will become more intuitive. Then when faced with a longer text, much of the summarizing procedure can be performed mentally, in the same manner that we process much of the information we receive from our world every day. Meanwhile, this method offers a way to approach a text that will allow a writer to begin to recognize, prioritize, and condense information.

## ANALYZING MACROSTRUCTURES:
## AN EXAMPLE ANALYZED

We will be dealing with an article from the *New York Times,* entitled "Doctors Say Baby with Baboon Heart Is Doing 'Remarkably Well' "[4] (see figure 7.1). We will be creating summaries for various purposes. First, assume you wrote this article or that you are a collaborator on a project which involves producing press releases about this event. Then, you can comfortably assume that you can copy, edit, and alter the text as needed. This actually reflects real-world writing situations, since most writers either write summaries and abstracts of their own work or are part of a writing team where they are authorized to work with the original author's words.

The first summary will be a press release for a newspaper, designed to inform a general reading audience about this significant medical breakthrough. We begin by deleting material readily recognized as irrelevant to a summary intended to inform the general public about this medical advancement. Refer to figure 7.2 to see what material is deleted. The rationale for each deletion is given below.

*Paragraph 1*

- The generic reference to doctors is insignificant.
- The baby's name is an alias, and therefore irrelevant.
- The day of the week is insignificant.

*Paragraph 2*

- The length of time of operation is unimportant.

*Paragraph 3*

- The second reference to Bailey is unnecessary, and since he is the only one quoted, the reference to other doctors is unnecessary.
- "Speaking" and "addressing" reporters at a news conference are redundant acts; remove one reference. Furthermore, the reporters had to have received this information at a news conference; therefore, the entire reference to the news conference can be deleted.
- Since this article is being edited to generate a more concise statement about the medical advancement made, all references to ethics can be dropped.

*Paragraph 4*

- Irrelevant paragraph on ethics. (There is a more specific reference to the baboon, in paragraph twenty-one, so essential information will not be lost by deleting paragraph four.)

*Paragraph 5*

- The reference to the doctor's age is insignificant.
- The background material on the decision to perform the procedure can be considered unnecessary for this specific type of summary.
- Ethical information is not necessary.

*Paragraph 6*

- The opinion presented here is unnecessary; paragraphs one and two more precisely summarize the baby's condition.

*Paragraph 7*

- The appeal to emotions and the anecdotal material is unnecessary.

*Note:* Do not be uncomfortable deleting sections of quoted material, so long as you do not alter the meaning. In all articles that we read, what people said has already been excerpted. You are simply further excerpting or deleting information.

# Doctors Say Baby With Baboon

By LAWRENCE K. ALTMAN

Special to The New York Times

[1] LOMA LINDA, Calif., Oct. 28— Doctors said the 16-day-old infant known only as Baby Fae remained in critical but stable condition today but was "doing remarkably well" after receiving the heart of a baboon at Loma Linda University Medical Center here last Friday.

[2] Nevertheless, "she may be in for a long battle in the weeks ahead," said Dr. Leonard L. Bailey, the pediatric surgeon who performed the five-hour transplant operation.

[3] Dr. Bailey and two other members of the transplant team spoke at a news conference to address some of the technical and ethical aspects of what he called a "highly experimental" operation.

[4] As he spoke, about a dozen demonstrators marched outside. About half of them protested the sacrifice of a healthy animal to prolong the life of a sick human. The other half supported the bold experimental procedure.

## Discussions of Ethics

[5] Dr. Bailey, a 41-year-old surgeon, had spent seven years doing the animal and laboratory research needed before the attempt was made on a human. He said the operation was undertaken only after months of discussion among the university's ethics committees and hours of discussion with the parents of Baby Fae.

[6] He said the doctors on his team "were pleased she is doing well today."

[7] "If you had the opportunity to see this baby and her mother it would help convince you of the propriety of what we are trying to do here," Dr. Bailey said. "The baby looks better than it ever has."

[8] The baby nearly died on her sixth day of life because of a birth defect called hypoplastic heart syndrome, which gave the baby virtually only half a heart and no chance to live.

[9] Dr. Bailey said of the demonstrators that he was "sympathetic with the issue of animal rights."

[10] "However," he went on, "I am a member of the human species. I deal with dying babies every day. I am more sympathetic with them. I am an animal lover but I love babies too."

[11] Dr. Bailey said that he had chosen to do the controversial operation now because his team had gone as far as it could in experiments on primates and other animals.

[12] Until now, with rare exceptions, babies born with the condition did not survive beyond two weeks. The only option available to parents of children with the condition has been surgery to relieve its effects. Such surgery entails great risk and has uncertain results.

## A New Drug for Transplants

[13] Dr. Bailey said he believed his was the only group in the world that was experimenting with a new drug, cyclosporin-A, for animal heart trans-

Figure 7.1. Reprinted, by permission, from *The New York Times* (October 29, 1984).

# *Heart is Doing 'Remarkably Well'*

plants in infants. The drug combats the body's normal rejection of foreign tissue such as transplanted organs. [14] Baby Fae received one dose of cyclosporin-A before the operation but had not received any more as of this afternoon, Dr. Bailey said. The team was concerned about the potential toxic effects of the drug, he said, adding that Baby Fae's blood is monitored frequently to detect any adverse effects.

[15] Dr. Bailey said that Baby Fae was receiving a steroid drug but no heart drugs. He said the team hoped to wean the baby from the mechanical ventilator that has helped her breathe. [16] The surgeon said his team planned to perform five such operations and then to evaluate the results to determine whether it should go ahead or retreat to the laboratory before trying the procedure again on humans.

### Private Research Funds

[17] Dr. Bailey said editors of scientific journals and sources of research grants had rejected his papers and requests for research funds. [18] "They weren't watching the babies die as I was," he said. [19] So Dr. Bailey and his colleagues pursued their research using private funds from Loma Linda and from the fees collected by surgeons at the medical center, he said. Much of the research was done with more than $1 million "out of our own back pockets," he said. [20] Dr. Sandra L. Nehlsen-Cannarella,

an immunologist who is director of transplantation immunology at the Montefiore Medical Center and Hospital of Albert Einstein College of Medicine in the Bronx, was invited to participate in the experimental operation. She described the atmosphere in the operating room when the baboon heart was transplanted:

"At the moment the heart began to beat, there was absolute awe. It was just an incredible event to see that little heart start up."

[21] The heart was taken from a female baboon between seven and eight months old, weighing 7½ pounds. [22] The researchers said that they had found that about half of an unspecified number of humans had pre-formed antibodies against baboons; so, if Baby Fae needs a blood transfusion, additional tests will have to be done on the donated blood. Dr. Bailey also said Baby Fae's doctors would have to study in greater detail than usual the immunizations that she received to prevent similar adverse reactions. [23] Dr. Jack Provonsha, director of the university's bioethics center, discussed the need to sacrifice a primate for experimental purposes. "It is difficult to look at a primate's hand and not feel kinship," he said. "It would be nice if we could use artichoke hearts. Primates are closer to us on the evolutionary scale. But the fact is the heart ties in with a mythological feeling and has more meaning than it probably ought to have."

# Doctors Say Baby With Baboon

By LAWRENCE K. ALTMAN
Special to The New York Times

[1] LOMA LINDA, Calif., Oct. 28— ~~Doctors said the~~ 16-day-old infant ~~known only as Baby Fae~~ remained in critical but stable condition today but was "doing remarkably well" after receiving the heart of a baboon at Loma Linda University Medical Center ~~here last Friday.~~

[2] Nevertheless, "she may be in for a long battle in the weeks ahead," said Dr. Leonard L. Balley, the pediatric surgeon who performed ~~the five-hour~~ transplant operation.

[3] ~~Dr. Bailey and two other members of the transplant team spoke at a news conference to~~ address some of the technical ~~and ethical~~ aspects of ~~what he called a~~ "highly experimental" operation.

[4] ~~As he spoke, about a dozen demonstrators marched outside. About half of them protested~~ the sacrifice of a healthy animal to prolong the life of a sick human. ~~The other half supported the bold experimental procedure.~~

## Discussions of Ethics

[5] ~~Dr. Bailey, a 41-year-old surgeon, had spent seven years doing the animal and laboratory research needed before the attempt was made on a human. He said the operation was undertaken only after months of discussion among the university's ethics committees and hours of discussion with the parents of Baby Fae.~~

[6] ~~He said the doctors on his team~~ ~~were pleased she is doing well today."~~

[7] ~~"If you had the opportunity to see this baby and her mother it would help convince you of the propriety of what we are trying to do here," Dr. Bailey said. "The baby looks better than it ever has."~~

[8] The baby nearly died on her sixth day of life because of a birth defect [called hypoplastic heart syndrome,] which gave the baby virtually only half a heart and no chance to live.

[9] ~~Dr. Bailey said of the demonstrators that he was "sympathetic with the issue of animal rights."~~

[10] ~~"However," he went on, "I am a member of the human species. I deal with dying babies every day. I am more sympathetic with them. I am an animal lover but I love babies too."~~

[11] ~~Dr. Bailey said that he had chosen to do the controversial operation now because his team had gone as far as it could in experiments on primates and other animals.~~

[12] Until now, with rare exceptions, babies born with the condition did not survive beyond two weeks. The only option ~~available to parents of children with the condition~~ has been surgery to relieve its effects. Such surgery entails great risk and has uncertain results.

## A New Drug for Transplants

[13] Dr. Bailey said he believed his was the only group in the world that was experimenting with a new drug, [cyclosporin-A], for animal heart

Figure 7.2. Medical Advancement (1st round deletion). Reprinted, by permission, from *The New York Times* (October 29, 1984).

# *Heart is Doing 'Remarkably Well'*

transplants in infants. The drug combats the body's normal rejection of foreign tissue such as transplanted organs. [14] Baby Fae received one dose of cyclosporin-A before the operation but had not received any more as of this afternoon, Dr. Bailey said. The team was concerned about the potential toxic effects of the drug, he said, adding that Baby Fae's blood is monitored frequently to detect any adverse effects. [15] [Dr. Bailey said that Baby Fae was receiving a steroid drug but no heart drugs. He said the team hoped to wean the baby from the mechanical ventilator that has helped her breathe. [16] The surgeon said his team planned to perform five such operations and then to evaluate the results to determine whether it should go ahead or retreat to the laboratory before trying the procedure again on humans.]

### Private Research Funds

[17] Dr. Bailey said editors of scientific journals and sources of research grants had rejected his papers and requests for research funds. [18] "They weren't watching the babies die as I was," he said. [19] So Dr. Bailey and his colleagues pursued their research using private funds from Loma Linda and from the fees collected by surgeons at the medical center, he said. Much of the research was done with more than $1 million "out of our own back pockets," he said. [20] Dr. Sandra L. Nehlsen-Cannarella, an immunologist who is director of transplantation immunology at the Montefiore Medical Center and Hospital of Albert Einstein College of Medicine in the Bronx, was invited to participate in the experimental operation. She described the atmosphere in the operating room when the baboon heart was transplanted:

"At the moment the heart began to beat, there was absolute awe. It was just an incredible event to see that little heart start up."

[21] The heart was taken from a female baboon between seven and eight months old, weighing 7½ pounds. [22] [The researchers said that they had found that about half of an unspecified number of humans had pre-formed antibodies against baboons; so, if Baby Fae needs a blood transfusion, additional tests will have to be done on the donated blood. Dr. Bailey also said Baby Fae's doctors would have to study in greater detail than usual the immunizations that she received to prevent similar adverse reactions.] [23] Dr. Jack Provonsha, director of the university's bioethics center, discussed the need to sacrifice a primate for experimental purposes. "It is difficult to look at a primate's hand and not feel kinship," he said. "It would be nice if we could use artichoke hearts. Primates are closer to us on the evolutionary scale. But the fact is the heart ties in with a mythological feeling and has more meaning than it probably ought to have."

*Paragraph 8*

- The name of the disease, while providing precise information, may be too technical for the general reading audience. As I am not yet sure how I want to present the reason that the transplant was performed, I will leave it for now and will determine if it needs to be deleted to fit the needs of my particular audience later. I have placed it in brackets to signal that the necessity of retaining this material is questionable.

*Paragraph 9*

- Ethical information is irrelevant.

*Paragraph 10*

- Emotional justification is irrelevant.

*Paragraph 11*

- Justification of decision for performing procedure is irrelevant.

*Paragraph 12*

- Delete "available to parents of children." "Only option" is sufficient.

*Paragraph 13*

- Bracket name of drug used to signal that it may be deleted later as being too technical for the intended audience.

*Paragraph 14*

- Delete all subsequent references to baby's alias.
- The issue is whether the drug should have been used at all considering the possible side effects; the dosage doesn't matter.

*Paragraph 15*

- This material on the baby's treatment is not explained well. It is not precise enough for the expert, and lay people probably won't understand the significance of steroids or weaning the child from the ventilator. But since it is material that is pertinent to the medical advancement, I have placed it in brackets and will consider editing or deleting it in a later round.

*Paragraph 16*

- Future plans do not tell us about this particular advancement, but do tell us where this research may lead, so it is worth saving at this time.

*Paragraphs 17–19*

• Funding issues are irrelevant.

*Paragraph 20*

• Personal response of participant/observer is unnecessary.

*Paragraph 21*

• Sex and weight of baboon is insignificant.

*Paragraph 22*

• Again, this material is not explained well—not precise enough for the expert and too technical for the lay person. But since it is material that is pertinent to the medical advancement, I have placed it in brackets and will consider editing or deleting it in a later round.

*Paragraph 23*

• Ethical statement is irrelevant.

The first round of local deletion produces the following summary:

A 16-day-old infant remained in critical but stable condition today, "doing remarkably well" after receiving the heart of a baboon at Loma Linda University Medical Center.

But "she may be in for a long battle in the weeks ahead," said Dr. Leonard Bailey, the pediatric surgeon who performed the transplant operation. He addressed some of the technical and ethical aspects of the "highly experimental" operation.

The baby nearly died on her sixth day of life because of a birth defect [called hypoplastic heart syndrome], which gave the baby virtually only half a heart and no chance to live.

Until now, with rare exceptions, babies born with the condition did not survive beyond two weeks. The only option for a child born with the condition has been surgery to relieve its effects. Such surgery entails great risk and has uncertain results.

Dr. Bailey said he believed his was the only group in the world that was experimenting with a new drug [cyclosporin-A] for animal heart transplants in infants. The drug combats the body's normal rejection of foreign tissue such as transplanted organs. The baby received cyclosporin-A. The team was concerned about the potential toxic effects of the drug, he said, adding that the baby's blood is monitored frequently to detect any adverse effects.

Dr. Bailey said that the baby was receiving a steroid drug but no heart drugs. He said the team hoped to wean the baby from the mechanical ventilator that has helped her breathe.

The surgeon said that his team planned to perform five such operations and then to evaluate the results to determine whether they should go ahead or retreat to the laboratory before trying the procedure again on humans.

The heart was taken from a baboon between seven and eight months old.

[The researchers said that they had found that about half of an unspecified number of humans had pre-formed antibodies against baboons; so if the baby needs a blood transfusion, additional tests will have to be done on the donated blood. Dr. Bailey also said the baby's doctors would have to study, in greater detail than usual, the immunizations that she received to prevent similar adverse reactions.]

## *Reorganization*

Before any additional steps can be taken—generalization, construction, or further deletions—material must be reorganized and grouped so that logical related concepts and statements are situated as near to one another as possible. Note that there is no construction at this stage, only reordering. During this step we must look at how well the text is organized. To determine how to group information, write down a phrase or sentence that summarizes information presented in each paragraph or read the whole essay and write down phrases or sentences that capture the main ideas on a separate piece of paper. Then rearrange the paragraphs so that related sentences and paragraphs are next to one another. Having jotted down the main ideas I recognized, I have decided to group the statements into three paragraphs. The first deals with the facts of the operation. The second deals with the technical aspects of the child's potential recovery and the doctors' concerns over her recovery. The last paragraph is simply a statement of the doctors' and researchers' future plans.

A 16-day-old infant remained in critical but stable condition today, "doing remarkably well" after receiving the heart of a baboon between seven and eight months old, at Loma Linda University Medical Center. The baby nearly died on her sixth day of life because of a birth defect [called hypoplastic syndrome], which gave her virtually only half a heart and no chance to live. Until now, with rare exceptions, babies born with the condition did not survive beyond two weeks. The only option with the condition has been high-risk surgery to relieve its effects. Such surgery has uncertain results.

But "she may be in for a long battle in the weeks ahead," said Dr. Leonard Bailey, the pediatric surgeon who performed the transplant operation. He addressed some of the technical aspects of the "highly experimental" operation. Dr. Bailey said he believed his was the only group in the world that was experimenting with a new drug, [cyclosporin-A], for animal heart transplants in infants. The drug combats the body's normal rejection of foreign tissue such as transplanted organs. The baby received cyclosporin-A. The team was concerned about the potential toxic effects of the drug, he said, adding that the baby's blood is monitored frequently to detect any adverse effects. Dr. Bailey said that the baby was receiving a steroid drug but no heart drugs. He said the team hoped to wean the baby from the mechanical ventilator that has helped her breathe. [The researchers said that they had found that about half of an unspecified number of humans had pre-formed antibodies against baboons; if the baby needs a blood transfusion, additional tests will have to be done on the donated blood. Dr. Bailey also said the baby's doctors would have to study, in greater detail than usual, the immunizations that she received to prevent similar adverse reactions.]

The surgeon said that his team planned to perform five such operations and then to evaluate the results to determine whether they should go ahead or retreat to the laboratory before trying the procedure again on humans.

Now, using the construction step, closely related ideas are combined and any redundancy made evident by that combination is removed. As statements are combined, a bit of further reorganization may be necessary: the order of statements may need to be switched to improve clarity and to make construction easier. Construction helps point out additional deletions that can be made; such deletions are made at this time.

Construction and second round deletion:

*Paragraph 1*

- "Stable" and "doing well" are closely related concepts, as are "no chance to live" and "not living beyond two weeks"; combine and delete one member of each pair. There is now a simple statement of the child's condition; likewise, delete other closely related comments on her condition which can now be considered redundant.

- Combine sentences on surgery. Delete comment about surgery "relieving its effects"; this is obvious.

*Paragraph 2*

- Delete comment on "her battle" which repeats ideas in paragraph 1.
- Delete Bailey's self-aggrandizing statement about his group probably being the only one performing this procedure as not adding to the information on the procedure.
- References to team and researchers can be deleted; the statements can be rewritten to focus on the baby.
- Combine statements with baby as grammatical subject.
- Combine and reorder material on experimental drug to make clear how these details are important to the child's condition.
- Simply state the baby is being monitered; further detail is not useful (especially for a lay audience).
- State concern about pre-formed antibodies, but delete material concerning the number of potential donors who may have preformed antibodies as unnecessary detail (which is also too technical for the intended audience). (Reordering and combining will also make clear the reason her immunization record needed to be checked.)

*Paragraph 3*

- If you determine not to "go ahead," you obviously go back/"retreat"; redundancy can be deleted.

The resulting text is:

[1]    A 16-day-old infant remained in critical condition but was "doing remarkably well" after receiving the heart of a baboon between seven and eight months old, at Loma Linda University Medical Center. The baby nearly died on her sixth day of life because she had only half a heart [called hypoplastic heart syndrome] which gave her no chance to live. Babies born with the condition rarely survive beyond two weeks. The only option with this condition has been high-risk surgery which has uncertain results.

[2]   Dr. Leonard Bailey, the pediatric surgeon who performed the transplant operation, addressed some of the technical aspects of the "highly experimental" operation. The baby received [cyclosporin-A], an experimental drug, developed by Bailey's group for animal heart transplants in infants, that combats the body's normal rejection of foreign tissue such as transplanted organs. The baby is monitored frequently to detect any adverse effects to the drug, which has potential toxic effects. The baby was receiving a steroid drug but no heart drugs. Bailey said the team hoped to wean the baby from the mechanical ventilator that has helped her breathe. If the baby needs a blood transfusion, tests will have to be done on the donated human blood to make sure it does not contain pre-formed antibodies against baboons. The child's immunization record will also have to be checked to prevent similar adverse reactions.

[3]   The surgeon said that his team planned to perform five such operations and then to determine whether it should try the procedure again on humans.

Now that most of the clearly extraneous material has been removed, I must prioritize the remaining text in order to decide what to excise in subsequent rounds of deletion. Material of major significance will be kept; material of limited significance will be deleted. The needs of the audience and the purpose of the text are the best guides for determining how the text should be further edited. Since this summary is intended to inform a general reading audience about this medical breakthrough, medical terminology and names of the various drugs used can be considered insignificant. (Keep in mind, if the summary were for members of the American Medical Association or for a health journal such information would be imperative.) Some material on where the surgery was performed and who participated may also be left out, though the primary surgeon, Dr. Bailey, should be mentioned.

I further edit the text through subsequent rounds of construction, deletion, and generalization. (Generalization plays a more significant role in later rounds.) Many rounds may be necessary to produce a summary of acceptable length. Paragraphs one and three are relatively short, and I now need to utilize construction and generalization to further pare down paragraph two. As I combine statements and make generalizations, some deletions will inevitably occur. To further edit paragraph two:

- Remove the reference to the technical aspects of the operation. All statements should focus on the baby's condition. This creates a generalization, focused on the baby, that can be used to unify the whole paragraph.

- I delete much of the specific information on cyclosporin-A that is not appropriate for this audience and replace it with a general statement about an "experimental drug" used. The reference to toxic effects, which may be unclear to my audience, is replaced by a more general statement on a possible "adverse reaction."

- A ventilator is a type of life-support system, I replace the statements concerning this with a more general statement that the baby is on "life support." Again, such a statement will have more meaning for my audience.

- All the material on blood transfusions is a bit technical. Most readers will not know what pre-formed antibodies are or why the baby's immunization record matters; so I will again make a generalization that is more appropriate for my audience.

- I have also moved the material on life support to the end of the paragraph, since it is the least technical. It also deals with the baby's general condition in the present, after the procedure has been performed. This format presents the material more logically.

I now have the following summary:

> A sixteen-day-old infant remained in critical condition but was "doing remarkably well" after receiving the heart of a baboon which was between seven and eight months old. The baby nearly died on her sixth day of life, because she had only half a heart which gave her no chance to live. Babies born with this condition rarely survive beyond two weeks. The only option has been high-risk surgery which has uncertain results.
>
> Dr. Leonard Bailey, the pediatric surgeon who performed the transplant operation, spoke on the baby's condition. The baby received an experimental drug, developed by Bailey's group for animal

heart transplants in infants, that combats the body's normal rejection of foreign tissue such as transplanted organs. The baby is monitored frequently to detect any adverse effects to the drug. She may require additional blood transfusions. If so, precautions will have to be taken to ensure that the heart is not rejected. The baby is still on life support.

The surgeon said that his team planned to perform five such operations and then to determine whether it should try the procedure again on humans.

My summary is now under 200 words, which is acceptable for most purposes. What if I have to produce a shorter summary? Rigid length constraints are often placed on abstracts, summaries, and articles in various professional journals, and authors must comply. While a skilled writer may not need to employ the macrostructure strategy to produce a summary, he might find it a valuable aid when he has to edit a text that is still 10, 20, or 30 words over the maximum allowable length. In such a situation, a writer most commonly prioritizes the remaining material and decides what else to delete. Remember that there are other options suggested by this procedure: combination and generalization also will reduce the number of words in a text, but will allow for some retention of content that deletion permanently eradicates. If I had to further reduce my summary (some journals ask for summaries under 150 words), I might say "young baboon" instead of giving the age and leave out the reference to the baby almost dying on her sixth day of life. I might also delete the sentence about the baby being on life support; letting the first sentence, which says she is in critical condition, stand as the only statement of her current status. The last paragraph may also be deleted, if I am only concerned with the procedure that has just been performed. These changes would produce a summary that is less than 150 words. While I am deleting relevant material, I now consider this material to be of lower priority. Further generalization and combination may also be useful.

[1]  A sixteen-day-old infant remained in critical condition but was "doing remarkably well" after receiving the heart of a young baboon. The baby nearly died, because she had only half a heart which gave her no chance to live. Babies born with this condition rarely survive beyond two weeks. The only option has been high-risk surgery which has uncertain results.

[2]  Dr. Leonard Bailey, the pediatric surgeon who performed the transplant operation, stated that the baby received an experimental drug, developed by his group for animal heart transplants in infants, that combats the body's normal rejection of foreign tissue such as transplanted organs. The baby is monitored frequently to detect any adverse effects to the drug. She may require additional blood transfusions. If so, precautions will have to be taken to ensure that the heart is not rejected.

It's possible that you may not agree with the material that I changed in each round. You may have been more conservative as you performed each round of deletion, or you may have efficiently combined various steps. In either case, the goal is to produce the desired final summary or abstract. It is not how many times you repeat the steps that matters; it's your results.

Obviously in dealing with this particular article, some medical knowledge is useful for determining how to generalize and what to delete.[5] Familiarity with the material you are working with always makes generating summaries and abstracts easier. In most cases, you will have the necessary prerequisite knowledge, and if you don't, this procedure will still help you to identify major concepts and significant points. Often, if the macrostructure cannot be identified, you have identified a point where the text breaks down and becomes obscure; therefore, this procedure may help to identify major ideas that are not clearly explained.

## MACROSTRUCTURES FOR DIAGNOSING TEXTUAL WEAKNESSES

In the above application, problems in creating part of the macrostructure arose when dealing with original paragraphs fifteen and twenty-two. These paragraphs are very technical, and the information is only lightly touched upon. For the lay audience who reads a daily newspaper, this material is probably quite meaningless, because the significance of medical comments about "pre-formed antibodies" and the use of steroids are not explained. Any reader who tries to generate a macrostructure, to determine the theme and major points of the text, will have problems with these paragraphs. Should these technical paragraphs be retained at a the higher level? Are they of major importance or are they insignificant? If they are of major importance, how so? By answering this final question, the reader attempts to supply the information the writer has omitted. If the reader cannot ascertain needed information and answer such questions, the writer has failed to produce a totally coherent text.

When it is difficult to extract a macrostructure from a text, because it seems to break down at certain points, you may have identified points at which global coherence is a problem. The inability to create a completely satisfying summary, or to generate a macrostructure, usually signals a flawed text. Most competent writers will clearly state their thesis and generate coherent paragraphs; thus the top and bottom levels of the macrostructure pyramid will be in place. Problems arise in the levels in between. Often, the text is flawed by the manner in which concepts and ideas are linked to one another from paragraph to paragraph. The writer may need to reorder the paragraphs and clarify the links between concepts (often by using the correct junctive) so that the global design is easier for the reader to ascertain.

Take, for example, the article we have been working with. This article is written in a journalistic style, so the paragraphs tend to be short and choppy; therefore, writing a phrase down which summarizes each paragraph won't work well. Instead, I wrote down a few main ideas I found in the essay and identified the paragraphs in which I found that information:

| | |
|---|---|
| Basic information about the procedure and child | [1], [2], [6], [8], [12] |
| Technical medical details | [8], [13–15], [22] |
| Progress and plans of the research team | [11] and [16] |
| Funding | [17–19] |
| Professionals' reactions and observations | [7], [20], [23] |
| Ethical controversy | [3–5], [9], [10], [21], [23] |

Clearly, the article could be organized more coherently. If this were my article, I would rearrange the ideas beginning with basic factual information and expand my text to consider the reactions of those closest to the situation and then examine the reactions of the public as a whole.

The order of ideas might go like this: basic information, technical details, progress and plans of team, professional reactions, and ethical issues. This organizational strategy indicates that funding is a peripheral issue that cannot be easily integrated into the essay; consequently, I would leave that topic out.

Missing information, lack of clear organization, gaps in development, and/or the need for a different organizational design may all be easier to identify and correct using such a macrostructure analysis.

## MACROSTRUCTURE ANALYSIS FOR REVISING TEXTS

We have just examined how macrostructure analysis may help to identify organization and development problems in completed texts. Obviously, it would be best if the writer corrected such problems during the revision process, before the text was finished. Macrostructure analysis may be the dynamic revising tool you need.

Often the revision process involves strengthening the global coherence of a text. Remember that most common problems result from not clearly linking concepts to one another from paragraph to paragraph. As a result, the logic of your essay will be unclear. Revision will usually involve reordering the paragraphs and clarifying the links between concepts. Such revision will make it easier for the reader to determine what you are trying to convey.

When you are writing, most importantly, get your ideas down on paper. Let the ideas flow freely onto the page. Don't worry about getting the text perfect the first time; when you revise you can come back to the text and work on order and development. Once you have a draft which you believe contains all the information you want to convey to your audience, you can begin revising.

First, as we discussed earlier in the chapter, identify your audience and your purposes. Is the draft you produced appropriate for the audience and purpose you originally identified? Or has your audience or your purpose shifted? If so, you may have to rethink who it is you are writing for and what you wish to say to them.

Next, read what you've written and write a macrostatement that identifies the unifying idea of each paragraph in the margin next to that paragraph (or list the macrostatements sequentially on a separate piece of paper). If you have problems coming up with a macrostatement for each paragraph, you have probably identified paragraphs that are too short and/or that lack a unifying idea. If that is the case, you will need to either combine short paragraphs into longer ones that develop a significant point, or you may need to use the techniques for developing ideas and expanding paragraphs suggested at the end of the coherence chapter. Your macrostatements may be phrases or whole sentences. I call this process of identifying the ideas developed in the essay an "after the draft outline." Once you have created your outline, you can read down the list of macrostatements and analyze the overall, global coherence of your essay. This list is very useful for examining a number of coherence issues. You can reassess the thesis (or gist) of your paper based on the points you have actually developed. Do your macrostatements support and develop your thesis? If not, you may want to reformulate your thesis based on what you have actually said. Do your macrostatements follow a logical progression? Look at your list of macrostatements and ask yourself: Have I included peripheral information (paragraphs) that I should delete? Have I left out any vital piece of information that my reader will need? Are my macrostatements (and paragraphs) in the right order, or would moving a paragraph (or paragraphs) make my argument stronger and easier to follow? In other words, to revise for better organization and development, a writer needs to delete superfluous information, add missing pieces, and reorganize the information so that the paragraphs are in the right order. You may want to revise a text two or three times; you don't have to get it perfect the first time. Revise until you are happy with the results.[6]

Macrostructure analysis can become an integral part of your revising process. It can help you to strengthen an essay's overall organization and development.

## APPLICATION

Since you are now familiar with the Baby Fae article, try writing a summary that highlights the ethical argument. (Such information would be of interest to a group of animal rights' activists or a group of religious fundamentalists who do not believe that such surgical intervention is right. At this time, do not try to bias your summary toward any one group's perspective, but simply summarize information that such groups would find useful for writing their own articles.) Create a summary that stays a close to the writer's original words as possible. Assume that you are writing for a general reading audience.

# 8

## *Pragmatics:*
## *Language in Use*

Until the late 1950s, linguistics, like the study of literature, concentrated on the text, divorced from its producers and consumers. While in the earlier part of the century, Saussure had identified speakers and hearers as fundamental elements of the communication circuit, they still received little attention. And, as we have seen with Chomsky, the first attempts to deal with speaker and listener treated them more as abstract entities with perfect language competence, rather than as individuals with varying degrees of communication competence whose individual attitudes and intentions color their discourse. But with the emergence of pragmatics, the study of language in use, speakers and their audiences began to receive attention. In pragmatics, speakers and listeners—and by extension writers and readers—are still somewhat idealistically defined; what is studied is their right and ability to participate in certain discourse situations, and their ability to successfully communicate according to prescribed language conventions. Here, the type of communication seems to define the participants, rather than the participants' personalities determining the communication. It is the fact that the speaker "makes a promise" or "issues a command" (two types of speech acts), rather than the fact that the listener distrusts or dislikes the speaker, whom he might perceive to be a threat or adversary, that determines the type of speech act and dictates this type of analysis. It was not until the development of sociolinguistics that linguists began to study how an individual's personal background and social status—as well as the psychological and physical setting for communication—influence the many different language interactions. Yet, pragmatics was a dramatic step forward, since it was the first effort by linguists to methodically deal with the fact that the participants are integral to the communication circuit.[1]

## SPEECH ACT THEORY

The beginning of pragmatics as a field of linguistic research can be traced to the pioneering work of John Austin and John Searle. Austin proposed a new methodology, called speech act theory, for dealing with utterances.[2] A speech act is an utterance that has a particular, singular purpose, such as commanding, questioning, or stating a fact. Speech act theory is concerned with the description of the performance of the speech act: a speech act is performed by a speaker (or writer) and directed at a listener (or reader).

It is John Searle's improved version of speech act theory that is used by most linguists today.[3] Searle divides the speech act into two components: 1) the locutionary act is what the speaker means; 2) the illocutionary act is the type of performance the speaker is executing, such as a command, promise, or declaration, and his utterance is delivered with a certain illocutionary force.

> Example: *utterance* = "Get out of my way!"
> *locution* (meaning) = move yourself from blocking me
> *illocutionary force* = an order (a type of directive)

The locutionary act is a statement that most commonly contains a subject and predicate. However, a speech act can be much longer than a simple sentence; it should not be defined by grammatical units, but simply as the amount of text it takes to create a particular speech act or to accomplish a particular purpose. The locutionary act can never stand alone; it is always delivered with a certain illocutionary force. For example, "the chair is wet" can be delivered as a simple assertion (an assertive as discussed below) or as an "indirect" warning (a type of directive) meant to advise you not to sit there. Illocutionary force, which determines the type of illocutionary act, can be signaled by word order (e.g., inverted word order signals a question), the verb chosen as well as the mood of the verb, the pitch or intonation contours of the utterance (e.g., a rise in pitch indicates a question and a drop in pitch indicates a command), and by punctuation in writing. Only when illocutionary force is coupled with words is a recognizable utterance generated.

## The Speech Act

1. The locutionary act is the saying of the message, the literal meaning. For example, "take out the garbage" means the listener is to remove the trash from the house and place it in the trash can outside.

2. The illocutionary act is defined by the force with which the utterance is delivered. The illocutionary act is recognizable by language conventions; we recognize questions, orders, and promises by such things as the word order, intonation patterns (or punctuation in writing), and certain key words (e.g., saying "I *promise*" when making a promise). The illocutionary force with which a locutionary act is delivered will determine how the utterance is interpreted; thus "take out the trash," may be a request or an order depending on the tone of the speaker.

While all speech acts have two components, speech acts themselves are divided into five classes.

## A Taxonomy of Speech Acts

*Assertives*

PURPOSE: The speaker commits himself to the truth of the expressed statement.

EXAMPLE: I believe that an ecumenical government is in our distant future.

### Directives

PURPOSE: The speaker attempts to get the hearer to do something.

EXAMPLE: I want you to complete the job immediately.

### Commissives

PURPOSE: The speaker commits himself to some course of action.

EXAMPLE: I promise I will take you to the movies.

### Expressives

PURPOSE: The speaker expresses the psychological state that is specified by a sincere desire to successfully carry out the speech act or the expression of an attitude toward the subject matter being conveyed by the utterance.

EXAMPLE: I resent your taking the dessert you know I wanted.

### Declarations

PURPOSE: When the speaker delivers such a speech act successfully, a correspondence between the words and world is created. These acts bring about some change in status or condition of the object being referred to. For example, the swearing in of the president-elect makes him the president. Many declarations are ritualistic, like weddings, and require a special set of circumstances—specific places and authorized participants.

EXAMPLE: I now pronounce you husband and wife.[4]

Speech acts are, by nature, conventional, understandable only because they follow a set of language conventions agreed upon by the society speaking a given language. For example, we recognize questions by the rise in pitch and by the inversion of word order. And we recognize that when a speaker asks a question, we are being asked to perform a task or to furnish some information. Our ability to successfully comprehend various speech acts is in part determined by our facility with grammar, as well as by our knowledge of the less tangible aspects of communication. Delivering the speech act that suits your purpose is not enough. As we shall see, the speech act must also be spoken under the appropriate conditions. If speech acts were not conventional, we would be unable to understand and properly respond to a speaker or writer. Fortunately, every native speaker acquires and develops a working knowledge of speech acts before adulthood.

## APPROPRIATENESS CONDITIONS FOR SUCCESSFUL COMMUNICATION

If any speech act is to be successfully executed the appropriate conditions must be in place. In order to "know" what "appropriateness conditions" apply, the participants must have communicative competence. In other words, everyone who participates in a language community must learn what conditions are necessary to successfully carry out the speech act. As communicators, a knowledge of these conditions can often help us to determine why a text succeeds or fails in communicating the speaker's or writer's intended message.[5]

### Appropriateness Conditions

1. The appropriate participants and circumstances must be activated:
   —the speaker has the right to make the utterance at the time;
   —the audience has the right to respond appropriately at the time;
   —the utterance is appropriate to the ongoing discourse in terms of subject matter.
   EXAMPLE: A verdict can only be given in a courtroom, at the end of a trial, and can only be delivered by the foreman of the jury.
2. A conventional procedure must be established.

EXAMPLE: A welcome can only be given at the beginning of a conversation. An apology is only appropriate when you have insulted or injured another's feelings.

3. Procedures must be correct and complete. If decorum and/or conventions of the speech are breached, then the speech act is nullified.

EXAMPLE: If during an antidrug program given to high school students, the main speaker began to sing "Lucy in the Sky with Diamonds," his effectiveness would be destroyed. If a minister began to read a eulogy during a marriage ceremony the vows would be deconsecrated.

4. The speaker must be sincere in his desire to communicate his message, and the audience must be sincere in wanting to understand what the speaker means. Both speaker and audience must believe that all other appropriateness conditions have been sincerely met.[6]

In most cases, native language speakers intuitively know when appropriateness conditions are being observed. But these conditions often elude foreign speakers, since they are not directly addressed in language classes. This is perhaps the most difficult aspect of learning a foreign language. In general, foreign language courses and texts deal only with vocabulary and grammar, and not with the interpersonal communication situation. This is why a nonnative speaker may err in speaking too informally to his boss, ordering him to "Gimme a match," or in speaking too formally to a close friend when asking him, "If it is not too much of an inconvenience could you please allow me to borrow a match from you?"[7] We tend to require that people learn these less tangible aspects of language use from experience, rather than through formal language training. Yet, such knowledge is fundamental to the success of any speaker in a new language community. People must be aware of the appropriateness conditions associated with each speech act in order to understand what choices (words, pitch, degree of politeness, etc.) are appropriate in a given set of circumstances. It is important to recognize that different speech acts have different appropriateness conditions that allow for certain participants, circumstances, and settings: in turn, the appropriateness conditions determine the kinds of speech acts allowed. When you go to a friend's house for dinner, it is inappropriate to sit down at the table and order as if you were in a restaurant. And though a Marine sergeant may issue a command to his children at home, they may ignore him, though his men in the barracks would not. Thus, participants and situations limit the number and types of speech acts we may expect, and they provide important clues about how we are to interpret and respond to a speech act. The importance of language conventions—including appropriateness conditions and pragmatic conventions—to our ability to use and understand our own language cannot be ignored.

The set of appropriateness conditions provided above is general enough to be useful for evaluating all speech act situations; specific details can be added to describe each situation. What happens if the appropriateness conditions are not observed? Communication breaks down. If the speaker or listener is insincere and does not really want to participate in the communicative act, we say there has been an "abuse" of the speech act. A "misfire" is the result of inappropriate participants, circumstances, or incorrect or incomplete procedures. In all these cases, the result is an unsuccessful speech act. Success is measured by the fact that the audience has successfully understood the message as it was intended by the speaker (or writer). This can only happen if the appropriateness conditions are observed.

## INDIRECT SPEECH ACTS

An indirect speech act occurs when the speaker communicates more to the hearer than he literally says. Often, the clue that a speaker is using an indirect speech act is that the action specified by the indirect speech act, performed literally, would be inappropriate in some way. For instance, if someone asks you, "Can you tell me what time it is?" He is probably not insulting your intelligence by asking if you are mentally capable of telling time, as the literal question would imply. Rather, he is asking if you would mind making the effort to look at your watch and tell him the time. Indirect speech acts are often used to soften the speaker's manner of addressing the listener. "Tell me what time it is" is an order; using "can" makes it a (less abrasive) request. People who know each other well rarely need to use the more formal directives and commissives previously discussed; therefore, they often use indirect speech acts. In addition to softening the speaker's manner, indirect speech acts often add emphasis or express an attitude toward what is being said, as in "*I do declare,* he's a liar." Among the most common methods of transforming direct speech acts into indirect speech acts are: 1) questioning a condition associated with the act, for example, "can"; 2) explicitly stating the speaker's obligation, for example, "must"; 3) asking permission to perform the act, for example, "may"; 4) stating an emotional attitude associated with performing the act, for example, "want" or "desire." By saying, "I believe Prof. Jackson will give a test tomorrow," when you heard him make that announcement, you are placing the sincerity condition in the foreground, explicitly bringing your belief that your statement is true to your listener's attention. Calling a condition into question is commonly used to transform orders into requests or favors: "can" turns orders into requests. All "can" questions—"can you pass the salt?", "can you take out the garbage?"— are not questions of one's physical ability, but conventionally interpreted as more polite ways of asking someone to do something for you.

If the message conveyed in an indirect speech act is to be successfully communicated, the speaker must rely on the listener sharing the same language conventions and necessary background knowledge. The hearer will use such knowledge to infer what the speaker has left out. To decode an indirect speech act the hearer must: 1) have a strategy for establishing the existence of an ulterior point; this is done, for example, by recognizing that one of the appropriateness conditions is being given special emphasis; 2) have a strategy for determining what the ulterior point is. The listener's ability to decipher the indirect speech act comes from understanding language conventions and from knowledge about the world that the speaker and listener (or writer and reader) share.

## INDIRECTION

A great deal of the discourse we participate in every day is in the form of indirect speech acts. Perhaps we can put to good use what we have learned about indirect speech acts to study an associated phenomenon, "indirection." Indirection is popular in advertising, bureaucratese, and as a device used by children to manipulate their parents into agreeing to things to which they would not normally agree. Consequently, indirection is often a deliberately manipulative act, less benign than the simple indirect speech act. When analyzing indirect speech acts, we are usually looking at single sentences; however, indirection is a quality of a complete text. For instance, beware the adolescent who begins a conversation by asking you if punctuality is a quality you believe she should strive for. She may ask you if you believe she should do her best to arrive at school, at work, and at appointments on time. She may next request that you replace her dilapidated three-speed with the latest twenty-five–speed mountain bike. You could say that the appropriate conditions for the conventional procedure of asking a favor have been flouted. You may be surprised that the same child who could not understand you when you said "take out the garbage" has now shown dazzling communicative competence. Of course, you can always respond by telling your precocious child to simply set her watch ahead five minutes and then she'll always be on time. In a more serious vein, look at the Pentagon's directive 5122.f which states the government's position on releasing information to the general public; this directive states that the Secretary of Defense for Public Affairs is responsible for:

1. Provid(ing) the American people with maximum information about the Department of Defense consistent with national security.

2. Initiat(ing) and support(ing) activities contributing towards good relations between the Department of Defense and all segments of the public at home and abroad. (J. W. Fulbright, *The Pentagon Propaganda Machine*)[8]

The first statement begins with an assertion that the Pentagon sincerely believes the public has a right to know and sincerely believes that the government has a duty to tell the public what it needs to know. But this is immediately followed by the disclaimer "consistent with national security," which would seem to make it virtually impossible to release "maximum information." The second statement also begins by giving precedence to "good" public relations; but this statement is disquieting because of a covert, implicit message that good relations take precedence over truth, since releasing unpopular information would destroy the public image for which the Pentagon is striving. The result? We question the sincerity claim placed in the foreground in the first statement, and then we become suspicious of all information released to us by the Pentagon.[9]

Rather than explicitly stating what we mean, indirect speech acts serve to imply meaning. In everyday discourse indirect speech acts are used in friendly, benign exchanges, such as asking for favors or making requests. They are often used to create a mood of cooperation; they are forms of friendly coercion. But indirect speech acts and global, textual forms of indirection can also lead to problems. If you are sincerely trying to convey material intended to inform or instruct your audience, then it is best to avoid any form of indirection as it can lead to misdirection and miscommunication. An indirect speech act always requires extra cognitive processing. This places obstacles in the way of successful communication, particularly in cases where the listeners or readers are unfamiliar with the nuances and conventions of the type of discourse the speaker or writer is using. For example, a nonnative speaker may have problems understanding the polite form of English questions, and a humanities major may have problems reading a *Scientific American* article on recombinant DNA. Listeners or readers are required to make inferences, and these inferences may lead them to entertain possible interpretations the speaker or writer would prefer that the audience not consider. Indirection can create confusion. Listeners or readers may miss the point and grow irritated, if they feel they are unable to understand what is being communicated, or if they feel that they are being manipulated.

Sometimes the writer or speaker deliberately misdirects or creates confusion. In the case of the Pentagon directive, the writer may be banking on the reader missing the point of the communiqúe. This would mean that the sincerity condition was blatantly violated. In that case, there was no true desire to successfully and effectively communicate information. The intent of the writer becomes of paramount importance here (though this is not an issue traditionally dealt with in speech act theory). Obviously a conscious desire to deceive through indirection has serious consequences; it disrupts communication. Such issues, concerning the obligations of the speaker, are the subject of the work of Paul Grice.

## GRICE'S COOPERATION PRINCIPLE

Paul Grice proposed that if the speaker and hearer wish to communicate successfully and effectively, then they must cooperate. He calls this shared goal the Cooperation Principle. The Cooperation Principle is supported by a set of maxims—presented by Grice as a set of instructions—which, if observed, according to Grice, will guarantee successful execution of speech acts and effective communication.

### Maxims of the Cooperation Principle[10]

Maxim of Quantity:
  1. Make your contribution as informative as is required.
  2. Do not make your contribution more informative than is required.

Maxim of Quality:
  1. Do not say what you believe to be false.
  2. Do not say that for which you lack adequate evidence.

Maxim of Relation:
  1. Be relevant.

Maxim of Manner:
  1. Avoid obscurity. (Obscurity refers to vagueness; meaning is unclear.)

2. Avoid ambiguity. (Ambiguity refers to the possibility of two or more possible meanings for a word or span of text.)
3. Be brief.
4. Be orderly.

Maxim of Consistency:
1. Do not create internal inconsistencies.
2. Do not create paradoxes (except for intentional rhetorical effects.)
3. Avoid oxymorons.

Grice's maxims must be upheld if successful, unobscured communication is to occur. But the maxims are often deliberately flouted and violated in bureaucratese and advertising, where the writer often intends to impede or prevent complete access to the material. (The Pentagon directive is an example of a violation of the maxim of consistency, since the Secretary of Defense cannot release maximum information and protect national security at the same time, nor can he release maximum information at all times and maintain a positive public image.) Thus, the audience is subtly, and sometimes none too subtly, manipulated and coerced.

Legal documents are excellent texts to analyze for breaches in the Cooperation Principle. While the language of lawyers seems obscure, lawyers rightly contend the jargon is necessary in order to be precise and to avoid and close loopholes. Yet, this obscurity also serves to prevent lay people from understanding contracts and legal records, and therefore forces them to enlist the services of lawyers, when, for example, they have to sign leases. Look at the following statement typically found in a lease:

> If title is not merchantable and written notice of defect is given by Leasee to Leasor on or before closing date, the Leasor shall use reasonable effort to correct said defect prior to date of closing.

Lay readers, who are not lawyers, may sense that the maxim of manner is violated here; the language is deliberately obscure, and the same message could probably be stated more briefly and simply. The readers may also feel that the writer has violated the maxim of quantity since the document does not provide them with enough information to interpret the meaning of the statement. You will find that when one maxim is violated, often other maxims are violated too. The maxims sometimes behave like a row of dominos: topple one and the others follow. As for the lease, though the language is obscure as far as the lay person is concerned and one or more maxims appears to be violated, the state will call the document precisely written and legally binding.

Advertising also deliberately flouts the maxims. Take all those pain reliever commercials where we are told that four out of five doctors recommend brand A. What we are not told is how many doctors were surveyed—thousands, hundreds, or ten? We are also not told if these doctors get free samples from the company that is promoting the drug. If a doctor takes free samples from the company and hands them out to his patients, is that considered an endorsement? The maxim of quantity is violated in all such ads; we are not given enough information to make an informed judgment as to the validity of the claims of the advertiser. Gricean analysis can be quite useful in such cases, revealing how speakers and writers deliberately obscure material. Let's look at one final example of violating the Cooperation Principle dealing with reports by our major TV networks that possible assassination attempts were to be made on high U.S. government officials.

> Looking over the networks' 24 reports about hit teams aired on the evening news between Nov. 25 and Dec. 25, 1981, it was possible for viewers to be told that:
>
> —The number of hitmen being searched for was, variously, three (ABC), five (CBS), (NBC), six (ABC), 10 (ABC, CBS), 12 (CBS) or 13 (NBC).
> —The assassins had entered the U.S. From Canada (ABC, CBS).

—The assassins were in Mexico (CBS).

—The assassins were not in Mexico (ABC).

—Carlos "The Jackal" was a possible hit-team member (CBS, NBC).

—The personal habits of various hit-team members included the wearing of cowboy boots and Adidas, and the smoking of English cigarettes (CBS, NBC).

—The hit teams were composed of three Libyans (ABC, NBC), three Iranians (CBS, NBC), two Iranians (ABC), three Syrians (NBC), one Palestinian (ABC, CBS, NBC).

—One team member, Achemed Duma, visited Phoenix, Arizona (ABC).

The information for these reports came from the following on-camera interviews with sources willing to be identified: none.

Instead, television reports quoted (among others) "sources," "officials," "security officials," "Government sources," "Capitol Hill sources," "It's been learned" and "ABC News has learned."

Indeed, ABC jumped on the story with both feet. On Thanksgiving Night, Nov. 26, Washington anchor Frank Reynolds stated that it was "known" that Libyan agents were "in this country for the purpose of assassinating the highest officials of the U.S. Government."

Unfortunately, the only person ever to assure a TV audience of that unique certainty was Reynolds. CIA director William Casey never said it. Neither did President Reagan or Secretary of State Alexander Haig. In fact, the head of the FBI, William Webster, told ABC's Sam Donaldson on Jan. 3, 1982, "We've never confirmed" any hard evidence about a hit team inside the United States. And ABC senior correspondent John Scali, who first broadcast reports about the Libyan plot on ABC insists, "No one ever told me there was hard evidence." (John Weisman, "Why American TV Is So Vulnerable to Foreign Propaganda")[11]

Virtually all of Grice's maxims are violated in these network reports. What is the relevance of personal habits—the wearing of Adidas or cowboy boots? Does this mean all American are to be suspicious of, and should report, anyone who looks Middle Eastern and who is dressed in such a fashion? And what does it matter that Dumas "visited" Phoenix? (Note the obscure past tense of the reference.) Obviously, these are examples of violations of the maxim of relation. Information on the number of hit men and the nationality of the members violate the maxims of manner (be orderly), quality (do not say that for which you lack adequate evidence), and consistency. Not only do the three major networks disagree, but they continually changed their own reports, though surely they would call this "updating" their numbers. If listeners were to assume that a factual event was being reported here, one that could be researched and verified, comparing network versions would certainly confound and disenchant them. Amassing all the data presented by all three stations reveals that the reports *in toto* break the maxims of quality and manner. To say the hit team is or isn't in Mexico is ambiguous and reveals that someone obviously lacks evidence to make any such statement. The most flagrant violations, and the most contemptuous, are those of the maxims of quality: all three networks are guilty of fabrication, or of broadcasting reports for which they lack adequate evidence. (The most damning piece of evidence is that both NBC and CBS reported Carlos "the Jackal" was a hit team member. The Jackal, as known to the general populace, is a fictional assassin created by Robert Ludlum for his *Bourne* trilogy. This is a flagrant violation of the maxim of quality.) By releasing such information, the networks also flagrantly break the maxim of quantity, giving more information than is required. In fact, no information needs to be disseminated to the public, because there is no real story, and the networks have actually spun tall tales and pulled "information" out of thin air.

Returning to the appropriateness conditions for speech acts, we could also say that appropriateness conditions have also been breached. One of the most basic conditions, sincerity, has been violated. Reynolds could not sincerely believe in the message he was conveying. And secondly, the broadcasters have exploited the conventional procedure. Newscasts compose a conventional genre that Americans are taught will always convey factual—not fictional or speculative (unless duly represented as such)—information. These broadcasts took advantage of the viewers' belief that the networks had completely and correctly complied with the established protocol for news reporting.

The Cooperation Principle and its maxims are quite helpful in determining how writers—especially in advertising, technical writing, journalism, and other types of professional writing—may either unintentionally or deliberately obscure material and impede communication. In cases where language is deliberately obscured to coerce or manipulate the reader (as in advertising, in forms of doublespeak, and in professional jargon), analyzing the text using a Gricean method can be quite helpful in determining how skilled writers manipulate their language. [12]

## WHAT PRAGMATICS OFFERS THE WRITER

Pragmatic approaches are perhaps most useful to the writer who is revising a text or analyzing a finished piece of prose. As we have seen, Gricean analysis can be used to study how the media can manipulate its audience, and it can be used to explain why a text may fail to communicate the writer's intended meaning. The maxims are easy to learn and use since they are clearly written as a set of simple instructions. Don't worry about determining whether you have "violated the maxim of quality"; rather, follow the instructions to check to see if a statement is irrelevant or if you lack the evidence to support a claim. Such observations should help you to refocus your argument. The set of maxims, as a whole, offers the writer a set of guidelines, especially useful during the revising process, by which to identify potential problematic statements.

Pragmatics acknowledges the conventional, social component of the language situation. Successful writers must be aware of the pragmatic features of communication, such as those that we have discussed here, if they are to write texts that will successfully convey their messages. Experienced communicators and writers in specialized fields often forget that novice writers and readers must be taught the conventions of that field. For example, the consumer who purchases his first computer has to be taught how to read a computer instruction manual; he must learn what he can expect from the manual and how best to use it. As writers, we owe it to our audience to become familiar with the conventions and circumstances—the pragmatic dimensions—of the situation for which we are writing. For whom are we writing? What expectations will they have?[13] What are the conventions of the genre in which we are writing? We must ask ourselves such questions and consider the pragmatic aspects governing the type of discourse in which we are engaging, if we want to produce texts that are acceptable for the given situation and that meet the needs of our readers.[14]

## LIMITATIONS OF PRAGMATIC APPROACHES

Pragmatics occupies an interesting niche in linguistic studies. It is the first field within linguistics to attempt to examine—though in an idealistic, abstract manner—the interpersonal parameters of language. But at the same time, speech act theory has tried to remain a precise, logic-based approach by which theorists can construct structural descriptions of classes and types of speech acts. These goals present a paradox for linguists: how are they to account for interpersonal and circumstantial aspects of language that are infinitely diverse, and at the same time construct an analytical, systematic approach for dealing with speech acts (i.e., a taxonomy that would classify all utterances). A mind-boggling task indeed, and the results? Speech act theory has generally dealt with 1) single speech acts or a single exchange between speaker and hearer such as question-answer, request-reply, or 2) fairly conventional speech act situations and texts such as the first few exchanges of a telephone call, greetings, ordering from a menu, and highly structured, short, simple narratives (such as those told by children).

The paradox presented by pragmatic studies inspired the inception of a new linguistic branch, sociolinguistics. The sociolinguist's main concern is the social, interpersonal, and situational aspects of language. As we look at sociolinguistics in the next chapter, you will see that Austin's appropriateness conditions can be considered the germinating seed of this new branch of linguistics. In sociolinguistics, the conditions are expanded and delineated in great detail to allow for a more serious inquiry into the more elusive interpersonal and social aspects of language.

## APPLICATIONS

1. What appropriateness condition is broken in each of the following cases?
   a. Someone says, "I thank you for what you are about to do."
   b. A husband comes home and announces he has just accepted an invitation to work out with his boss at the health club tonight, having forgotten he had promised to take his wife out on the town over a week ago. She is wearing a lavish evening dress and obviously spent two hours on her makeup and hair. After he makes his announcement, she replies, "Oh, go right ahead. It's no big deal. I really don't mind."
   c. A teacher, knowing that a student has been unable to finish the essay due today, calls on that student to read his essay in front of the class.

2. Street signs often rely on conventional knowledge. Tourists, in particular, might be momentarily confused by such signs as:[15]
   a. Sign posted in German's Black Forest: "It is strictly forbidden on our Black Forest camping site that people of different sex, for instance, men and women, live together in one tent unless they are married with each other for that purpose." What maxim is violated?
   b. Sign in a Japanese hotel: "You are invited to take advantage of the chambermaid." What maxim is violated?
   c. Sign on a trash receptacle in England: "Please litter." What appropriateness condition(s) does the sign depend on if the reader is to properly decode the message?

3. The following excerpt is from a nationally distributed survey by the Republican National Committee on Reagan Administration Defense Strategy. The directions and four selected questions from the original seven questions are given here. All questions required the respondent to check off yes, no, or undecided.
   a. What maxims are violated in the following text?

*Directions:* Answer each question, then return this form in the postage-paid envelope. So as not to prejudice your responses, please do not read the Republican positions listed at the end of this survey until you have completed your answers. Only total results will be released to Reagan Administration and Party officials.

> 1) Do you support appropriations for modernizing our defenses which became dangerously obsolete as a result of cutbacks by the Carter/Mondale administration?
>
> 2) Do you support a nuclear freeze by the United States, whether or not the Soviets do the same?
>
> 3) Do you agree with Democrats who say that Soviet/Cuban efforts to topple pro-West governments in Central America pose no direct threat to U.S. security?
>
> 4) The Soviets have amassed the largest naval force in the world and have increased the number of submarines patrolling the U.S. coast. Should the U.S. Navy receive more funding to replace our aging sea force and build more Trident nuclear submarines?

b. Are any appropriateness conditions compromised by this survey?

# 9

## Sociolinguistics: Language and the Community of Individuals

A rule-governed system is just one base of knowledge we rely upon when constructing our discourse.[1] In other words, grammar alone does not offer all the information we need to know in order to speak or write in every given situation. Why, for example, is it appropriate to yell "hello" to attract a friend's attention when he is standing across the street, but not to greet a priest at the beginning of mass in the same manner? Other tacit knowledge, besides grammar, is necessary if we are to communicate effectively in the numerous situations that we find ourselves in every day. The interpersonal situation itself provides a context which limits the types of verbal and written exchanges that will occur. Sociolinguistics addresses the questions of how we appropriately gauge interpersonal and situational factors to ensure that what we say and write will be interpreted as we intend. Sociolinguistics attempts to identify and understand the multitude of complex human factors affecting communication: factors such as how who we are, what we believe, and what attitudes we hold affect what we say and how we say it. Moreover, sociolinguists also study how our gestures, behaviors, tone, and style of speaking and writing contribute to the act of communication.

## THE SOCIAL SITUATION AND THE SPEECH COMMUNITY

In previous chapters where the text was our primary concern, our ability to successfully communicate seemed to be determined by our mastery of the rule-governed system of our language. A study of discourse from such a perspective not only emphasizes grammar, it concentrates on the referential aspect of language, how language refers to real world objects and events. The emotional aspect of discourse is ignored: the psychological state of the speaker and listener (i.e., participants' personal and societal motives for interacting and attitudes affecting their willingness to communicate) as well as the tone and manner of the speaker (e.g., serious, jesting, or sarcastic) receive no attention. When we looked at the people communicating, they remained idealized. Consequently, we looked only at conventionally defined intents and goals, such as asking a favor or making a promise. Underlying such a traditional approach are the assumptions that all people involved in the act of communicating have the same language competence[2] and belong to an idealized, homogeneous language community. This means that every person who speaks (American) English, speaks the same English: we all can and do use the same grammatical structures (except when we inadvertently make a mistake), and we use these same structures all the time, at home, at work, at play. However, as we know from experience, this is not the case.

Language always serves to further the needs of the people engaged in communication, whether by comforting, instructing, seducing, or informing. Even if you speak to yourself, in which case you are both sender and audience, you are satisfying a personal need to express your emotions or to "hear yourself think." Sociolinguists acknowledge that each language speaker has a repertoire of styles or "ways of speaking" that serve various needs; these styles vary depending on who the speaker is, where the speaker is (the locker room or the boardroom), and who the intended recipient is (a lover or boss). We are seen as participating in many speech communities and adapting our language for each particular situation and audience. For example, a black inner-city youth attending Princeton may be able to "rap" with the kids down the street during summer vacation but will speak more formal "Standard English" when his professor calls on him in class. Situations in which we communicate are not governed by an established set of rules; rather they serve as contexts that help to define and circumscribe the kinds of discourse that will take place.

The speech situation is both a physical setting—the time and place—as well as a psychological setting. The psychological setting is socially determined and can be considered the overall mood or atmosphere—serious, festive, formal, casual, and the like. While the number of possible discourses that can possibly occur seems as infinite as the number of verbal and written exchanges we engage in, once a speech situation is identified, not all imaginable combinations of topics, channels, genres, and tones and manners of addressing an audience can occur. Once either the situation or participants are identified, the infinite variables become finite; then, only certain combinations of discourse features are possible. Now, we can begin to describe the particular speech situation.

## S-P-E-A-K-I-N-G

Dell Hymes identified a set of fundamental, interpersonal components of communication. These elements are presented under the mnemonic SPEAKING which stands for:

- S—Situation: This includes both the physical setting—time and place—as well as psychological setting—mood or atmosphere—e.g., serious, festive, formal, casual, and the like.
- P—Participants: This includes the person who sends the message (speaker or writer) as well as the audience (the listener[s] or reader[s]). This may include (demographic) information about their social status and position (held or desired), ethnicity, age, sex, vocation, as well as information about their attitudes.

E—Ends: This includes the goals that those engaged in the communication intend to accomplish and any unexpected outcomes.

A—Act Sequence: This includes the content—what is said (topic)—and form—how it is said (grammatical usage and word choice)—of the message.

K—Key: This includes the tone and manner in which the communication is performed, including serious, mocking, ironic, sarcastic, and perfunctory.

I—The Instrumentalities: These include the channels and styles. Channel is the mode of delivery, including spoken, sung, written, telegraphed, or signed. Style is a measure of how formal or intimate the speaker's language is based upon the situation and who is being spoken to.

N—Norms of Interpretation: This includes the determination of what behaviors are acceptable in particular speech communities. For middle-class Americans this includes such things as inserting fillers when you hesitate (e.g., "uh," "you know"). For blacks this may include recycling back to the beginning of an utterance (a practice many whites unjustly view as a defect in speech). This also includes issues of how much eye contact is appropriate between participants, how close they may stand or sit, and whether they can touch each other while speaking; these factors vary from class to class, and culture to culture.

G–Genre: These are the categories by which we recognize spoken and written types of discourse, including editorials, proposals, lectures, romance novels, mystery novels, letters, etc.[3]

S-P-E-A-K-I-N-G offers the writer a compendium of considerations beyond the contextual material of the text. These considerations are best formulated as a series of questions the writer can contemplate while writing and evaluating the text's effectiveness:

S: Is the text appropriate for the situation?

P: Who is your intended audience? (Demographically characterize them and consider their needs.)[4] Is the communication geared for the intended audience? Is the vocabulary appropriate to their level of knowledge? Is the information presented in a manner they will understand? For example, giving computer specifications in a user's manual is inappropriate, since the user will not understand that material and may develop anxiety about using computers, if he is led to believe that using the computer requires such technical knowledge.

E: Are the goals of your communication clear? Do you make clear what you want the audience to do, learn, or consider after reading your text? Have you anticipated unexpected responses they may have to what you have written? For example, if you inadvertently insulted your readers' intelligence by giving too much elementary information, you may cause them to react hostilely toward you and your proposal.

A: Are the grammar and form of the communication correct and appropriate for the audience? Are the topics easy to identify?

K: Is your tone appropriate? Do you sound condescending or unsure of yourself? Is humor appropriate? Do anecdotes and digressions add to the presentation or make you sound unprofessional?

I: Is the style and degree of formality chosen appropriate for the audience? For example, the formal style of a scientific journal article should be toned down before it is delivered at a conference (perhaps adding more personal pronouns and using less statistical information). An oral presentation is less formal than a written article.

N: Is there anything, in the manner in which you present your information, that may offend your audience, such as assumed familiarity or (unintended) sexism or racism?

G: Have you chosen the correct genre for your intended audience and observed the rules of the genre in which you are writing? For example, in a conversation people take turns speaking. If you do not allow the other person to speak, he may become irritated. Or, if you write a business letter to colleagues at your place of business, they may consider the letter a threat, since a less formal interdepartmental memo is perceived to be the appropriate mode of communication.

These questions touch upon major sociolinguistic concerns and will help writers to consider the interpersonal facets of effective communication.

## PARTICIPANT INTERACTION—STYLES OF ACCOMMODATION

In addition to choosing a style of writing appropriate for our audience, we must also base our choice of style on how we wish to be perceived. As a writer, you select a manner in which to present yourself that will accommodate your own intentions and your audience's needs and their possible responses to what you intend to communicate. We can say that the writer chooses a style of accommodation. In choosing a style, you must consider how your tone, manner, and attitudes as well as the readers' loyalties, mood, and attitudes will affect the communication.[5] Accommodation theory emphasizes the fact that communication is an interactive process; the participants' attitudes toward each other and the rapport they develop, or lack thereof, have a direct effect on the outcome of the communication.

You will choose a style of accommodation based on what you perceive to be your rights and responsibilities in the communicative exchange as well as what rights and responsibilities you have assigned to your readers. You will also choose a "face to put forth," a "public face," to win your audience's approval, and at the same time you will need to maintain a "private face" to protect your right to write what you see fit. A writer must find the appropriate style to gain audience approval without compromising self.[6] Face is most evident in the formality of address and the degree of politeness the writer uses. Face is indicated by the forms of address, sentence length, vocabulary, and syntax. (Passive syntax is erroneously believed to be more formal, when it simply distances the audience by creating obtuse prose.) Writers and readers also choose the "footing" on which they engage one another. As a writer, you take on a role determined by the amount of authority you wish to claim for your work. You can present yourself as a "reciter" who simply reports someone else's words or as the "author" who selects the information presented and who claims to be an authority on what is said. The audience can also take on a number of different roles, including passive listener or active challenger. The tone and manner (key and instrumentalities) you adopt in your writing offer cues about the footing you perceive yourself to be on with your readers.[7]

Accommodation theory does not provide a writer with a series of rules for instant success in communication. Yet, using this approach, a set of questions can be devised that will help you to gauge the rapport you have established with your audience. These questions are best asked during the prewriting and revising stages.

1. What do you expect the attitude of your audience to be: passive, challenging, skeptical, or eager for your communication?
2. How have you presented yourself in the text? Does the face and footing you choose for yourself encourage the attitude you wish to elicit from your audience? Is the manner in which you present yourself appropriate? (Are you authoritative without seeming overbearing?)
3. What attitude does your text encourage? Do you have to attempt to change the attitude of your audience to make them willing to engage the information presented in your text? (Information that may help you to negotiate with your audience appears later in this chapter, in the section on plans.)

You should keep the relationship between the writer and reader in mind when you design texts. Though you may not have to explicitly deal with readers' attitudes in the text, the forms of address ("we" includes the audience, whereas "you" can be at times inviting and at other times accusatory and distancing) and the syntax and grammar you choose (precise grammar and passive syntax signify formality and distance the audience) offer implicit cues about the face you have chosen and the footing you believe you are on with your audience. This, in turn, will affect how readers will respond to your text. As a writer, how you perceive your audience and want them to view you are always revealed by the manner in which you present yourself and your material.

## EVALUATORS AND INTENSIFIERS—CLUES TO THE SPEAKER'S OR WRITER'S ATTITUDE

Evaluators and intensifiers are words and phrases that indicate and contribute to the key and style (instrumentalities) of a piece of prose. Evaluators and intensifiers are not part of the factual content of what the writer is presenting and are, therefore, not essential to the development of the topic of discourse. Rather, they are a form of commentary that weaves throughout the text, indicating which points are being emphasized, highlighting the writer's attitude toward the information being presented.[8] For example, if a friend says to you, "I have a *great* job," he has not given you any factual information about what he does; he has simply expressed his satisfaction with his job. Many evaluators and intensifiers can occur within sentences: a shift in verb tense, repetition of a word or phrase, qualifying words and phrases such as "best," "very"; emphatics such as "do" (in "I *do* want to go" or "I *do* believe it"), and comparators ("-er," "-est," "more," and "most" forms of adjectives); negatives such as "no" and "not"; and modal verbs such as "may," "could," and "might." How you use evaluators and intensifiers will give the reader a sense of your level of confidence, sincerity, and attitude toward both the information you are conveying and your audience. Evaluators and intensifiers are a prominent feature in advertising and marketing, in speeches and persuasive arguments.

Consider how a shift in tense works as an evaluator. In expository writing, a shift in tense may signal that the writer is digressing or has added material that is nonessential: if the text is written in present tense, the writer may shift to past tense to offer an anecdote, testimonial, or some type of background information. A shift in tense may also signal that the writer is giving heightened significance to a particular point: if the text is written in past tense, a shift to present (e.g., "and that is the truth") conveys the writer's conviction or attitude to the reader. Advertisers often shift to future tense within an advertisement to make a promise to the consumer (often a promise that cannot be substantiated, as in "this will be the best peanut butter you've ever tasted").

Consider, for example, the following fabricated testimonial ad:

> Try new, improved Dudzee detergent. I did and the results were stupendous. It's not like all the other detergents you can buy, because it only takes a tablespoon of Dudzee to give you the cleanest load of wash you have ever seen. Your whites will be whiter, your colors brighter. When you try it, I am sure you will be amazed by whiter whites and brighter brights.

The only facts in this ad are: there is a new detergent called Dudzee, and only one tablespoon is required to do a load of wash. The testimonial style—signaled by the shift from present tense in the first sentence to past tense in the second—is rhetoric intended to sell the product. Repetition is obviously used; "whites," "whiter," and "brighter" are repeated to try and convince you that this detergent is better than others. "Whiter," "brighter," and "cleanest" are examples of comparative forms. "Improved" also creates a comparison, but what Dudzee is an improvement over or how it has been improved is not stated. (In fact, "new" and "improved" could be considered contradictory.) Such deletions of necessary information, or hedging, are common evasive tactics of advertising. Another comparison is made using the negative "it's *not* like all the others," and again the criteria for comparison is missing. Certain qualifying phrases such as "you have *ever* seen" add emphasis, since such a phrase packs more of a punch than "you have seen." The testimonial ends by shifting from present to future tense; the statement "you will be amazed" is the final attempt to coax the consumer to buy the product. While the majority of the advertisement, the testimonial, is in past tense, the main message of the advertisement, buy the product, is highlighted by the use of present and future tense in the first and last sentences ("try new, improved Dudzee" and "you will be amazed").

The use of intensifiers and evaluators in writing is extremely important. They create a tone that may engage the audience or put people off. The appearance of too many evaluators buries the information, and the prose may sound too tentative, too dramatic, or incredulous. Overuse of qualifying words and phrases and emphatics such as "probably," "possibly," "perhaps," "maybe," and "I do believe" reveals indecisiveness, undermines authority, and inadvertently weakens prose. A writer can also use evaluators to create a tone that sounds overbearing and arrogant; for example, "it would be absolutely absurd to consider any position other than mine," or "I am assuredly correct in making that statement." Such phrases strewn throughout a text can be disastrous; the reader may quickly decide to seek a less pompous and egotistical writer's perspective on the subject. There is also a problem if too few qualifiers occur. By failing to insert the necessary or correct qualifier, a writer becomes guilty of overgeneralization: saying that a fact is true of "all" when it is, in fact, true of a "few," "some," or "most."

By recognizing how evaluators are used in prose, we can begin to analyze how the rhetoric of advertising, propaganda, and persuasive writing works. Evaluators can be exploited by skilled writers in order to hedge, when they lack sufficient facts or when the facts appear to support a perspective other than their own. By saying "maybe," "perhaps," "it is possible," or "we believe" writers protect themselves from charges of libel, since they do not assert that the statements they have made represent the truth. (For example, a writer could state that "it is possible that the president has defected to Russia." Anything is possible, though some things are highly improbable. Often this is how gossip columns and rag sheets get away with printing many of their scoops and stories. See also the excerpt from "Why American TV Is So Vulnerable to Foreign Propaganda" in chapter 8.) If writers astutely use evaluators, they can make highly suspect comments and even avoid legal recourse. The choice of how you qualify your information is, in the end, a personal and ethical one.

All writers use evaluators and intensifiers in their prose to stress or emphasize certain points. These devices can be used responsibly, or they can be used to manipulate readers. Be conscious of how you use evaluators and intensifiers; consider how the appearance of these devices will affect how your audience will read and respond to your text.

## DEALING WITH EXPERIENCE: SCRIPTS AND SCHEMAS

Scripts and schemas provide us with "structures of expectations" that help us to deal with the experiences we encounter everyday. We call up these structures—that are based on old experiences and stored in long-term memory—to deal with typical, daily events and common occurrences, such as ordering in a restaurant, writing a lab report, or inviting someone out. Structures of expectations are built on cultural and institutional information that we have collected throughout our lives about the appropriateness of various actions and words in different situations; they are a store of shared social knowledge that people in a given culture carry in their memories. When we experience a series of situations that seem alike, we recognize actions and utterances that we have repeated and that were socially acceptable; we then store information in memory about how to act in that type of situation as a generalized episode. In other words, a structure of expectations is a compendium, which takes the form of an abstracted or generalized situation, created by first experiencing and then processing specific, similar events. Once a structure has been formed, the next time we encounter a similar situation, we do not have to work as hard to interpret or process the new information being presented because we can call up the scripts and schemas stored in memory to guide us. Because scripts and schemas are evoked based on our ability to recognize that an experience shares significant features with previous ones, scripts and schemas only help us to handle stereotypical or commonly encountered situations. In addition, since our scripts and schemas are based on shared cultural understanding about our world, these structures not only help us to determine which of our actions will be viewed as socially acceptable, but also help us to determine what we can appropriately say or write.

### *Scripts*

Scripts are designed specifically to help us predict and interpret an event sequence, a series of actions and utterances, that could be collectively called an activity. For example, the "eating out at a restaurant" event includes ordering, having food brought to you, eating, and paying the check. A script is a programmatic, standard sequence that typifies a given activity or situation such as answering the phone or buying groceries. A particular script is activated when certain key concepts of a situation are recognized. These key concepts generally involve specifically identifying the situation or a key action (i.e., picking up groceries in a grocery store) and/or identifying the roles of the participants (i.e., the clerk at the checkout and the purchaser). Scripts are intended to describe how people actually behave when engaged in the events (their behavior) as well as how we expect them to behave (their attitude).[9]

Quite commonly, a situation may invoke more than one script, but this is a minor problem that is quickly resolved as we process information about the situation. Imagine that you are traveling in Europe for the summer, not only to see Europe but also hoping for some romantic adventure. You enter the dining car of the Oriental Express as it lumbers through the picturesque and romantic Swiss Alps. You sit down to have lunch, and a single person of the opposite sex asks to join you. You gesture toward the seat next to you, as your mind races through the potential scripts for the conversation that may soon ensue. Possible scripts include "getting acquainted conversation," "traveling conversation," "ordering and eating lunch conversation," and "romance conversation." Often, at the beginning of a communicative encounter a variety of scripts are possible, and the participants' attitudes and behavior will largely determine which script is finally chosen. In general, one script is chosen to predominate for a given amount of time, though later the participants may shift to another. Continuing our story, you may both order your food, then shift to a "getting acquainted script" to determine if the potential for a romantic encounter exists. Attitudes and behavior come into play: Does your new acquaintance signal interest in romance by making flirtatious comments, drawing nearer as you speak, or suddenly edge away from you as if resenting your advances? Having asked a few questions to get acquainted, you may have discovered that your fellow traveler is simply a well-dressed, fast-talking socialite who freeloads off of various relatives. You may decide you do not want to pursue this relationship any further. Changing your tone of voice, shifting the topic of discourse, and inching away will all convey the message that you are shifting scripts. You may then pull out your maps and your trip diary and engage in the "traveling conversation script" or comment on the food and engage in "lunch conversation," signaling that a romance script is no longer an option.[10]

Scenarios are scripts for written texts. Whereas scripts deal with communication in general, writers use scenarios to design texts that are easier for readers to understand.[11] In other words, a writer can implicitly evoke a schema that the reader probably has already stored in memory or explicitly develop a scenario in the text to help the reader form a new scenario (or expand upon an already existing scenario). The scenario, like a script, is determined by the situation—who the audience is and the purpose of the text—and it will provide parameters concerning what the writer should include in that type of text and situation. For example, many of us are familiar with the scenario for scientific journal articles:

### Scenario for Scientific Articles[12]

1. Introduction (and review of literature) section(s):
   a) a statement of the problem to be investigated including a hypothesis that indicates the investigators' proposed solutions
   b) reasons for looking at this particular problem
   c) review of earlier attempts to deal with the problem
2. Methodology section
   a) materials—a list of instruments and/or conditions necessary to test or implement the solution
   b) procedure—a step-by-step guide for performing the experiment or implementing the solution
3. Data and Results section—a presentation of testing and/or of the researchers' implementation of a solution, including statistical analysis
4. Discussion and/or Conclusion section(s)—includes interpretation and qualification of results, inferences, and theoretical im-

plications. This section will usually place the solution into a larger context beyond the specific question addressed by this particular experiment. It may also include directions for further research and discuss consequences of research in terms of its impact on other research.

If the writer is successful in evoking a scenario, then the reader will rely upon that scenario while reading the text.

A scenario approach is particularly useful in designing and revising technical documents such as instructional manuals. In using the scenario approach, emphasis is placed on anticipating the audience's needs: what will the reader need to know to perform the activity? To generate or elicit scenarios for readers, the writer should organize text headings (and topic sentences) around the action.[13] Organizing headings and topic sentences around the action emphasizes the reader's role and the actions to be performed, and identifies the particular situation in which the actions take place. Writers should also try to anticipate the reader's questions and consider turning these questions into headings. While experienced writers intuitively know when and what relevant information is missing, when intuition fails, the following list may be helpful in determining how to revise a text to include information a reader may require:

1. Information on the reader's role and actions about to be performed.
2. Identification of the results or goals desired.
3. A sequentially organized list of actions that explains how to accomplish the goal. This may include an explanation of the reasons for and the consequences of each action, and alternative paths for achieving the goal if the primary sequence fails.
4. Information about preconditions necessary to begin the activity or to use an object. This may include explaining why the action is to be performed.
5. Information on how to use the equipment needed.
6. Information on common problems that might arise.

7. An overview, before the detailed list of actions, that sets up a series of expectations and subgoals.
8. Analogies that explain how the activity or object being used resembles other, more familiar ones, as well as examples of how the object can be used.[14]

(A reader may need all or only some of this information, depending on his prior knowledge and his investment in the activity.)

## Schemas

A schema is a dynamic and complex knowledge structure that is activated to help us deal with a given situation.[15] As with a script, a schema is activated to deal with a typical situation, and a key concept (or concepts) is required to activate the whole schema. But unlike scripts, which deal with sequential activities or events and represent information in that same way, information stored in schemas is organized hierarchically and/or spatially. A schema is like a three-dimensional spider's web where each juncture of threads contains a bit of information. Consider a web for "geometry." Each node would give information on a particular term, such as axioms, corollaries, theorems (stored together in one part of the web as aspects of proofs), isosceles triangles, hexagons, or planes (stored together in another part of the web as figures).

Hierarchical and spatial schemas are believed to be the method by which experts store knowledge in their particular field, since such schemas are more flexible and efficient, allowing for a greater number of relations among the items of information, and therefore providing a greater number of ways of accessing the stored information. This results in faster processing and comprehension of incoming information. Since experts store knowledge in various kinds of visual, spatial arrays, they often prefer that information be presented in graphic forms such as tables, matrices, maps, graphs, hierarchies, and networks that mirror the schemas in their minds.[16] A form is chosen that suits the specific type of information. For example, tables may be the best method for exhibiting the various qualities of one item or for comparing a limited set of items. Expertise develops from working with material until it becomes familiar, while simultaneously forming or expanding schemas by which to store that material. The schemas formed are dynamic; they continue to develop as new material is added to them. Lay people and novices do not possess schemas for understanding unfamiliar material in specialized fields. As they are repeatedly exposed to information, and as that information begins to be recognized as familiar, they will being to develop schemas.

Often a writer may find it useful to include a visual representation of material in the text to reinforce the written material. Because a visual display (a table, graph, schematic picture, etc.) is often easier to comprehend than a written explanation, such a display may help the novice to begin to form schemas like the experts'. But keep in mind that the selection of the type of visual display is extremely important, since choosing the wrong graphic array can impede comprehension—irritating the expert and confusing the lay person—just as choosing the correct graphic can facilitate comprehension.

## PLANS: WHEN SCRIPTS AND SCHEMAS FAIL

In a new situation, we cannot depend on structures of expectations formed for situations and events we have already encountered. When we lack a script or other structure of expectations, plans are the default or backup strategies we use to approach the new situation. To create a plan, we first ascertain our goal in the given situation, and we then attempt to construct a strategy for achieving it.

We do in fact have some standard plans that we use for approaching certain types or categories of problems. Plans not only help us to determine our choice of actions in a given situation, they may also suggest writing options useful for dealing with a situation or problem. Let us look at a useful plan for negotiating a goal. We all find that we often need strategies for negotiating various situations. You may want to convince your spouse to go to the movie you want to see, get your kids to do chores, or persuade a friend or colleague to help you finish a project. Writers involved in negotiating projects and proposals may also find a plan for negotiation useful. In such cases, the writer is often trying to get the reader to accept a plan or to agree to act in the manner suggested in the text. Plans are arranged sequentially (like the plan for negotiating a goal below), beginning with strategies that assume that the speaker (or writer) and audience are willing to cooperate and in which the speaker (or writer) and audience deal politely with one another. If the first strategy fails you proceed to the second, and continue down the list—trying more confrontational strategies—until you find the strategy that enables you to get your audience to do what you desire. This plan can be used for oral presentations and negotiations as well as for written texts:

### Plan For Negotiating a Goal

*Ask:* If your audience is predisposed to accept your proposal or request for action, you may simply ask them to act.

*Invoke a theme:* Refer to some facet of the proposal that is already known to the audience and that will reappear as a main topic of the discourse.

*Inform of a reason:* Provide a reason why your audience should cooperate with you (a mutual need, profit, etc.).

*Bargain:* Offer to do something for your audience, or give them something they need in return for their cooperation. ("If you buy the car," the salesman says because he wants to get his commission, "I'll throw in a stereo for free.")

*Threaten:* Threaten to carry out an action that will displease the audience.

*Overpower:* Overrule the audience's objection and simply carry out the action as you wish.[17]

The footing that the parties are on will have a bearing on how well a plan may work and which particular steps are actually options for the speaker or writer. A superior can simply ask that a task be done and expect that it will be completed. A subordinate cannot threaten or overpower a superior. To threaten or overpower you must be in a superior position or at least able to create a convincing pretense. You must also be willing and able to carry through on your threat, and if you intend to overpower your audience, you must be able to perform the action without their help.

It is virtually impossible to backtrack in this system. Once you have committed yourself to a specific step, or escalated to a confrontational strategy, it is nearly impossible to back down. Thus, while it is possible to start with any strategy in the plan, it is important not to start with a strategy more forceful than required. It is never a good idea to threaten your audience, if asking or invoking a theme will get you what you want, since by threatening you create animosity and may find your audience rejecting your proposal. Friends often simply need to be asked. In a professional situation, start by offering a rationale or reason for what you are proposing. Remember, you are wasting time and your communication will be less effective, if it is more elaborate than necessary.

Consider a situation in which you have been a dissatisfied customer: perhaps a company miscalculated your bill, a product you bought broke within a week, or the serviceman failed to show up on the day you specifically took off work so that your furnace could be repaired. Angered, you might call the company's customer service center, and in a rage, you bark your complaint at the person on the other end of the phone. But that person may have been quite willing to help you, even if you had restrained yourself. If you start in the plan at the level of a threat, and the customer service representative is sympathetic and quite willing to assist you, then you will find yourself quite embarrassed by your own rudeness and by the fact that it is quite difficult to return to a polite, cooperative conversational exchange when you have already threatened the other party. In addition, the representative may become less cooperative in response to your abrasive manner.

In any given situation, we will always try a script or schema first, since plans require more mental effort. However, once a plan is reenacted a few times, it has the potential to become a script or schema itself.

## EVOKING STRUCTURES OF EXPECTATIONS THROUGH TEXT DESIGN

Headings are an efficient way to elicit schemas that your audience may already have learned. If they will need to work on forming a new schema or will need to resort to a plan, systematically organized headings will still be an enormous aid. In many cases, headings that state who is doing the action (agent) and/or what the action is,[18] or that identify the object of inquiry or the topic, are appropriate. But if the reader is not expected to perform a task or achieve a goal, agent and action headings may not be useful. Moreover, in a longer text that contains hierarchically developed sections, while a topic heading may be useful for the topmost, superordinate level, you may need to break the text into more discrete, smaller units with more specific headings.

Just as concrete language more successfully communicates a message than abstract language, so concrete headings are preferable to abstract ones, since they elicit structures of expectations already stored in memory. Case in point, the conventional headings found in scientific journal articles do little to help readers process information, other than identify the genre and indicate the order in which material will be presented. Since these headings are abstract and conventional and do not relate to the specific material presented in any given article, they offer virtually no information. A heading such as "methodology" calls up no specific schema for any particular type of information (as for a specific type of experiment which would be useful in this case), only a weak set of expectations about the "kind" of material that will follow (procedural information). A more specific statement like "Procedure for DNA Extraction" stimulates the readers' knowledge of procedures pertaining to the contextual information to follow (DNA extraction) as well as the type of information (procedural). Naming the type of procedure described in the methodology section, specifying the kind of research or the researchers consulted for the literature review (i.e., "the rhetorical and linguistic research in discourse analysis"), naming the primary object of study or stating the hypothesis under study as a heading for the data section may all be of aid to the reader. Scientific and technical writing will continue to evolve over the next few decades, and if writers continue to implicitly evoke traditional scenarios by continuing to present material in sections as prescribed by those scenarios while also designing concrete headings referring to the information being discussed, then future readers will be able to comprehend the information more efficiently.

To conclude, here are some tips on how to create headings. While structuring around agent and action or topic is often useful, here is a more useful generalization: design headings so that the reader can identify main sections or major points; your headings should emphasize the information to which you want the reader to pay the most attention. You will want to design concrete, specific headings that suit your needs; the types of headings you choose will depend on the type of text and its purpose. Next, try to anticipate the questions the reader may have concerning that type of information.[19] Here are some aspects you may want to consider in trying to determine what kinds of headings to use:

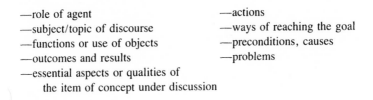

—role of agent                              —actions
—subject/topic of discourse                 —ways of reaching the goal
—functions or use of objects                —preconditions, causes
—outcomes and results                       —problems
—essential aspects or qualities of
      the item of concept under discussion

Third, make your headings parallel whenever possible: if some headings are imperatives make them all imperatives; if some are one word make them all one word; if some headings are descriptive noun phrases (i.e., the gas-propelled model) make them all descriptive noun phrases. The best way to check whether your headings are concrete, meaningful, and parallel is to write them down on a separate sheet of paper and evaluate them as a set.

In considering how to design structures of expectations, we have to consider how information is processed. Thus, in concluding this study of how linguistic theories and applications can facilitate the process of writing and revising, we have come full circle, returning to the basic premise with which we began this study: skillful writing is measured by how successfully the writer communicates information to the audience through the text.

## APPLICATIONS

1. Consider the following form letter that was sent to a number of customers:

   > Dear cardholder:
   > For account history reasons, we will not renew your card when it expires. During our review of your account, we considered many factors. If you have any questions about the decision, contact the customer service department during business hours.

   Such a letter was sent both to people whose cards were being pulled due to bad credit histories and to those who simply had not used their cards for an extended period of time. To the latter group who received the letter, the implication that something was wrong with their credit could be quite upsetting.

   a. Using S-P-E-A-K-I-N-G, analyze the problems of sending this brief letter to people who have simply not used their cards for an extended period of time.

   b. Consider the following rewritten letter, specifically designed for the group of people who have not used their cards for quite some time.

   > Dear cardholder:
   > Regretfully, we have decided not to renew you card when it expires. We have made this decision since your credit history indicates that you have not used your card for an extended period of time. If you have any questions, please call one of our representatives between 8:00 and 5:00, Monday through Friday.

   How does it compare to the original letter in dealing with the customer who does not have a bad credit rating? (Use the questions in the section on "Participant Interaction—Styles of Accommodation" to help you.)

2. Determine what level of the plan for negotiating goals is best to start at in the following situations.

a. You, as a writer, have been asked to submit a proposal to the Audubon Society to elicit their support in stopping the building of a dam that will jeopardize and/or destroy the habitats of endangered wildlife species living in that area.

b. You, as a writer, are asked to submit a proposal to stop the construction of the dam to the electric company that will be building, running, and profiting from the dam.

c. An employee has been late to work for the fifth time this month. During the past three months he was continually late. He was warned three times that such behavior could cost him his job. (Consider the previous warnings as "informing [him] of a reason" to come to work on time.) Now you, his employer, must deal with the situation.

d. The airline has lost a piece of your luggage. It was supposed to arrive on a later plane and be delivered to your home later that day. It is the next morning and your bag still hasn't arrived. You call the airline's lost and found, wanting your luggage.

3. Identify the evaluators and intensifiers in the following excerpt from Jesse Jackson's speech to the National Democratic Convention, July 19, 1988.

[1]    America is not a blanket woven from one thread, one color, one cloth. When I was a child growing up in Greenville, South Carolina, and grandmomma could not afford a blanket, she didn't complain and we did not freeze. Instead she took
[5]    pieces of old cloth—patches—wool, silk, gaberdine, crockersack—only patches, barely good enough to wipe off your shoes with. But they didn't stay that way very long. With sturdy hands and a strong cord, she sewed them together into a quilt, a thing of beauty and power and culture. Now, Democrats, we must
[10]   build such a quilt.

    Farmers, you seek fair prices, and you are right—but you cannot stand alone, your patch is not big enough. Workers, you fight for fair wages, you are right—but your patch of labor is not big enough. Women, you seek comparable worth and pay equity,
[15]   you are right—but your patch is not big enough. . . .

    But don't despair. Be as wise as my grandma. Pull the patches and the pieces together, bound by a common thread.

When we form a great quilt of unity and common ground, we'll
have the power to bring about health care and housing and jobs
[20] and education and hope. . . . We the people can win.

4. Design a script or schema for a type of text you commonly
   write: a form of correspondence (memo or business letter), a
   proposal or report, an editorial or piece of persuasive writing.
   a. Using S-P-E-A-K-I-N-G questions, analyze your audience
      and you relation to them.
   b. Consider what material needs to be covered, what scripts or
      schemas your audience can call upon, and what headings
      (if appropriate) you could employ that would be of use to
      your audience.
   c. Once you have written a document, using accommodation
      theory and the information presented on plans and evalua-
      tors in language, analyze the way you present yourself and
      the way you deal with the audience. Are there any changes
      you should make that you have discovered by doing this
      analysis?

This application may actually serve as a guide for a "sociolinguistic" evaluation and revision of most texts.

# *Answers*

## CHAPTER 2—PROCESSING INFORMATION

The first thing to consider is who the intended audience is—company employees. Their goal will be to quickly identify what coverage they have. How should the material be organized? Paragraph structure makes accessing necessary information by scanning the text difficult. Therefore, some kind of chart is preferable.

Should the text be data-driven or conceptually driven? Since we have a list of items here (best presented in a chart to make it easy for the employee to refer to items pertaining to his situation) the text should be primarily data-driven. Yet, it will help to have an introduction that identifies the purpose of the text and the material that the chart will provide, as well as headings that group items. To reiterate a main point of this chapter, even material that is primarily data-driven requires some conceptualization or conceptually driven processing, if the reader is to understand why the information is significant.

## Employee Insurance Coverage

This brochure explains the insurance coverage available to our employees. It explains who is eligible, what life, medical, and dental insurance is available, and the costs and coverage of the plan.

### Who is Eligible?
—All full-time employees are automatically covered. No contribution is required.

—Part-time employees, spouses, and children can be covered. Cost is $40 per month per person.

—Children must be added into coverage within thirty days of birth.

### Life Insurance
—All employees automatically receive $12,000 term life that is paid by employer.

—Optional term life: Employees can purchase additional life insurance that equals up to 200 percent of the employee's annual salary. The employee pays fifty cents per $1,000 of the total life insurance amount.

—Life insurance may be purchased for your spouse and children at an additional cost.

### Medical Insurance
Coverage: Hospital stays, diagnostics, hospice, and home health care

Exclusions: Preexisting conditions, acupuncture, and chiropractic services

Deductibles: $50 for each hospital admission

### Dental Insurance
Coverage: Preventive treatment 100 percent
         Major care 80 percent
         Orthodontics 75 percent

Exclusions: Preexisting conditions and occlusions

Deductibles: $50 on major dental care

The text begins with a conceptually driven overview. The text progresses from identifying whether or not the employee has coverage to what kind of coverage. The data-driven information is arranged under headings that conceptually group the material making specific items easier to locate.

Headings use key terms of the text; therefore, they are useful for the reader. Note that "Life," "Medical," and "Dental" subheadings are parallel (all are single word adjectives modifying and identifying the type of insurance); again, this makes the text easier for the reader to use. Under Medical Exclusions and Dental Coverage, information is listed in a logical order from most frequently requested services to the least frequently requested.

Elaborative rehearsal is not an issue for this text. But if the writer wanted employees to become familiar with their own coverage, and if this text were more complicated (as portfolios explaining insurance coverage usually are), the writer could design a worksheet for the employees to fill out and record their own personal coverage.

## CHAPTER 4—ALTERNATIVE GRAMMARS (PART II)— CASE GRAMMAR

1. Point out that the passage is written entirely in passive voice. The writer can be taught to recognize the "to be" + verb constructions and the "by" constructions in order to identify this problem on his own. Then, explain how to correct the problem by performing the following procedure: 1) cross out all instances of "by"; 2) cross out all "to be" verbs in "be" + verb constructions; 3) reverse the order of the noun phrases so the subject of the preposition "by" comes first in the sentence. The result is:

> The company's technical writer wrote the manual. The technical writer now should supervise the editing that needs to be done. The marketing team must then give approval of the final document.

Beyond using transformational grammar to eliminate passive voice, you might point out the weakness of the verb "give" that can be replaced by the active verb "approve," rather than nominalization "approval," to produce: "The marketing team must then approve the final document." Beyond that, you could discuss sentence combining and reducing repetitious elements. This eliminates the primer, simple style of the sentences, to yield:

The company's technical writer wrote the manual, and he should supervise the editing that needs to be done. The marketing team must then approve the final document.

2. line  2: organelles = Agents, since they perform an act—
         "colonizing"
         Also a possession belonging to "me"
   line 3:  me = Patient acted on by organelles
         them = Patient acted on by virus
   line 4:  virus = Agent
         they = Agent "conveying"
   line 5:  organelles = Patient infected by phages

A few brief lines, analyzed using case grammar, tells us a great deal about the power of Lewis Thomas' prose, as well as why this passage doesn't sound like an excerpt from a cell biology textbook. Organelles, the main subjects and agents, are combined with verbs that are reserved for animate beings. Hence, cells and cell parts become autonomous entities or beings that are then treated anthropomorphically. Each of our bodies becomes a colony of little individuals, and this personification is essential to Thomas' style and vision of biology. Organelles are agents, capable of acting independently of the human organism of which they are parts. And it is organelles, not the person, that are attacked by viruses and that in turn spread the virus to other organelles. Hence, the organelles become the agents to blame when we become sick.

Roles and relationships between sentence elements are clearly presented here. Agent and patient are the primary roles used in this passage. The number of variables—phrases and the number of roles they take on—is tightly controlled and roles are used consistently. When there is a shift in the role of a noun, it is within a clearly developed progression: the agent "organelles" becomes patient of the "virus," and then the agent spreading disease to other organelles.

3. Begin by commending the writer for trying to sound professional. Also impress upon the writer that adopting an impersonal, passive tone in order to sound authoritative and objective actually makes her letter unclear and undermines her authority, since she distances herself

from her own accomplishments. By asserting herself and claiming responsibility for her achievements (as the agent performing the actions), she will sound more authoritative and forceful and that is the kind image she should want to convey.

First, have the writer identify the primary noun and verb phrases (the subject material) of each sentence.

S1) letter — is responding

S2) advertisement — stated
 entry-level position — sought

S3) experience — makes me qualified

S4) I — have researched

S5) experience — demonstrates

S6) thank you

S7) I — hope
 position can be discussed

Proceed by discussing the issue of agency. Point out that the verbs "responds," "sought," "demonstrates," and "discussed" all require personal agents. A letter can't respond, a person does. An experience can't demonstrate, a person must. Ask the writer who the agent is: obviously, it is the writer herself. Discuss how, through revision, she can become a presence in the text, and then proceed by helping her to correctly identify the agent of each sentence.

S1) I am responding

S2) You seek

S3) experience makes me qualified (This passive does work since the activity done can be highlighted as the subject of the sentence.)

S4) I have (done) researched

S5) I (have) demonstrate(d) or my experience shows/reveals

S6) thank you

S7) we can discuss

(Note that there are also some grammatical problems concerning verb tense and aspect; correct forms that differ from the writer's are added in parentheses. This would have to be discussed, but cannot be explained by case grammar.)

Once correct agency is assigned, the rest of the sentence structure will generally fall into place. Again, you can discuss what nouns can go with what verbs or other noun phrases in the sentence. This results in the proper assignment of patient or object.

S1 and 2) I am responding to the ad for "who"—a paralegal. It is not an object but a person that is sought; thus the ad is for a person, paralegal, not a "paralegal position."

S3) "my experience qualifies me"

(Also, get rid of the weak unnecessary word "make.")

S5) "I have demonstrated my ability by . . . " or, change the verb to go with the inanimate subject "experience": "my experience reveals."

Another possibility is: "my experience is evidence of."

S7) We can discuss "what"—the position.

To Whom It May Concern:

I am responding to your advertisement for a Paralegal. The advertisement stated that you seek an entrance-level paralegal to review and organize documents.

Four years of experience as a paralegal qualifies me for this position. I have (done) research for various employers and organizations on many legal issues. Thus, I have demonstrated my ability to (do) research and organize complex data. (Or, my experience is evidence of my ability to (do) research and organize complex data).

Thank you for your consideration. I hope we can discuss the position in the near future.

Little grammatical knowledge is required to do a majority of the revision. Simply identifying subjects and verbs, or main points, will get the writer started. Questions of "who" is doing "what" (for "whom") become ways of assigning proper roles. Through revision utilizing case grammar, the letter has been significantly improved. Still, one other problem needs to be addressed. "I have researched" is not proper English usage; the writer has to use "done," and write "I have done research." The necessity of "do" with particular constructions is an aspect of grammar that can't be dealt with using case grammar, but that needs to be addressed.

To some of us, this letter still may not sound very eloquent. But, more importantly, it is still in the writer's own words. (This is particularly important if you know that the intended audience—e.g., a prospective employer or a teacher—is expecting to read the writer's own words.) Further tinkering with the vocabulary and sentence structure will turn this into the editor's work and misrepresent the writer. Working solely with the grammatical problems will help the editor to focus on only those corrections necessary to convey the writer's intended meaning.

## CHAPTER 5—ANALYZING AND IMPROVING COHERENCE

1. FIRST PARAGRAPH:

1   Water from rain and snow can seep thousands of feet underground.
2   In some volcanic areas it is then heated by contact with deeply buried hot rocks.
3   Temperatures of this water can attain 400°F (204°C) or higher—much above the temperature of boiling water at the surface.
4?   Such "superheating" is possible because of the high underground water pressure.
3   When the water becomes heated, it expands and rises toward the surface.

In the first paragraph, coherence breaks down in the fourth sentence. Is this a level four sentence? It is hard to determine because the reference to "such superheating" is unclear; the "such" implies that we know what is being referred to from a previous reference, but we do not. A sentence needs to be included that states "when water is heated to 400°F or higher in volcanic areas the phenomenon is called superheating." In addition, the last sentence chronologically/sequentially follows sentence two, or you could say it presents material too specific for this first paragraph and needs to be moved to the next paragraph.

What I would suggest is making the first paragraph a general introduction to the material. I would then move the last sentence of the first paragraph to the next paragraph (since it sequentially connects to the first sentence of that second paragraph), which is a paragraph that specifically and chronologically discusses how superheating produces hot springs and geysers. I would rewrite the first paragraph as follows:

> Water from rain and snow can seep thousands of feet underground. In some volcanic areas it is then heated by contact with deeply buried hot rocks. Temperatures of this water can attain 400°F (204°C) or higher—much above the temperature of boiling water at the surface. When water is heated to 400°F or higher in volcanic areas we call the process "superheating." Such "superheating" is possible because of the high underground water pressure.

The first paragraph now serves as a level one introduction to the second paragraph. Now, let's look at the second paragraph (having added the last sentence of paragraph one):

> 2   When the water becomes heated, it expands and rises toward the surface.
> 3   Near the surface where pressures become sufficiently low, some of the water boils to steam, producing hot springs.
> 1   In most hot springs, the steam and the heat energy of the hot water are lost by steady, quiet escapes to the surface.
> 1   A few springs, however, deliver so much energy to the surface that it cannot all be lost by steady escape.
> 3?   From time to time, steam bubbles become too abundant to escape quietly through the water;
> 3?   instead the steam lifts the water, sweeping it upward and out of the vent.
> 4   As this occurs the pressure at deeper levels is lowered, boiling action increases, and a chain reaction is started that leads to an eruption.
> 2   These hot springs that erupt and intermittently deliver large amounts of energy to the surface are called geysers.

The third sentence is actually the topic sentence of this paragraph and connects the general introduction of the first paragraph to the information in the second ("quiet escapes" is another way of saying "underground water pressure"). The sentence should be moved. A better order is:

> In most hot springs, the steam and the heat energy of the hot water are lost by steady, quiet escapes to the surface. [Once] the water becomes heated, it expands and rises toward the surface. Near the surface where pressures become sufficiently low, some of the water boils to steam, producing hot springs.

Now the subsequent sentences become a more specific explanation, chronologically developed, of how hot springs and geysers are produced. (I have changed "when" to "once" in sentence two for better coherence.)

The "a few springs" sentence starts a parallel section which compares how geysers are produced to how hot springs are produced. The "however" indicates that this sentence is coordinate to the preceding one. I would add "however" to highlight the comparison of geysers to hot springs that follows. But the sentence beginning "from time to time" breaks the paragraph coherence. Some piece of information seems to be missing. "Steam bubbles" have never been mentioned before, and the reader has to infer how they are connected to the previous material. I would add a level two sentence that would connect the ideas of the "in most hot springs" sentence to the information in the "from time to time" sentence, a sentence like "this build up of energy produces steam bubbles." We can then refer to "the" steam bubbles, since we now have a definite reference to an aforementioned concept. This last sentence completes the comparison of geysers to hot springs begun in the "a few springs, however" sentence; therefore, it is level two. The paragraph now reads:

> In most hot springs, the steam and the heat energy of the hot water are lost by steady, quiet escapes to the surface. Once the water becomes heated, it expands and rises toward the surface. Near the surface where pressures become sufficiently low, some of the water

boils to steam, producing hot springs. However, a few springs deliver so much energy to the surface that it cannot all be lost by steady escape. This build up of energy produces steam bubbles. From time to time, [the] steam bubbles become too abundant to escape quietly through the water; instead the steam lifts the water, sweeping it upward and out of the vent. As this occurs the pressure at deeper levels is lowered, boiling action increases, and a chain reaction is started that leads to an eruption. These hot springs that erupt and intermittently deliver large amounts of energy to the surface are called geysers.

Finally, I would also add a transition sentence at the end of the first paragraph that says that "superheating" produces hot springs and geysers, since a transition sentence connecting the details of the second paragraph to the ideas of the first is missing. (The reader can probably figure this out, but tourists who pick up the brochure at the geyser site want to read and understand information quickly.) This results in a more effective and efficient text.

My revision has preserved the writer's original words and meaning, while making the information easier to comprehend. Christensen's rhetoric has helped me to identify where coherence breaks down: if I look specifically for sentences that are vaguely or improperly linked, our adaptation of his method suggests how to reorder the sentences and improve coherence. (Remember: recognizing the breaks in coherence is more important than assigning the same levels as I have.) My final version is:

Water from rain and snow can seep thousands of feet underground. In some volcanic areas it is then heated by contact with deeply buried hot rocks. Temperatures of this water can attain 400°F (204°C) or higher—much above the temperature of boiling water at the surface. When water is heated to 400°F or higher in volcanic areas we call the process "superheating." Such "superheating" is possible because of the high underground water pressure. "Superheating" produces hot springs and geysers.

In most hot springs, the steam and the heat energy of the hot water are lost by steady, quiet escapes to the surface. Once the water becomes heated, it expands and rises toward the surface. Near the surface where pressures become sufficiently low, some of the water boils to steam, producing hot springs. However, a few springs deliver so much energy to the surface that it cannot all be lost by steady escape. This buildup of energy produces steam bubbles. From time to time, [the] steam bubbles become too abundant to escape quietly; instead the steam lifts the water, sweeping it upward and out of the vent. As this occurs the pressure at deeper levels is lowered, boiling action increases, and a chain reaction is started that leads to an eruption. These hot springs that erupt and intermittently deliver large amounts of energy to the surface are called geysers.

| Reuters, | an English company, is the European International Press Association. | Their |
|---|---|---|
| given | new | given |

| public image is less than 5% of the company. 95% is financial information reporting. | They |
|---|---|
| new | given |

| are 140 years old, doing business in 160 countries. | Their | reputation is built on ethics. | Their |
|---|---|---|---|
| new | given | new | given |

| charter is to deliver unbiased, fair, equitable and untempered news. NOTE: | Their | policy has |
|---|---|---|
| new | given | new |

| been to pay | their engineers | for 8 hours a day—4 hours | to do today's business and 4 hours to |
|---|---|---|---|
| new | given | new | new |

| create anything | they | want. Needless to say, | they | defy convention. All the patented |
|---|---|---|---|---|
| new | given | new | given | new |

| technology is priced cost effectively. | Reuters | is the largest single communication service in the |
|---|---|---|
| new | given | new |

| world. Security has to be key, due to the fact that the price of gold bullion is traded between two |
|---|
| new |

| countries that are literally at war; and no one using | this Reuters system | knows who did what, |
|---|---|---|
| new | given | new |

| when, and to whom for how many Oreos! Need I say more? |
|---|
| new |

The only givens in this passage are "Reuters" and the pronouns "they" and "their." As we discussed earlier in this chapter, the repetition of a name and of pronouns does not really serve to create coherence, unless main points are also coherently connected. (Engineers and systems are givens carried over from early paragraphs, but again little is done to connect subsequent mentions to earlier ones or to develop the ideas further.) If we look at how the idea and concepts connect from sentence to sentence, we also see that there is a notable lack of coherence. Given-new shows that most sentences do have an orienting given, "they," but this orientation is almost useless. The givens are not the key concepts (security, creativity, ethics, etc.); therefore, they are of no help to the reader. Actually, using the given-new contract would be a good way to approach this letter. Focus on repeating key concepts and ideas as givens.

b. The third paragraph begins with a level one sentence. But after that each sentence seems to leap a level of connectedness (something along the lines of 1-3-5-7). In other words, it is virtually impossible to assign levels to this paragraph because the sentences are unconnected.

The fact that you can't even use Christensen on the text tells you something about the lack of coherence here. It doesn't simply tell you that there is a breakdown of coherence at a particular point; it tells you that there is no coherence at all.

c. The biggest problem here is that Reuters is never clearly defined. The coherence techniques can help us to identify the fact that there are disjunctions, or gaps, in the text, but these techniques cannot tell us what information needs to be added. In addition, the main points are obscured; what the writer intends to say must be determined before the issue of connecting points coherently can even be addressed. The letter needs to be evaluated in terms of overall, global coherence—the development of a single point or delivery of a clear message. What are the main points here? Coherence techniques cannot help us deal with such questions of global meaning. But once the main points have been identified, techniques we have discussed for improving coherence may be useful.

## CHAPTER 6—ACHIEVING COHESION

1. *Reference:* Pronouns "its," "their," "them," and "these" are used. Carson avoids substitution (which is the weakest form of cohesion).

*Ellipsis:* An example of ellipsis can be found in the second sentence: "soil is" is deleted from the clause beginning "born of. . . . " In addition, "chisels of frost and chisels of ice" has been compacted through ellipsis.

*Lexical cohesion:* Obviously "soil" and "life" are the most frequently repeated words. Note that they are used in a variety of positions to avoid dull, lifeless prose. "Soil" is the object of the preposition "on" in the first sentence and the subject in the second; "life" is the subject at the beginning of the first sentence in the phrase "agriculture-based life," and the object of the prepositional clause, "of a marvelous interaction of life," toward the end of the second sentence.

"Life" is also used as a component of other words, "nonlife," and in its adjective form, "living." Used as an adjective, "life" then shifts position in the sentence; it functions as a modifier rather than a noun (as subject or object) as in "living things." In addition, the terms "living things" and "living plants and animals" can be considered synonyms for "life," which add a bit of variety to the terminology of the passage.

*Junctives:* The contrastive junctive "yet" occurs in the first sentence, connecting this paragraph to one that actually came before it in the complete text. "It is equally true" works as an additive junctive phrase. "As" is used as a temporal junctive (meaning at the same time) to begin the clause "as waters running. . . . " Carson also uses "for" as a conditional junctive to connect the second sentence to the first and "then" as a temporal junctive to connect the last sentence. She uses "and" in the third sentence to connect the event of "chisels [which] split and shattered" to the "parent materials [which] gathered together."

The ideas themselves are coherent, and the cohesive devices reinforce and highlight the relationships.

2. Note that the use of the junctives "because" and "since" signals a conditional relationship. The author tries to use the junctives to create conditional linkage, but the ideas do not connect in that manner. An unhappy marriage does not lead to doing abortions, and true stories are not necessarily tragic.

In the third sentence the use of "one" (substitution) and "them" (reference) to refer back to abortion(s) is confusing, due to shift from single to plural form and to the fact that "them" is separated by twenty-five words from its true antecedent (and "one" intervenes in between "abortion" and "them"). Another reference problem results from the ambiguous use of the relative pronoun "which." Does "which" in the third sentence refer to money or to "doing them for money"? The writer clearly has a problem using the relative pronoun "which," since in the second sentence she uses it to add a clause that is in no way connected to the two preceding clauses. This jeopardizes coherence. The improper use of "which" and of junctives suggests the writer does not understand how her ideas connect and reveals that there is an underlying coherence problem that needs to be addressed before the writer can choose the correct junctives.

The writer uses cohesive devices to connect clauses which do not contain coherent ideas. This text illustrates the fact that simply utilizing cohesive devices does not guarantee a coherent text.

## CHAPTER 7—ANALYZING MACROSTRUCTURES

### Deletions—On Ethics, intended for a general reading audience:

*Paragraph 1*
- Same deletions as for summary of medical advancement.

*Paragraph 2*
- Delete "battle" and length of operation which are not important to an ethics argument. (The seriousness of the baby's condition is germane to the ethics argument, but there are clearer, more specific statements on this made later in the article.)

*Paragraph 3*
- Delete reference to unquoted doctors.
- Delete redundancy of conference and address.
- Delete reference to technical advancement not germane to this summary.

- Delete reference to highly experimental operation that repeats information in paragraph four, and that makes the same statement but is focused on the ethical issue.

*Paragraph 4*

- Delete specific references to Bailey speaking and to the march which are trivial. All that matters is the presence and opposing position of the demonstrators.

*Paragraph 5*

- Delete reference to doctor's age as trite.
- Delete "parents of Baby Fae" and just use "parents." Obviously it is the parents of the baby involved.
- Delete all subsequent references to baby's alias.

*Paragraph 6*

- Opinion of condition is irrelevant.

*Paragraph 7*

- Anecdotal and emotional statements are irrelevant.

*Paragraph 8*

- Basic facts are needed for clarity, but delete medical jargon which is unnecessary.

*Paragraph 9*

- All that is really necessary in this paragraph is the doctor's statement of "his sympathies." Note that this relates back to material presented in paragraph four and would probably be much more useful next to that paragraph.

*Paragraphs 10 and 11*

- Delete "he went on" as unnecessary.
- Delete "primates and other" since "animals" is inclusive of all groups.
- These two paragraphs are at the heart of an ethical discussion.

*Paragraphs 13–15*

- Delete all information on treatment which can be considered inconsequential to this discussion. Animal rights advocates can draw a significant conclusion from the last sentence in paragraph fifteen: if the child is on life support and if her state is this critical, then the decision to sacrifice a healthy animal was un-justified. Therefore, this material should be retained as it may be useful in an ethical discussion. (It takes a bit of medical knowl-edge to recognize how this statement could be manipulated for various purposes, but you can still produce a good summary without it. I have bracketed some information that may be impor-tant, yet problematic for the writer/editor.)

*Paragraph 16*
- Though this paragraph does not deal with the ethics of the situa-tion at hand, it is relevant to a discussion on the ethics of ongoing animal research. Retain this material.

*Paragraphs 17 and 19*
- Delete information on funding issues.

*Paragraph 20*
- Delete lengthy credentials and just establish the speaker's author-ity.
- Delete redundancy referring to both the atmosphere in the operat-ing room and during the heart transplant.

*Paragraph 21*
- Delete weight and sex of baboon, which are insignificant.

*Paragraph 22*
- This paragraph poses the same problems as paragraph fifteen. There is the implication that further complications are quite pos-sible; the baby may die, and then the animal was sacrificed for nought. I choose to save the material before the semicolon be-cause it helps to make that point. That material will need to be rewritten later for clarity. (If you lack the medical knowledge to recognize the significance of this statement and choose to delete it, you can still generate an acceptable summary. Remember, most readers won't understand this anyway; therefore, this mate-rial will quite possibly have to be deleted later. Again, I have bracketed the information because it may be problematic for the writer/editor.)

*Paragraph 23*

- "Experimental purposes" is a useless statement of the obvious; therefore delete it.
- Delete reference to artichoke hearts which is simply silly.
- The mythical significance of the heart is not the issue for those who opposed the procedure. The issue is the sacrifice of a healthy animal. This statement is a *non sequitur*; therefore delete it.

For the text resulting from these deletions see the figure "Ethics" on page 200.

I must now reorganize this material. While the article will focus on ethics, before engaging in such a discussion, facts about the procedure performed on the baby must be given. I have reorganized the text into four paragraphs. (By jotting down the "gist" or a macrostatement about each paragraph, I can identify four major sections in this article.) I will now begin creating a summary using these four gists/macrostatements to organize my piece; each gist will be the focus of a paragraph.

In the first paragraph, information on the baby's present condition is given. Since her condition is tenuous, the question of whether the baboon should have been sacrificed becomes crucial, leading into an ethical discussion. Paragraph two details Bailey's work, adding to the ethical controversy. Paragraph three presents both sides of the controversy and offers comments by authorities. Paragraph four looks toward the future, suggesting that the ethical controversy will continue.

Reorganization:

> A 16-day-old infant, after receiving the heart of a baboon between seven and eight months old, weighing 7 ½ pounds, remained in critical but stable condition today, but was "doing remarkably well," said Dr. Bailey, the pediatric surgeon at Loma Linda University Medical Center. The baby nearly died on her sixth day of life, because of a birth defect which gave the baby virtually only half a heart and no chance to live. Until now, with rare exceptions, babies born with the condition did not survive beyond two weeks. The only option has been high-risk surgery to relieve its effects. Such surgery entails a great risk and has uncertain results. [The researchers said that they had found that about half of an unspecified number of humans had

# Doctors Say Baby With Baboon

By LAWRENCE K. ALTMAN

Special to The New York Times

[1] LOMA LINDA, Calif., Oct. 28— ~~Doctors said the~~ 16-day-old infant ~~known only as Baby Fae~~ remained in critical but stable condition today but was "doing remarkably well" after receiving the heart of a baboon at Loma Linda University Medical Center here last Friday.

[2] ~~Nevertheless, "she may be in for a long battle in the weeks ahead," said Dr. Leonard L. Bailey, the pediatric surgeon who performed the five-hour transplant operation.~~

[3] Dr. Bailey ~~and two other members of the transplant team spoke at a news conference to~~ address some of the ~~technical and~~ ethical aspects ~~of what he called a "highly experimental" operation.~~

[4] ~~As he spoke,~~ about a dozen demonstrators ~~marched outside. About~~ half of them protested the sacrifice of a healthy animal to prolong the life of a sick human. The other half supported the bold experimental procedure.

## Discussions of Ethics

[5] Dr. Bailey, ~~a 41-year-old surgeon,~~ had spent seven years doing the animal and laboratory research needed before the attempt was made on a human. He said the operation was undertaken only after months of discussion among the university's ethics committees and hours of discussion with the parents ~~of Baby Fae.~~

[6] ~~He said the doctors on his team~~ ~~were pleased she is doing well today."~~

[7] ~~"If you had the opportunity to see this baby and her mother it would help convince you of the propriety of what we are trying to do here," Dr. Bailey said. "The baby looks better than it ever has."~~

[8] The baby nearly died on her sixth day of life because of a birth defect ~~called hypoplastic heart syndrome, which~~ gave the baby virtually only half a heart and no chance to live.

[9] Dr. Bailey said ~~of the demonstrators that he was~~ "sympathetic with the issue of animal rights."

[10] "However," ~~he went on,~~ "I am a member of the human species. I deal with dying babies every day. I am more sympathetic with them. I am an animal lover but I love babies too."

[11] Dr. Bailey said that he had chosen to do the controversial operation now because his team had gone as far as it could in experiments on ~~primates and other~~ animals.

[12] Until now, with rare exceptions, babies born with the condition did not survive beyond two weeks. The only option available to parents of children with the condition has been surgery to relieve its effects. Such surgery entails great risk and has uncertain results.

## A New Drug for Transplants

[13] ~~Dr. Bailey said he believed his was the only group in the world that was experimenting with a new drug, cyclosporin-A, for animal heart trans-~~

Figure 7.3. Ethics (1st round deletion). Reprinted, by permission, from *The New York Times* (October 29, 1984).

# *Heart is Doing 'Remarkably Well'*

~~plants in infants. The drug combats the body's normal rejection of foreign tissue such as transplanted organs.~~ [14] ~~Baby Fae received one dose of cyclosporin-A before the operation but had not received any more as of this afternoon, Dr. Bailey said. The team was concerned about the potential toxic effects of the drug, he said, adding that Baby Fae's blood is monitored frequently to detect any adverse effects.~~ [15] ~~Dr. Bailey said that Baby Fae was receiving a steroid drug but no heart drugs. He said the team hoped to wean~~ [the baby from the mechanical ventilator that has helped her breathe.]

[16] The surgeon said his team planned to perform five such operations and then to evaluate the results to determine whether it should go ahead or retreat to the laboratory before trying the procedure again on humans.

### Private Research Funds

[17] Dr. Bailey ~~said editors of scientific journals and sources of research grants had rejected his papers and requests for research funds.~~ [18] "They weren't watching the babies die as I was," ~~he said.~~ [19] ~~So Dr. Bailey and his colleagues pursued their research using private funds from Loma Linda and from the fees collected by surgeons at the medical center, he said. Much of the research was done with more than $1 million "out of our own back pockets," he said.~~ [20] Dr. Sandra L. Nehlsen-Cannarella, ~~an immunologist who is~~ director of transplantation immunology ~~at the Montefiore Medical Center and Hospital of Albert Einstein College of Medicine in the Bronx,~~ was invited to participate in the experimental operation. ~~She~~ described the atmosphere ~~in the operating room~~ when the baboon heart was transplanted:

"At the moment the heart began to beat, there was absolute awe. It was just an incredible event to see that little heart start up."

[21] The heart was taken from a female baboon between seven and eight months old, weighing 7½ pounds. [22] [The researchers said that they had found that about half of an unspecified number of humans had pre-formed antibodies against baboons;] ~~so, if Baby Fae needs a blood transfusion, additional tests will have to be done on the donated blood. Dr. Bailey also said Baby Fae's doctors would have to study in greater detail than usual the immunizations that she received to prevent similar adverse reactions.~~

[23] Dr. Jack Provonsha, director of the university's bioethics center, discussed the need to sacrifice a primate ~~for experimental purposes.~~ "It is difficult to look at a primate's hand and not feel kinship," ~~he said. "It would be nice if we could use artichoke hearts.~~ Primates are closer to us on the evolutionary scale. ~~But the fact is the heart ties in with a mythological feeling and has more meaning than it probably ought to have."~~

pre-formed antibodies against baboons. The baby is still on mechanical ventilation that helps her breathe.]

Dr. Bailey had spent seven years doing the animal and laboratory research needed before the transplant attempt was made on a human. Dr. Bailey said that he had chosen to do the controversial operation now because his team had gone as far as it could in experiments on animals. He said the operation was undertaken only after months of discussion among the university's ethics committees and hours of discussion with the parents.

About a dozen demonstrators marched, half of whom protested the sacrifice of a healthy animal to prolong the life of a sick human. The other half supported the bold experimental procedure. In a news conference, Dr. Bailey addressed some of the ethical aspects of the "highly experimental" operation. He said he was "sympathetic with the issue of animal rights. However I am a member of the human species. I deal with dying babies every day. I am more sympathetic with them. I am an animal lover but I love babies too. They weren't watching the babies die as I was," he said. Dr. Sandra Nehlsen-Cannarella, a transplant immunologist, invited to participate in the experimental operation, described the atmosphere as the heart was transplanted: "At the moment the heart began to beat, there was absolute awe. It was just an incredible event to see that little heart start up." Dr. Jack Provonsha, director of the university's bioethics center, discussed the need to sacrifice a primate. "It is difficult to look at a primate's hand and not feel kinship. Primates are closer to us on the evolutionary scale."

The surgeon said that his team planned to perform five such operations and then to evaluate the results to determine whether it should go ahead or retreat to the laboratory before trying the procedure again on humans.

Obviously, these paragraphs are choppy. But related statements are now situated next to one another, which will make it easier to work with this material and to finally produce a coherent summary. Now I proceed to construction and a second round of deletion.

## Construction:

*Paragraph 1*

- "Stable" and "doing well," as well as "no chance to live" and "not living beyond two weeks," are closely related; combine and delete one member of each pair. Continue to combine and delete any perceived redundant comments on the baby's condition.

- Combine sentences on surgery.
- Bracketed material is not yet well related to the rest of the paragraph. For now, I will leave it; generalization will be necessary to clarify the relationships.

*Paragraph 2*

- Delete redundant references to operation and combine clauses about "undertaking operation."

*Paragraph 3*

- Bailey's comments about being "sympathetic to animal rights" and being a lover of babies and animals are closely related; combine and retain only one.

## *Second round of deletion:*

*Paragraph 1*

- Reduce amount of information on age of baboon and child.
- Delete reference to Loma Linda. Replace "university ethics committees" with "Loma Linda ethics committees."
- Delete sentence on "living two weeks," since imminent death due to the heart condition is obvious from other sentences.
- Comment on effects of surgery is obvious; therefore delete it.
- Name of condition unnecessary and too technical for audience.

*Paragraph 2*

- Delete any perceived unnecessary words.

*Paragraph 3*

- Delete "member of human species" comment which is peripheral to main issue.
- Delete reference to bold experiment and reference to speaking at a news conference on ethics as unnecessary. (His comments are obviously on ethics.)
- Comment by Provonsha is neither scientific nor ethical, delete as insignificant.

*Paragraph 4*

- If you are determined not to "go ahead" you obviously "re-treat"/go back; remove redundancy.

The resulting text is:

[1]   A 16-day-old infant remained in critical condition after receiving the heart of a young baboon, according to Dr. Bailey, the pediatric surgeon. The baby nearly died, because she had only half a heart, which gave her no chance to live. The only option was high-risk surgery which has uncertain results. [The researchers said that they had found that about half of an unspecified number of humans had pre-formed antibodies against baboons. The baby is still on mechanical ventilation that helps her breathe.]

[2]   Dr. Bailey had spent seven years doing the animal and laboratory research needed before the transplant attempt was made on a human. His team had gone as far as it could in experiments on animals, and only after months of discussion among Loma Linda's ethics committees and hours of discussion with the parents, did they perform the operation on a human.

[3]   About a dozen demonstrators marched, half of whom protested the sacrifice of a healthy animal to prolong the life of a sick human. The other half supported the procedure. Dr. Bailey said he was "sympathetic with the issue of animal rights. I deal with dying babies every day. I am more sympathetic with them." Dr. Jack Provonsha, director of the university's bioethics center, discussed the need to sacrifice a primate. "It is difficult to look at a primate's hand and not feel kinship. Primates are close to us on the evolutionary scale."

[4]   The team planned to perform five such operations and then to evaluate the results to determine whether it should try the procedure again on humans.

## Generalization

There are two points in the text where generalization is extremely useful. In paragraph three, the context for Dr. Provonsha's comment is a bit vague and must be inferred. I delete the figurative language and deduce the position underlying it, arriving at: "Dr. Provonsha, director of the university's bioethics center, believes that because primates are close to humans on the evolutionary scale, it is difficult to accept the sacrifice of the baboon, but he still supports the procedure."

I would also generalize the material in brackets in paragraph one to read: "the baby is still on life support, and there is still the possibility of future complications."

## Further Editing

If I had to shorten the summary to below 200 words, I would delete paragraph four on future plans and just deal with the present ethical situation. (If I had the space, I would include this material as it offers a good reason for debating the ethical issues now.) I could delete all but the most basic information in paragraph one and delete the reference to the time spent making the decision. Paragraph two can be pared down through further construction and generalization. (I also chose to combine paragraphs one and two.) You can prioritize any further deletions and decide which ones you would do first to get down to the length appropriate for your summary. My summary is now less than 150 words, suitable for most publications:

> A 16-day-old infant remained in critical condition after receiving the heart of a young baboon, said Dr. Bailey, the pediatric surgeon. The baby nearly died, because she had only half a heart. Despite the uncertain outcome, the Loma Linda's ethics committee and the parents consented to the high risk surgery, which was her only chance for survival. The team had spent seven years doing animal research and had gone as far as it could with animals, before operating on a human.
>
> About a dozen demonstrators marched: half protested the sacrifice of a healthy animal; half supported the procedure. While Dr. Bailey is sympathetic to animal rights, he is more concerned with saving infants. Dr. Provonsha, director of the university's bioethics center, believes that because primates are close to humans on the evolutionary scale, it is difficult to accept the sacrifice of the baboon, but he still supports the procedure.

You may find you perform a different number of rounds of deletion, reorganization, construction, and generalization. You may have changed or deleted words, phrases, and sentences in a different order. This does not matter, so long as you are able to utilize these techniques to produce a summary or abstract. (Since we may have different backgrounds in science, you may have made some different editing choices.) Using these techniques, you should have been able to produce a summary *similar* to mine in content: there should have been a statement on the situation that has given rise to the controversy (a healthy young baboon sacrificed for a baby which would have died due to a heart condition); there should be some attention to both those in favor and those opposed.

## CHAPTER 8—PRAGMATICS: Language in Use

1a. The procedures are not correct and complete: you do not thank someone for doing something before they have done it.

 b. The sincerity condition is breached; the wife is not sincere in saying that not going out is no big deal.

 c. This is an interesting example. We could say that appropriate participants and circumstances are not activated since the student cannot respond appropriately to the request. The teacher has taken advantage of a conventional procedure of "teacher calling on student to perform." On the other hand, some teachers might argue that no appropriate conditions have been breached since the teacher has the right to call on the unprepared student to teach him that he is expected to come to class prepared.

2a. The maxim of quantity (don't give more information than is required) is violated by the statements "people of different sex, for instance men and women" and "married with each other." The maxim of manner (avoid obscurity) is also violated by the statement "live together in one tent unless they are married with each other for that purpose."

 b. The maxim of manner is violated; there is an unintended sexual allusion here (ambiguity) and the intended meaning is obscured.

 c. Appropriate circumstances must be activated; the sign *must* be on a trash receptacle. Also you may consider conventional procedure, in that the reader of the sign will know through cultural experience that "please li ter" is not an invitation to throw trash around the area but a request that you *not* litter and instead place the trash in the receptacle.

3a. The directions flout the maxim of quantity—do not make your contribution more informative than is required—by telling us not to look at the answers at the end; our answers are, in fact, prejudiced by knowing that the Republican position is given at the end of the survey.

Question 1 violates the maxims of quantity and quality. Telling us that "the defenses became obsolete as a result of cutbacks by the Carter administration" is opinion; there is a lack of adequate information (especially as the statement is presented here) to make that claim. In addition, this information has no bearing on whether the respondent should believe that defenses should be modernized; the contribution is more informative than required.

Question 2 violates the maxim of quality by the use of the tagged-on statement "whether or not the Soviets do the same." The respondents support of a nuclear freeze should be independent of this information.

Question 3 violates the maxim of relation—whether the Democrats back the position or not is irrelevant. What is interesting about this question is its coercive tactics. If you align yourself with the Democrats you are made to feel that you are anti-American. The question also violates the maxim of manner (avoid obscurity): exactly what are "pro-West" governments? Are they all democratic, or do they simply engage in friendly relations with the United States? The United States is known to support certain dictatorships which are friendly to the United States, even if the people are oppressed. This question could also be considered a violation of the maxim of quality, since there is not enough information on what constitutes a pro-West government.

Question 4 violates the maxim of quality, that our "sea force is aging," implies that it is inadequate to do the job. That is a matter of opinion. Adequate information is lacking to support this claim. Note that there are no statistics comparing the sizes of the fleets;

this can be considered to be another violation of the maxim of quality and perhaps also of the maxim of manner, since facts are obscured. Another instruction under the maxim of manner is also violated—be orderly. Why does supporting equalizing the sea forces mean that we should build more "nuclear" submarines? There is no logical connection.

b. Now let's look at the appropriateness conditions at work in this survey.

*Sincerity:* Is there a sincere effort to collect unbiased opinions? Hardly. We are told what the "right" answers are according to administration policy; these answers can be found at the end of the survey. (This could also be considered a violation of the conventional procedures for conducting surveys.) The survey writers try to coerce us into accepting the party line. The questionnaire is worded in such a way that if we disagree with the party position we are made to feel like subversives or traitors.

*Participants:* Who received this survey? Republicans only? Middle and upper class? We have no idea who the polling group was.

*Procedure:* Consider the fact that we are told that only completed results were released to the Reagan administration. Who would send such a survey in? A majority of those who would actually send it in would probably agree with party policy. And did the Reagan administration see the survey or only the results? Were they simply told that x number of people out of those polled support the party position? Did the people who received the results actually look at the survey and see that it is designed to ascertain only results acceptable to the party? Are they aware of the coercive tactics that were used?

Analysis of this survey should make us a little more skeptical when we hear or read the results of polls, particularly if we are not given information on how the poll was administered or interpreted.

## CHAPTER 9—SOCIOLINGUISTICS—LANGUAGE AND THE COMMUNITY OF INDIVIDUALS

1a.  S—The situation is writing to inform customers that their cards are being canceled. The setting is business. The psychological setting is serious; though the degree of seriousness—the implications of cancellation—depends on whether you have a bad credit history or not. Unfortunately, this distinction is not dealt with in the communiqué.

P—Here we can identify the first problem. Two different groups of customers (participants) have been treated as one. The first group needs to know their credit history is bad; therefore, their credit is being canceled. The second group's cards are being canceled, simply because they have not provided revenue for the company. The letter does not clearly discriminate between the two groups, and insults and antagonizes the second group. To avoid this problem, two different letters should have been drafted and sent out.

E—The sender's goal (end), letting the customers know that the card will not be renewed, is clear. But the responses of both groups have not been anticipated. The sender has not considered that the customers of the second group will be offended by the suggestion that they are bad credit risks.

A—The form of a business letter is appropriate; it provides a record that the customer has been officially notified.

K—Tone is a bit harsh and suggests that all people who receive the letter have done something wrong, hence creating the possibility that some people will be wrongfully accused of being bad credit risks. A letter such as the one below is better suited for those who simply have not used their cards recently:

Dear cardholder:
     Regretfully, we have decided not to renew your card when it expires. We have made this decision since your credit history indicates that you have not used your card for an extended period of time. If you have any questions, please call one of our representatives between 8:00 and 5:00, Monday through Friday.

Note the increased use of personal pronouns "you," "our," and "we" which creates a friendlier tone. The reason for the action is clearly stated so no offense is given, nor should any be taken, and this also makes the letter seem less abrasive and ostentatious.

> I—A slightly less formal letter may be appropriate (see rewrite above).
>
> N—There is nothing here that violates norms of interpretation for a business letter notifying customers that their credit is to be canceled. Yet, the attitude conveyed by the letter is not appropriate in dealing with those customers who do not have bad credit.
>
> G—The business letter (genre) is acceptable.

The business that sent this communiqué may have felt it was saving time by only sending out one letter. But considering the number of complaints they may receive from irate customers, it may have been more efficient to draft two letters.

b. The writer of the revised letter anticipates that the audience may be startled and offended by the communiqué. By using personal pronouns, a qualifier such as "regretfully," and by offering to explain the decision if the customer will "please contact us," the writer encourages the customer not to overact. The writer still informs the customer of the situation, but encourages friendly relations, which may encourage the customer to do business with the company again.

2a. Audubon will probably be most sympathetic with your proposal. You could assume you just need to ask for help. But simply asking is really only appropriate in casual social situation, or if you are asking subordinates to do a task for you, in which case you do not have to give them a reason. If you are writing a formal proposal, or if you are asking for a commitment to a project that requires a large amount of money and/or manpower, you should invoke a theme and inform of a reason.

b. In this case invoking a theme will not be enough. You will have to inform [them] of a reason why they should consider halting construction. A reason still may not be enough. More than likely, you will have to try bargaining. If they will lose revenue by not building their dam, they will probably require something of equal value in return for halting construction. (But you shouldn't bargain until you have tried steps that require less commitment on your part and know that you can't get what you want without offering something in return.)

c. If the employee has been warned before, and you are the superior, you can threaten to fire him. If you find the employee worth keeping because of the value of his expertise, you could try bargaining and offering him some kind of perk if he establishes and maintains a record of coming to work on time—the behavior you desire.

d. In this case you, the initiator of the discourse, are probably already irate. Do not begin with a threat, or by trying to overpower the party on the other end. (Though you can write letters and complain to the Federal Aviation Association, these threats will do nothing to resolve the immediate situation.) In a phone conversation the other party can always hang up; threats have little effect.

Since the party you are speaking to on the phone works in the lost and found, she is there to serve you and is conversant with this type of problem. You do not want to attack her, since she may become unwilling to help you. Simply invoke a theme, tell her of your particular situation, and ask for help.

3. The speech is primarily written in the present tense. The shift to past tense (line two) introduces an anecdote which intensifies and reinforces the message of the speech. Jackson also shifts to future tense: "we must build," "we'll have the power," "the people can win." Note also the modal "must" is more forceful than "should" or "could."

Negatives such as "did not freeze" (4–5) are more powerful than simply stating the same idea in the positive, such as "we were warm enough."

Repetition: "you are right" and "your patch is not big enough" (10–14).

Qualifiers: "barely good enough" (5) and "not big enough" (11–14).

Comparison: "be as wise as my grandma" (15).

The identification of evaluators and intensifiers helps to identify some of the rhetorical flourishes that make this such a powerful speech (though obviously, in looking at the written transcript, we cannot examine how aspects of voice and tone affected the delivery).

# Notes

1. Nils Enkvist, "Text and Discourse Linguistics, Rhetoric, and Stylistics," in *Discourse and Literature,* ed. Teun van Dijk (Amsterdam: Benjamins, 1985), pp. 11–33.

## CHAPTER 1. LANGUAGE AND LINGUISTICS

1. The classic linguistic model of the communication circuit, more detailed than the one here, can be found in Ferdinand de Saussure, *Course in General Linguistics,* ed. Charles Bally, Albert Sechehaye, and Albert Riedlinger, trans. Wade Baskin (New York: McGraw Hill, 1966).

2. Of course, other languages do allow for more movement of individual words in a sentence. Often this is because the language is inflectional, meaning the prefixes and suffixes attached to words indicate their grammatical function in the sentence.

3. For C. F. Hockett's design principles of language, see "The Origin Of Speech," *Scientific American* 203 (1960), 89–96, and *A Course in Modern Linguistics* (New York: Macmillian, 1958).

4. For further information on the history of English, see for example, W. F. Bolton, *The Living Language: The History and Structure of English* (New York: Random House, 1982).

5. Unfortunately, the primary text we use to derive his theories was not written by Saussure himself, but was a corroborative effort of a small group of students who consolidated all their notes from his course offered in 1907–8, to create *Course in General Linguistics.* (I mention this not to undermine the importance of this work—it is indeed the seminal work of modern linguistic theory—but to qualify the nature of this text, which may not capture all of the subtleties of Saussure's own thoughts on his theories.)

6. Saussure, *Course in General Linguistics* pp. 65–69. This presentation of the nature of the linguistic sign is derived directly from Saussure's.

7. For information on Chomsky, see John Lyons, *Noam Chomsky* (New York: Penguin, 1978) for a good introduction. Chomsky's own works are much more difficult to read; see *Syntactic Structures* (The Hague: Mouton, 1957) and *Aspects of a Theory of Syntax* (Cambridge: MIT, 1965).

8. John Austin, *How to Do Things with Words* (Cambridge: Harvard, 1962).

9. John Searle, *Speech Acts: An Essay in The Philosophy of Language* (Cambridge: Cambridge, 1969).

10. The best introduction is Dell Hymes, *Foundations in Sociolinguistics: An Ethnographic Approach* (Philadelphia: Pennsylvania University Press, 1974). Peter Farb's, *Word Play: What Happens When People Talk* (New York: Bant 1975), is an interesting pop culture approach to these issues.

11. Claude Lévi-Strauss, *The Savage Mind* (Chicago: Chicago University Press, 1966); and Jacques Derrida, *Of Grammatology*, trans. Gayatri Chakravorty Spivak (Baltimore: Johns Hopkins, 1974).

## CHAPTER 2. PROCESSING INFORMATION

1. This model is based primarily on the model proposed by Walter Kintsch and his associates. See Walter Kintsch, *Memory and Cognition* (New York: Wiley, 1977); and Walter Kintsch and Teun van Dijk, "Toward a Model of Text Comprehension and Production," *Psychological Review* 85 (1978); 363–94; as well Donald Norman, *Memory and Attention: An Introduction to Human Information Processing,* 2d ed. (New York: Wiley, 1976); and such collections on human information processing as Daniel Bobrow and Allan Collins, ed., *Representation and Understanding: Studies in Cognitive Science,* (New York: Academic, 1975) and Thomas Bever, John Carroll, and Lance Miller, ed., *Talking Minds: The Study of Language in Cognitive Science,* (Cambridge: MIT, 1984).

2. George Miller, "Prose Comprehension and the Management of Working Memory" in *New Methods in Reading Comprehension Research,* ed. by David Kieras and Marcel Just (Hillsdale: L. Erlbaum, 1984), 327–46. Miller distin-

guishes between short-term memory which is used to learn lists and "working memory" which is used to perform tasks such as comprehension and problem solving: "working memory [is] a store that allows rapid access to its contents and long-term memory [is] a static repository in which information can be stored or retrieved but not actively processed" (332). Working memory requires elaborative rehearsal. Essentially, Miller describes working memory by the processes that occur there rather than by the nature of the storage site.

Earlier, Kintsch and Van Dijk in "Toward a Model of Text Comprehension and Production" described the "short-term memory buffer" as a part of the working memory.

3. F. I. M. Craik and R. S. Lockhart, "Levels of Processing: A Framework For Memory Research," *Journal of Verbal Learning and Verbal Behavior* 11 (1972): 671–84.

4. See for example, Anne Treisman, "Verbal Cues, Language and Meaning in Selective Attention," *American Journal of Psychology* 77 (1964): 215–16.

5. The large number of these words in every spoken and written text also partially accounts for our ability to read a page much faster than we could read each word aloud. When we read, we can quickly skim over function words which simply provide a logical framework within which we interpret concepts. Thus we read much more quickly than we can speak, since our eyes can move across the page much faster than we can speak.

We also do not read the individual letters of each word, but recognize the shapes and the first few letters of a word, and thus anticipate the rest of it; this in part accounts for reading speed. See Frank Smith, *Understanding Reading: A Psycholinguistic Analysis of Reading and Learning to Read* (New York: Holt, Rinehart, and Winston, 1971), esp. chap. 9.

6. Charles Osgood, "Toward an Abstract Performance Grammar" in *Talking Minds*, 147–80, points out that function words and word order contribute to creating a comprehensible text, but this material is inconsequential to processing information into long-term memory.

7. See for example, D. A. Norman and D. G. Bobrow, "On Data-Limited and Resource-Limited Processes," *Cognitive Psychology* 7 (1975): 44–64.

8. For a discussion of top-down and bottom-up processing, see for example S. E. Palmer, "Visual Perception and World Knowledge," *Explorations in Cognition*, ed. Norman, Rumlehart, and the LNR group (San Francisco: Freeman, 1975), 279–308.

9. Marilyn Adams and Allan Collins, "A Schema-Theoretic View of Reading," *New Directions in Discourse Processing*, ed. Roy Freedle (Norwood: Ablex, 1979), 1–22.

10. This process, called generalization, is unconscious when we learn our native language, but conscious when we learn a foreign language.

11. See George Miller, "The Magical Number Seven, Plus or Minus Two: Some Limits on Our Capacity for Processing Information," *Psychological Review* 63 (1956): 87–97.

12. See, for example, W. A. Bousfield, B. H. Cohen, "The Occurrence of Clustering in the Recall of Randomly Arranged Words of Different Frequencies-of-usage," *Journal of General Psychology* 52 (1955): 83–95. See also Donald Norman, *Memory and Attention*, 91–94.

13. See for example, Donald Norman, *Memory and Attention*, 106–8, or Kintsch and Van Dijk, "Toward a Model of Text Comprehension and Production," or Ronald Johnson, "Retrieval, Cues and Remembering Prose: A Review," *Discourse Processing*, ed. Flammer and W. Kintsch (Amsterdam: North Holland, 1982), 219–37. Together recency and superordination are called, by Kintsch, the "leading edge" phenomenon.

14. N. C. Waugh and Donald Norman, "Primary Memory," *Psychological Review* 72 (1965): 89–104, present experiments on the effect of serial presentation of data, and they discuss what was remembered best.

15. Margret Rihs-Middel, "Expectancy Structures in Prose Readings," in *Discourse Processing*, ed. A. Flammer and W. Kintsch (Amsterdam: North Holland, 1982), 76–86.

16. Spatial arrays take the forms of matrixes, hierarchies, graphs, maps, etc. Different types of spatial arrays are more effective for dealing with certain kinds of material. These various arrays complement schema by supplying key concepts and generalizations as well as factual, detailed information. More information on schemas can be found in Chapter 9. For more on spatial arrays, see Nancy M. Cooke and James McDonald, "A Formal Methodology for Acquiring and Representing Expert Knowledge," *Proceedings of the IEEE* 74 (1986): 1422–30, and Carol McGuinness, "Problem Representation: The Effects of Spatial Arrays," *Memory and Cognition* 14 (1986): 270–80.

17. Schnotz, Wolfgang, "How Do Different Readers Learn with Different Text Organizations?" *Discourse Processing and Comprehension*, ed. Roy Freedle (New York: Ablex, 1977), 87–97.

18. Many of these features are discussed by: Connie Bridge, Susan Belmore, Susan Moskow, Sheila Cohen, and Patricia Matthews in "Topicalization and Memory for Main Ideas in Prose," *Journal of Reading Behavior* 16 (1984): 61–80. See also Thomas Huckin, "A Cognitive Approach to Readability," 90–108, and Linda Flower, John Hayes, and Heidi Swarts, "Revising Functional Documents: The Scenario Principle," 41–58, both in *New Essays in Technical and Scientific Communication: Research, Theory, Practice*, ed. Paul Anderson, R. John Brockman and Carolyn Miller (Farmingdale: Baywood, 1983).

## CHAPTER 3. ALTERNATIVE GRAMMARS (PART I)— TRANSFORMATIONAL GRAMMAR

1. Traditional grammar is "prescriptive," dictating how speakers and writers are to use their language. By contrast, linguists propose "descriptive" grammars; such grammars do not prescribe how people are to use their language, but describe how people actually do speak and write.

2. Chomsky calls such utterances "well-formed," and he is only interested in accounting for grammatically well-formed utterances in his system. He does not account for the many sentences that are spoken by people every day and that, despite their incorrectness, are still understood by a listener.

3. Lexical entries are simply plugged in at the appropriate time, by using what remains a vaguely defined set of lexical insertion rules. In addition, how the words are chosen, what they mean, and how a nuance associated with a word in a specific context affects how a sentence is formed are not treated. Words, inflections, auxiliaries, and modals appears as demanded by deep syntactic structure description.

4. A compound sentence has two or more independent clauses. A complex sentence has a main clause and one or more subordinate clauses. See the section on "Compound and Complex Sentences" in this chapter for further explanation.

A passive sentence is one that reverses the order of the noun phrases found in an active sentence. The direct object of the active sentence becomes the subject, the active verb is replaced by a form of the auxiliary verb "be" (i.e., "is," "are," "was," "were"), and the subject of the active sentence may appear in a "by-phrase." For example, "The boy was bitten by the dog" rather than "The dog bit the boy."

5. Based on Noam Chomsky, *Syntactic Structures* (The Hague: Mouton, 1957); and *Aspects of a Theory of Syntax* (Cambridge: MIT, 1965). For other good basic information on transformational grammar see Traugott and Pratt, *Linguistics for Students of Literature,* New York: Harcourt, Brace, Jovanovich, 1980). For a thorough introduction see John Lyons, *Noam Chomsky* (New York: Penguin, 1978). This is a highly simplified model.

6. See Chapter 1 of this text. English is a two-tense system like German. This means perfectives such as "have been seen" and progressives such as "is working" are the result of verb phrases using auxiliaries and modals, rather than affixes to the main verb as are used in Romance languages.

7. All imperatives have the deep structure "you + verb," as in "you stop." As a further transformation, the imperative undergoes the deletion of the subject "you," and we get a command such as "stop!" Transformational grammar also includes descriptions of how to create content questions, or wh-questions ("who," "what," "where," and "why"), as well as yes-no questions. Yes-no questions require "do" (if no other auxiliary appears). Negative statements also require "do" (again, if no other auxiliary appears). Therefore, transformational grammar includes a transformational rule for the use of "do," called the "do-support" rule. Other important obligatory transformations include those that give rise to the proper word and affix order, such as the "affix-hopping rule." A complete description of the rules for transformational grammar can be found by consulting John Lyons, *Noam Chomsky* or Chomsky's own texts *Syntactic Structures* and *Aspects of a Theory of Syntax.*

8. This process is important when the person or object expressed in the

deleted phrase needs to be explicitly stated. If the person or thing responsible for the act is considered insignificant, then the passive structure may be preferred, in order to call greater attention to the act itself or the affected person or object. For example, "the stove was turned on" may be preferable to "the stove was turned on by the cook."

9. Having applied the obligatory and optional transformational rules necessary to generate the surface structure, the writer is now ready to apply the phonetic rules of English. Phonetic rules are not specified in transformational grammar, since phonetics is a separate field of linguistic study. Thus the transformational grammar description of an utterance ends here.

10. Transformational grammar does have its limits. Chomsky's intention is to explain our language competence. In doing so he creates an ideal speaker: one who only utters grammatical, well-formed sentences, who knows grammar perfectly, and who has no memory limitations. Indeed, when it comes to performance in the real world, there is no such thing as an ideal speaker. Many of our utterances are not perfectly well-formed; yet we are still understood. Transformational grammar cannot explain why listeners tolerate certain grammatical errors and understand what the speaker is trying to express, while refusing to tolerate other errors. Transformational grammar is not concerned with the fact that very few of us know grammar perfectly or use it correctly at all times. This severely limits transformational grammar's power to explain a majority of real spoken or written discourse.

In addition, transformational grammar cannot deal with nonliteral, nonfactual statements. A way to deal with figurative language, irony, or sarcasm has not been built into this system. Figurative use of language requires that we look at the context of the statement, while irony as well as sarcasm require that we examine the relationship of the speaker to the listener and the speaker's intentions. Such aspects of language cannot be explained by word definition and syntactic analysis and are only examined when linguists investigate how language is used in a given context. In actuality, since both traditional grammar and transformational grammar deal with sentences in isolation, neither can deal with nonliteral language.

## CHAPTER 4. ALTERNATIVE GRAMMARS (PART II)— CASE GRAMMAR

1. Charles Fillmore, "Lexical Entries for Verbs," *Foundations of Language* 4 (1968): 373–93, and "The Case for Case," *Universals in Linguistic Theory,* ed. Emmon Bach and Robert Harms (New York: Holt, Rinehart, and Winston, 1968), 1–88.

2. Based on Fillmore, with added roles based on: Algirdas Greimas, "La structure des actants du récit: Essai d'approche générative," *Word* 23 (1967): 221–38; Fredric Nef, "Case Grammar vs. Actantial Grammar: Some Remarks

on Semantic Roles," *Text vs. Sentence: Basic Questions of Text Linguistics*, Part 2, ed. Janós Petòfi (Hamburg: Helmut Buske Verlag, 1985), 634–53; and Mary Pratt and Elizabeth Traugott, *Linguistics for Students of Literature* (New York: Harcourt, Brace, Jovanovich, 1980), 187–204. The addition of roles based on Greimas has resulted in this type of classification also being called role grammar.

3. These two sentences are related by what is called indirect object movement. Both forms are acceptable; one is simply a stylistic variation of the other. We most commonly use the sentence structure that deletes "to."

4. Michael Gray, "What Really Happened at Three Mile Island," in *Popular Writing in America: The Interaction of Style and Audience*, ed. Donald McQuade and Robert Atwan (New York: Oxford), 353. Originally published in *Rolling Stone*, May 17, 1979.

5. William Laurence, "The Atomic Bombing of Nagasaki Told by a Flight Member," in *Popular Writing in America: The Interaction of Style and Audience*, 144. Originally published in *New York Times*, September 9, 1945.

6. Chomsky's transformational grammar could also be used to correct the passive sentences.

7. Cognitive psychological research supports this conclusion. Walter Kintsch, E. Kozminsky, W. Streby, G. McKoon, and J. Keenen, "Comprehension and Recall of Texts as a Function of Content Variables," *Journal of Verbal Learning Behavior* 14 (1975): 196–214, demonstrate that as the number of content variables—such as noun phrases occupying particular roles—in a stretch of prose increases, the prose becomes more difficult to follow and to comprehend.

8. Sartre's prose may be at least as easy, if not easier, to decipher, since he commonly uses concrete metaphors as analogies.

9. Hazel Barnes, "Introduction to Sartre's *Being and Nothingness*," in Jean-Paul Sartre, *Being and Nothingness* (New York: Washington Square Press, 1966), xii. (I have removed all tag phrases and evaluators here, which are unnecessary for this analysis.)

10. I am indebted to the work of my graduate assistant Katy Wegner who did the first analysis of this passage.

11. Ego is defined as "coming into being" in the preceding paragraph; thus, Ego as experiencer spatially expressed—"existing in the world"—also carries over as another role of Ego in this paragraph.

12. "We" exists on another level of discourse. It is not part of the description of the system; instead it is used to tell the reader how to engage in discourse about the system. Since personal pronouns are used sparsely in this passage, the appearance of "we" is abrupt and difficult to process.

13. For the experienced writer, this statement should be modified to: limit the role of each main noun phrase to one per clause (two at most if you are expressing a change in the element or comparing it to something else). If the prose contains complex sentences, treat each clause as a sentence.

14. Robert de Beaugrande, *Text, Discourse, and Process* (Norwood: Ablex, 1980), 80–87. Here is their list:

*agent:* entity that performs an action, and thus changes the situation
*affected entity:* (patient) entity acted upon by the agent and action
*objects/entities:* entities with stable identity
*instrument:* object used by entity to cause an event to occur
*location:* the place where
*time:* at which or in which state or event occurs
*situations:* in which entities are presented
*event:* occurrence which changes the situation or state of the entities
*action:* events which are caused by agent or entity
*state:* temporary condition of an entity
*relation:* detailed relationships such as mother-daughter, mentor-pupil
*attribute:* the characteristic state of an entity
*motion:* change of location
*form:* shape
*substance:* material composition of an entity
*part:* component of an entity
*cause:* necessary for event to happen
*enablement:* allows event to occur
*reason:* for occurrence of state or event
*purpose:* for state or event
*emotion:* sensory state experienced by entity
*communication:* transmitting knowledge between entities
*volition:* action of will or desire of entity
*cognition:* knowledge of entity
*possession:* relationship between an object and entity who owns or
    has it
*specification:* relations between a class and a smaller element, stating
    the narrower traits of the latter, or how it is a specific instance of the
    larger class
*value:* worth of entity in terms of other entities
*quantity:* number of which, also scale or measurement
*modality:* concept of necessity, probability, possibility, obligation
*equivalence:* equality, sameness, or correspondence
*opposition:* converse of equivalence
*co-reference:* different expressions used to activate the same entity

15. Case grammar was designed to work with individual sentences, but as we have seen, it can be applied to whole passages of discourse. (Fredric Nef had pointed out that case grammar could only explain sentences. He believed Greimas' roles, rather than Fillmore's case grammar, worked across a stretch of text. Fillmore's roles can in fact be easily modified to work on a passage of text,

and, in fact, the most practical solution is to combine the roles of both Fillmore and Greimas in order to arrive at the most useful set of roles for a particular type of prose.)

16. Lewis Thomas, "Organelles as Organisms," in *Lives of a Cell: Notes of a Biology Watcher* (New York: Viking, 1974), 85.

## CHAPTER 5. ANALYZING AND IMPROVING COHERENCE

1. Various theoreticians offer various versions of the given-new contract. Some of the most influential have been put forth by S. Haviland and H. H. Clark, "What's New? Acquiring New Information as a Process in Comprehension," *Journal of Verbal Learning and Verbal Behavior* 13 (1974): 512–21 and "Comprehension and the Given-New Contract," *Discourse Production and Comprehension,* ed. Roy Freedle (New York: Ablex, 1977), 1–40; W. L. Chafe, "Discourse Structure and Human Knowledge," *Language Comprehension and the Acquisition of Knowledge,* ed. J. B. Carroll and R. O. Freedle (Washington: Wiley: 1972) and "Givenness, Contrastiveness, Definiteness, Subjects, Topics, and Points of View," in *Subject and Topic,* ed. C. N. Li (New York: Academic, 1976), 27–55; M. A. K. Halliday, "Notes on Transitivity and Theme in English," *Journal of Linguistics* 3 (1967): 199–244, and "Modes of Meaning and Modes of Expression: Types of Grammatical Structure, and Their Determination by Different Semantic Function," in *Function and Context in Linguistic Analysis,* ed. D. J. Allerton, Edward Corney, and David Holdcroft (Cambridge: Cambridge University Press, 1979), 57–79. If you wish to read a good summary of many of the major theories, consult Gillian Brown and George Yule, *Discourse Analysis,* (Cambridge: Cambridge University Press, 1983), 169–89.

2. This manner of looking at given-new, based on the psychological status of the speaker and listener/reader, is Halliday's and is found in "Notes of Transitivity and Theme in English." The speaker treats as given material that which is recoverable from previous mention or inferable from context itself.

3. If the writer depends solely on elements of sentence structure for coherence, he is much likelier to abuse and reduce given-new to a mechanical formula, since he is creating cohesion, not necessarily coherence. Used in this fashion, the given-new contract becomes a test of cohesion, NOT coherence—dealing with linking forms, not ideas—then coherence may in fact be lacking. The writer must pay attention to the ideas, to what is being said, not just to repetition. (See chapter 6 for more on this point.)

4. See the example, "Some Uses and Abuses of Economic Multipliers," in the following section on Christensen's Rhetoric of the Paragraph. The passage rigidly adheres to the given-new formula. (Key terms used to achieve coherence are italicized; first use of a term = new, subsequent uses = given.) While this text has linear coherence and makes sense, it seems to ramble, since the true focus of the essay is not announced until the last sentence of the second para-

graph. Much of the first six to seven sentences seem to suggest that the article will focus on how the decision-makers perform their duties. The introduction, while linearly coherent, is somewhat misleading and perfunctory, and should be tightened to reflect the true focus of the article. Let this be a warning that sequential coherence is not enough, and that often it is useful to check coherence with more than one method (particularly a second method that deals with overall, global coherence, as discussed in chapter 7).

5. Halliday would say this line is inferred by the previous statement, by the implicit connection made here based on comparing the body's and the mind's responsibility for action. Also, by placing it first in the sentence, the speaker treats it as a given.

6. Lewis Thomas, "Autonomy," in *The Lives of a Cell: Notes of a Biology Watcher,* (New York: Viking, 1974), 75. Note that I have divided phrases into given and new since we do in fact process information by phrases, and thus this more accurately represents how we cognitively process given-new. Within the new phrases, Haviland and Clark consider pronouns to be given links that establish coherence. We can see from this example that the pronouns themselves make the new information easier to process, but are not alone enough to turn the new phrases into givens, since "you" is not sufficient to call up the earlier key concept of you controlling your actions.

7. Francis Christensen, *Notes toward a New Rhetoric* (New York: Harper and Row, 1967), 54–81, is devoted to the paragraph. Unlike the given-new contract, Christensen's rhetoric is generative. Using passages from various well-known writers, he takes the topic sentence—which is also usually the first sentence—and demonstrates how it can be elaborated, developed, and specified by the following sentences of the paragraph.

8. Charles Dickens, *A Tale of Two Cities* (1859; New York: Penguin, 1970), 35. The paragraph is written as a single sentence. If Dickens sat in a freshman composition class, his teacher would probably point out the series of comma splices and tell him that each clause is actually a sentence. Yet, as readers, we can see that Dickens' one-sentence paragraph serves as an excellent example of coordinating structure.

9. Kim Chernin, "The Boutique," *The Obsession: Reflections on The Tyranny of Slenderness* (New York: Harper and Row, 1981), 88–89.

10. "What is a Geyser?" in *Geysers,* U.S. Geological Survey (Government Printing 1986-491-402/01). This pamphlet is the type you would get at an information center when you visit an attraction such as Old Faithful.

11. Eugene Lewis, "Some Uses and Abuses of Economic Multipliers," *Wyoming Issues* 1 (1978): 7.

12. Teachers may find that Christensen's rhetoric can be used to design exercises that may help writers learn how to develop and expand their own paragraphs during the revision process. At first, develop exercises that give writers a skeletal paragraph to fill in.

EXERCISE:
The following paragraph needs to be further developed so that it more effectively expresses the main idea.

> People who watch soap operas are one of two types, "the break-takers," or "the addicts." The break-takers only watch one or two favorite shows as a diversion from household chores or as a break during the work day from their job. Addicts watch soap operas all day, everyday.

Rewrite the paragraph, adding sentences where indicated. You will be directed whether to add a subordinating or coordinating sentence.

1 People who watch soap operas are one of two types, "the break-takers," or "the addicts."
  2 The break-takers only watch one or two favorite shows as a diversion from household chores or as a break during the work day from their job.
    3 Add a subordinate sentence that further tells why people take a break from household chores or which further describes the household chore break-takers.
    3 Add a coordinate sentence that tells why people take a break from their work day, or that further describes the job break-takers.
  2 Addicts watch soap operas all day, everyday.
    3 Add a subordinate sentence that elaborates on who the addicts are, or how their addiction affects their daily routine.
      4 Add another subordinate sentence that build on the previous sentence.
1 Superordination: Add a general statement that concludes the paragraph.

> Write your new paragraph out in paragraph form. Compare the paragraph I have given you, which is 1-2-2, with your own paragraph that is 1-2-3-3-2-3-4-1. Discuss which is the better paragraph and why.

As writers become more comfortable with this procedure, teachers can design subsequent exercises that are less directive. (Give them a theme and then ask them to develop it with a specific structure such as 1-1-2-3-1, or give them a theme and a list of instructions to "add a subordinate sentence" or "add a coordinate sentence.")

Using exercises such as this was suggested by one of my graduate students, Will Grant in "Pre-Text—Re-Text—Post-Text: A Study in Revision Strategies," unpublished. Mr. Grant has tried this approach with his high school students with excellent results.

13. Rather than writing "vague" or "expand," teachers, editors, and writers responding to each others' work in workshops could better help one another by giving them such instructions.

This list is based on theoretical discussions of "entailment," how sentences can be logically connected. See, for example, Roger Schank, "The Structure of Episodes in Memory," 237–72 and David Rumelhart, "Notes on a Schema for Stories," 211–36, both in *Representation and Understanding: Studies in Cognitive Science,* ed. Daniel Bobrow and Allan Collins (New York: Academic, 1975).

14. One limitation of Christensen's work is that his observations on paragraph types are based solely on descriptive paragraphs. This may prejudice his statements on how typical paragraphs work. But as a diagnostic device, his methodology may be useful for looking at all paragraph types. Also, he is interested in using his methodology for teaching students how to write paragraphs, rather than as a check for paragraph coherence and as a tool for revision. As I previously stated, I believe that the methodology is better used to describe how already-written paragraphs are working, or not working.

## CHAPTER 6. ACHIEVING COHESION

1. Cohesion is first and foremost a feature of texts, whereas ideas by themselves exist as mental images that may be thought of in spatial or graphic terms rather than as linear texts.

2. Based on M. A. K. Halliday and Ruqaiya Hasan, *Cohesion in English* (London: Longman, 1976).

3. "Do" also has other functions in English; it is necessary in many questions and many negative sentences. In such instances "do" is not used for substitution but as an auxilary verb.

4. Elizabeth Rudolph, "Connective Relations—Connective Expressions—Connective Structures," *Text and Discourse,* ed. Janós Petòri (New York: de Gruyter, 1988), 97–133.

Other systems are possible; Halliday and Hasan, Dressler and de-Beaugrande, and others prefer to break adversarial relations into disjunction and contrajunction and to clump temporal and conditional into subordinate relations. I prefer Rudolph's system which is more appealing to a writer's sense of connections (as opposed to a theoretical linguist).

5. Joan Didion, "Slouching Toward Bethlehem," *Slouching Toward Bethlehem* (New York: Dell, 1968), 84.

6. Loren Eiseley, "The Star Thrower," *The Star Thrower* (New York: Times Books, 1978), 169.

7. Rachel Carson, "Realms of the Soil," *Silent Spring* (New York: Houghton Mifflin, 1962), 53.

8. Peg Yorkin, "Reviews from a Feminist Perspective," *Reports from the Feminist Majority* 2 (1990): 7.

# CHAPTER 7. ANALYZING MACROSTRUCTURES

1. This chapter is based on Teun van Dijk, *Macro-structures* (Hillsdale: Erlbaum, 1979).

2. For a start on defining audience issues see Arthur Walter, "Articles from the 'California Divorce Project': A Case Study of the Concept of Audience," *College Composition and Communication* 36 (1985): 150–59; Douglas Park, "The Meaning of 'Audience,'" *College English* 44 (1982): 247–57; and Walter Ong, "The Writer's Audience is Always a Fiction," *Publications of the Modern Language Association* 90 (1975): 9–21.

3. This procedure is based on Van Dijk's macrorules, *Macro-structures*, 28–73. Van Dijk proposes five macrorules for deriving macrostructures, which are listed here in the order in which they are performed:

> 1. *Weak deletion:* is the deletion of material not relevant to the larger issue or point. This is called the deletion of irrelevant detail.
>
> 2. *Generalization:* is the process of abstracting detail from specific statements in order to create a more general statement. This requires grouping facts and ideas, and developing a statement that subsumes the whole group.
>
> 3. *Construction:* joins sentences or clauses together in a single macro-statement. The clauses that are joined may come from different sections of a text. Construction is the joining together of two or more clauses or statements into one statement. (This distinguishes construction from abstraction; here, no detail or material is lost.)
>
> 4. *Strong Deletion:* is the deletion of material that is relevant at a local, specific level, but which becomes irrelevant, or peripheral at a more general level.
>
> 5. *Zero rule:* leaves a statement intact and raises it to a higher level of generalization. The zero rule is really a description of statements that are not edited but that are moved to a higher level without any adaptation.

I have found that reorganization is essential to the production of macrostructures, since often text must be reorganized to identify the best method for presenting the material in a logical order. Secondly, I have replaced Van Dijk's weak and strong deletion with deletion. As one moves up the pyramid of macrostructures to greater generalization it is not necessary to distinguish between strong and weak deletion, but to recognize that at each level, more local material is considered irrelevant or peripheral.

4. Lawrence Altman, "Doctors Say Baby with Baboon Heart Is Doing 'Remarkably Well,'" *New York Times,* October 29, 1984, A-15. Used by permission of *New York Times,* 1992.

5. For example, the sentence on the child's immunization record was not well explained in the article: does immunization mean she may have pre-formed

antibodies against the baboon that may still cause rejection, or does it mean she may have antibodies against transfused human blood? I have made generalizations based on what I believe the writer intended to say about the immunization record. In recognizing that I have to speculate about his intended meaning, I have identified a sentence which creates a coherence problem and which makes it difficult to edit the text. If I were to publish any form of this article, I would want to clarify this sentence.

6. This revision process is similar to the one suggested in Peter Elbow's *Writing with Power* (New York: Oxford, 1981), 32–38 and 128–38. Here is a summary of his procedure (see pages 38 and 138):

—Have your audience and purpose clearly in mind.

—Read over raw writing and mark important bits.

—Find your main point.

—Put the parts in order on the basis of your main idea.

—Make a draft.

—Possible detour: deal with a breakdown. (Add missing pieces. Reorder. Tighten and clarify by cutting.)

—Tighten and clean up your language.

—Remove mistakes in grammar and usage.

Like Elbow, I believe that correcting grammar, punctuation, and other mechanical errors should come last. Conveying your message in a clear, orderly fashion is most important.

## CHAPTER 8. PRAGMATICS: LANGUAGE IN USE

1. At this point in the development in linguistic studies, linguistics begins to relate to another field of language study, rhetoric. In both these fields, theorists recognize three primary elements: speaker (or by extension, writer), audience, and text.

2. John Austin, *How to Do Things with Words* (Cambridge: Harvard, 1962).

3. John Searle, *Expression and Meaning: Studies in the Theory of Speech Acts* (Cambridge, Cambridge University Press, 1979). Searle replaced Austin's three component speech act with a two component description. (He dispensed with the notion of the perlocutionary act, since effect or consequence is in fact signaled or determined by the illocutionary act. He also defines the locutionary act more precisely; locution is no longer based on the verb used.)

4. Each class also has a characteristic syntactic form.

assertives: I + verb (+ that) + S.
directives: I + verb + you + future volition verb (+ NP) (+ adv).
commissives: I + verb (+ you) + I + future volition verb + (NP) + (adv).
expressives: I + verb + you + I/you VP
                                    which yields
                            I + verb + I/you + gerundive.
declaratives:               I + verb NP₁ + NP₂ be V
                            OR which can be truncated to yield
                                    I + verb + S

S represents sentence or statement.
Elements in parentheses are optional.

In each case "I + verb" can be dropped, for example "I will take you to the movies."

5. Austin, *How to Do Things with Words,* Lecture II, 12–20.
6. Here, theorists deal in a very limited fashion with the speaker's and audience's attitudes and beliefs. Obviously, this is a very limited way of looking at the issues, since only the participants' attitudes and beliefs regarding their desire to participate in the communication of a single message are dealt with. How they may interpret and respond to the message, based on cultural background, or beliefs and attitudes, is not dealt with (those are issues for sociolinguistics).
7. Issues of status are culturally dependent. One culture may perceive a person as occupying a position of power or respect while another culture may perceive that position differently (e.g., some cultures afford a teacher a position of respect, while in America we tend not to). This will affect how the speaker addresses the hearer. Formality is also dealt with differently in various languages and cultures. Romance languages have different forms of formal or informal address; English does not.
8. J. W. Fulbright, *The Pentagon Propaganda Machine* (New York: Liveright, 1970), 32–33.
9. Such examples of indirection are obviously more complicated than the "can you tell me what time it is" speech act. To date, speech act theory has dealt primarily with simple indirect speech acts that are usually single conventional utterances, such as requests or promises, or very brief conventional exchanges between two people, such as an exchange of greetings. But we can see that appropriateness conditions do not apply only to isolated utterances; the principles used to discuss speech acts can be used to discuss and reveal interesting facets of complete texts.

10. Paul Grice, "Logic and Conversation," in *Syntax and Semantics III,* ed. Peter Cole and Jerry Morgan (New York: Academic, 1978), 41–58. The maxim of consistency is my own addition.

11. John Weisman, "Why American TV Is So Vulnerable to Foreign Propaganda," *TV Guide,* June 12, 1982, 7–8.

12. The problem with Gricean analysis of nonliterary prose is that it assumes all communication is straightforward and literal. Grice generally assumes that the speaker is observing the sincerity condition, and that the speaker is not trying to obscure meaning, create double entendres, or otherwise toy with the listener. Gricean analysis was not designed to deal with metaphor, puns, humor, or irony found in poetry and fiction, where we recognize that breaches of maxims—such as avoid ambiguity—do not necessarily impede communication. Already, linguists interested in literary analysis are finding ways to adapt Gricean analysis to deal with nonliteral types of language use. See Mary Pratt and Elizabeth Traugott's *Linguistics for Students of Literature* (New York: Harcourt, Brace, Jovanovich, 1980) or Mary Pratt's *Toward a Speech Act Theory of Literary Discourse* (Bloomington: Indiana University Press, 1977).

13. Audience analysis, a rhetorical field of study, offers practical information about how to analyze your audience. For good information on audience analysis you may want to consult the following: J. C. Mathes and Dwight Stevenson, "Audience Analysis: The Problem and a Solution," in *Designing Technical Reports,* ed. John Mathes (Bobbs-Merrill Educational Pub: Indianapolis, 1976); Walter Ong, "The Writer's Audience Is Always a Fiction," *Publications of the Modern Language Association* 90 (1975): 9–22; Lisa Ede, "Audience: An Introduction to Research," *College Composition & Communication* 35 (1984): 140–54; and Linda Flower, John Hayes, and Heidi Swarts, "Revising Functional Documents: The Scenario Principle," *New Essays in Technical Communication: Research, Theory, Practice,* ed. Paul Anderson, R. John Brockman, and Carolyn Miller (Farmingdale: Baywood, 1983).

14. Teachers and editors may find that critiquing problems in terms of how the text does not accommodate the circumstances, audience, or procedure being addressed often diffuses a potentially awkward situation in which an inexperienced writer perceives criticism as an attack on his ability. Approaching a text in this way may also diffuse some of the writer's anxiety, since this approach to evaluating writing emphasizes objective criteria which the writer can learn, rather than more vague, subjective criteria.

15. Richard Lederer, *Anguished English* (New York: Doubleday, 1987). The sign from the Black Forest is on page 96, and the sign from a Japanese hotel is on page 94.

# CHAPTER 9. SOCIOLINGUISTICS—LANGUAGE AND THE COMMUNITY OF INDIVIDUALS

1. Sociolinguistics has often suffered from being labeled a pseudoscience by some traditional linguists who pride themselves on developing and practicing an analytical field of study. Sociolinguistic inquiry cannot be performed using the formal or logic-based methodologies of traditional linguistics that were designed to study grammar and texts isolated from the communication situation. Much of human language behavior as it occurs in true social situations is difficult, if not impossible, to explain by a set of rules.

2. The complaint of sociolinguists against such traditional approaches is that language competence inadvertently becomes the same as performance. According to a traditional approach, we are all idealized language speakers and hearers. (If someone deviates from acceptable English it is unintentional; he has erred or is indolent.) There is no way to account for individual or group differences in such an approach. For the sociolinguist, competence has a interpersonal or cultural aspect that cannot be accounted for by grammar alone.

3. Hymes, Dell, *Foundations in Sociolinguistics: An Ethnographic Approach* (Philadelphia, Pennsylvania University Press, 1974), 54–62. I would like to define key and style a bit more precisely.

Many clues that the key is not serious are nonverbal, such as the wink of an eye or a gesture of the hand. Unusual emphases (i.e., pitch) of words or phrases in sentences may also be an indicator of key. The acceptable key for communication is largely determined by the situation; for example, if you are in a casual, playful situation teasing may be acceptable; in the boardroom it is not.

Style (Instrumentalities) is more precisely divided into dialect, register, and code. Dialect, such as Midwestern or Southern, is a feature of who you are and where you grew up. Register is determined both by the situation and the audience; it is primarily determined by the social atmosphere of the situation. For example, your style is different when you are out to dinner with a friend at McDonalds than when you are dining at a four-star restaurant with your boss. Your language will be more elaborate in formal situations and more restricted in casual situations, and you will choose the code appropriate for the situation. The elaborate code is defined as verbally explicit: grammar is precise; little or no contextual material is left out. This code is used in business, with professionals such as doctors and lawyers, as well as with people we do not know well or to whom we choose not to be close. The restricted code is more verbally implicit: material is left out, and the grammar is looser and less precise. Since this code is only used with intimates, we expect that they can mentally insert (infer) what we have left out.

For a less formal treatment of S-P-E-A-K-I-N-G for the nonlinguist see Peter Farb, *Wordplay: What Happens When People Talk* (New York: Bantam, 1975), 37–40.

4. See note 2, Chapter 7 and note 13, Chapter 8, for recommended research in audience analysis.

5. The research and approaches discussed in this section are based on descriptions of interactions of speakers and listeners in Dell Hymes' *Foundations in Sociolinguistics;* I have adapted this research for writers. Unlike S-P-E-A-K-I-N-G, accommodation theory looks at individuals negotiating communication rather than at participants having a role determine in a large social network. See for example, "Women and Politeness: A New Perspective on Language and Society," *Developments in Anthropology* 3 (1976): 240–41; Howard Giles, Donald Taylor and Richard Bourhis, "Towards a Theory of Interpersonal Accommodation through Language," *Language in Society* 2(1973), 177–92; and Lisa Simard, Donald Taylor, and Howard Giles, "Attribution Processes and Interpersonal Accommodation in a Bilingual Setting," *Language and Speech* 19 (1976): 374–87.

6. Penelope Brown and Stephen Levinson, "Universals in Language Usage: Politeness Phenomena," *Questions and Politeness: Strategies in Social Interaction* (Cambridge: Cambridge, 1976). Brown and Levinson deal with speakers and listeners.

7. Erving Goffman, *Forms of Talk* (Oxford: Basil Blackwood, 1981), see chap. 3, "Footing," esp. pp. 124–28. This approach was also designed to deal with speakers and listeners. Goffman observes that the tone of voice, the gestures, and the body language of the participants are cues to footing.

8. In William Labov and Joshua Waletzky, "Narrative Analysis: Oral Versions of Personal Experience," *Essays on the Verbal and Visual Arts,* ed. June Helm (Seattle: Washington University Press, 1967), 12–44, evaluators and intensifiers are discussed as elements of narrative.

9. See Roger Schank and Robert Abelson, *Scripts, Plans, Goals and Understanding: An Inquiry into Human Knowledge Structures* (Hillsdale: Erlbaum, 1977) for one of the best and most extensive works on scripts and plans. The following sections on scripts and plans are based on their work.

10. One problem with using scripts as a tool is that we don't know how much material is essential to a given script. What information is necessary, and what is expendable or superfluous detail? Should a restaurant-ordering script include the waiter's recommendations? In addition, how does one find a systematic means of limiting the extralinguistic knowledge, such as information on attitudes and gestures, necessary to carry out the sequence of events?

11. Commonly, scenarios are defined as written scripts. Linda Flower, John Hayes, and Heidi Swarts, "Revising Functional Documents: The Scenario Principle," in *New Essays in Technical and Scientific Communication: Research, Theory, Practice,* ed. Paul Anderson, R. John Brockman, and Carolyn Miller (Farmingdale: Baywood, 1983), 41–58, use the "scenario approach" to mean prose structured around agent, action, and situation.

12. Based on APA style.

13. Based on Flower, Hayes, and Swarts, "Revising Functional Documents: The Scenario Principle," 41–58.

14. Based on Roger Schank, "Rules and Topics in Conversation," *Cognitive Science* 1 (1977): 421–41.

15. For a detailed theoretical discussion of schemas see Marilyn Adams and Allan Collins, "A Schema-Theoretical View of Reading," in *New Directions in Discourse Processing,* ed. Roy Freedle (Norwood: Ablex, 1979), 1–21; and Daniel Bobrow and Donald Norman, "Some Principles of Memory Schemata," *Representation and Understanding: Studies in Cognitive Science,* ed. Daniel Bobrow and Allan Collins (New York: Academic, 1975), 131–50. For more complete practical definitions of schemas and their uses, see S. T. Fiske and P. W. Linville, "What Does the Schema Concept Buy Us?" *Personality and Social Psychology Bulletin* 6 (1980), 543–57; and Linda Flower and John Hayes, "Images, Plans and Prose: The Representation of Meaning in Writing," *Written Communication* 1(1984): 195–235.

16. Nancy M. Cooke and James McDonald, "A Formal Methodology for Acquiring and Representing Expert Knowledge," *Proceedings of the IEEE* 74 (1986): 1422–30; and Carol McGuinness, "Problem Representation: The Effects of Spatial Arrays," *Memory and Cognition* 14 (1986): 270–80, investigate forms of expert knowledge.

17. Schank and Abelson offer this plan as a "planbox for negotiating a goal," p. 90. I have deleted "beg or plead" from their list since I believe begging undermines trying more forceful strategies.

18. See Flower, Hayes, and Swarts, "Revising Functional Documents: The Scenario Principle," for suggestions on dealing specifically with technical documentation.

19. See, for example, Thomas Huckin, "A Cognitive Approach to Readability," in *New Essays in Technical and Scientific Communication: Research, Theory, Practice,* ed. Paul Anderson, R. John Brockman, and Carolyn Miller (Farmingdale: Baywood, 1983), 90–108; and Linda Flower and John Hayes, "Images, Plans and Prose: The Representation of Meaning in Writing," *Written Communication* 1(1984): 195–235.

# Bibliography

Adams, Marilyn, and Allan Collins. "A Schema-Theoretic View of Reading."
In *New Directions in Discourse Processing,* ed. Roy Freedle, 1–22. Norwood: Ablex, 1979.

Altman, Lawrence. "Doctors Say Baby with Baboon Heart Is Doing 'Remarkably Well.'" *New York Times,* October 29, 1984: A–15.

Austin, John. *How to Do Things with Words.* Cambridge: Harvard, 1962.

Ausubel, David. "The Use of Advanced Organizers in the Learning and Retention of Meaningful Verbal Material." *Journal of Educational Psychology*
51 (1960): 267–72.

Bartlett, Fredrick. *Remembering.* Cambridge: Cambridge University Press,
1932.

Beaugrande, Robert De. *Text, Discourse, and Process.* Norwood: Ablex, 1980.

Beaugrande, Robert De, and Wolfgang Dressler. *Introduction to Text Linguistics.* New York: Longman, 1981.

Bever, Thomas, John Carroll, and Lance Miller, ed. *Talking Minds: The Study
of Language in Cognitive Science.* Cambridge: MIT, 1984.

Bloomfield, Leonard. *Language.* New York: Holt, Rinehart, and Winston,
1933.

233

Bobrow, Daniel. "Dimensions of Representation." In *Representation and Understanding: Studies in Cognitive Science,* ed. Daniel Bobrow and Allan Collins, 1–34. New York: Academic, 1975.

Bobrow, Daniel, and Allan Collins, ed. *Representation and Understanding: Studies in Cognitive Science.* New York: Academic, 1975.

Bobrow, Daniel, and Donald Norman. "Some Principles of Memory Schemata." In *Representation and Understanding: Studies in Cognitive Science,* ed. Daniel Bobrow and Allan Collins, 131–50. New York: Academic, 1975.

Bolton, W. F. *The Living Language: The History and Structure of English.* New York: Random House, 1982.

Bousfield, W. A., and B. H. Cohen. "The Occurrence of Clustering in the Recall of Randomly Arranged Words of Different Frequencies-of-Usage." *Journal of General Psychology* 52 (1955): 83–95.

Bridge, Connie, Susan Belmore, Susan Moskow, Sheila Cohen, and Patricia Matthews. "Topicalization and Memory for Main Ideas in Prose." *Journal of Reading Behavior* 16 (1984): 61–80.

Brown, Gillian, and George Yule. *Discourse Analysis.* Cambridge: Cambridge University Press, 1983.

Brown, Penelope. "Women and Politeness: A New Perspective on Language and Society." *Developments in Anthropology* 3 (1976): 240–41.

Brown, Penelope, and Stephen Levinson. "Universals in Language Usage: Politeness Phenomena." In *Questions and Politeness: Strategies in Social Interaction.* Cambridge: Cambridge, 1976.

Carson, Rachel. *Silent Spring.* New York: Houghton Mifflin, 1962.

Chafe, W. L. "Creativity in Verbalization and Its Implications for the Nature of Stored Knowledge." In *New Directions in Discourse Processing,* ed. R. O. Freedle, 41–55. Norwood: Ablex, 1977.

Chafe, W. L. "Discourse Structure and Human Knowledge." In *Language Comprehension and the Acquisition of Knowledge,* ed. J. B. Carroll and R. O. Freedle. Washington: Wiley, 1972.

Chafe, W. L. "Givenness, Contrastiveness, Definiteness, Subjects, Topics, and Point of View." In *Subject and Topic,* ed. Charles Li, 27–55. New York: Academic, 1976.

Chafe, W. L., ed. *The Pear Stories: Cognitive, Cultural and Linguistic Aspects of Narrative Production.* Norwood: Ablex, 1980.

Chernin, Kim. *The Obsession: Reflections on the Tyranny of Slenderness.* New York: Harper and Row, 1981.

Chomsky, Noam. *Aspects of the Theory of Syntax.* Cambridge: MIT, 1965.
_____. *Syntactic Structures.* The Hague: Mouton, 1957.

Christensen, Francis. *Notes toward a New Rhetoric.* New York: Harper and Row, 1967.

Collins, Allan, and Elizabeth Loftus. "A Spreading-Activation Theory of Semantic Processing." *Psychological Review* 82 (1975): 407–28.

Cole, Peter, ed. *Radical Pragmatics*. New York: Academic, 1981.

―――. *Syntax and Semantics 9: Pragmatics*. New York: Academic, 1978.

Cole, Peter, and Jerry Morgan, ed. *Syntax and Semantics 3: Speech Acts*. New York: Academic, 1975.

Collins, Allan, Eleanor Warnock, Nelleke Aiello, and Mark Miller. "Reasoning from Incomplete Knowledge." In *Representation and Understanding: Studies in Cognitive Science*, ed. Daniel Bobrow and Allan Collins, 383–415. New York: Academic, 1975.

Cook, Walter. *Case Grammar: Development of the Matrix Model (1970–1978)*. Washington, D.C.: Georgetown University Press, 1979.

Cooke, Nancy M., and James McDonald. "A Formal Methodology for Acquiring and Representing Expert Knowledge." *Proceedings of the IEEE* 74 (1986): 1422–30.

Coulthard, Malcolm. *An Introduction to Discourse Analysis*. London: Longman, 1977.

Craik, F. I. M., and R. S. Lockhart. "Levels of Processing: A Framework for Memory Research." *Journal of Verbal Learning and Verbal Behavior* 11 (1972): 671–84.

Derrida, Jacques. *Of Grammatology*, trans. Gayatri Chakravorty Spivak, Baltimore: Johns Hopkins University, 1974.

Dickens, Charles. *A Tale of Two Cities*. 1859. New York: Penguin, 1970.

Didion, Joan. *Slouching toward Bethlehem*. New York: Dell, 1968.

Dijk, Teun van. "Connectives in Text Grammar and Text Logic." In *Grammars and Descriptions*, ed. Teun van Dijk and Janós Petòfi, 11–60. Berlin: Walter de Gruyter, 1977.

―――. *Macro-structures*. Hillsdale: Erlbaum, 1979.

―――. "New Developments and Problems in Textlinguistics." In *Text versus Sentence*, ed. Janós Petòfi, 509–23. Hamburg: Helmut Buske Verlag, 1979.

―――. *Text and Context: Explorations in the Semantics and Pragmatics of Discourse*. London: Longman, 1977.

Dressler, Wolfgang. *Trends in Textlinguistics*. New York: Walter de Gruyter, 1977.

Ede, Lisa. "Audience: An Introduction to Research." *College Composition & Communication* 35 (1984): 140–54.

Eiseley, Loren. *The Star Thrower*. New York: Time Books, 1978.

Eikmeyer, Hans-Jürgen. "Word, Sentence, and Text Meaning." In *Text and Discourse Constitution: Empirical Aspects, Theoretical Approaches*, ed. Janós Petòfi, 215–68. New York: Walter de Gruyter, 1988.

Elbow, Peter. *Writing with Power*. New York: Oxford, 1981.

Enkvist, Nils. "Text and Discourse Linguistics, Rhetoric, and Stylistics." In *Discourse and Literature*, ed. Teun van Dijk, 11–33. Amsterdam: Benjamins, 1985.

Enkvist, Nils, John Spencer, and Michael Gregory. *Linguistics and Style.* London: Oxford, 1964.

Epstein, Edmund. *Language and Style.* London: Methuen, 1978.

Fabb, Nigel, Derek Attridge, Alan Durant, and Colin MacCabe, ed. *The Linguistics of Writing: Arguments between Language and Literature.* New York: Methuen, 1987.

Farb, Peter. *Word Play: What Happens When People Talk.* New York: Bantam, 1975.

Fillmore, Charles. "The Case for Case." *Universals in Linguistic Theory,* ed. Emmon Bach and Robert Harms, 1–88. New York: Holt, Rinehart, and Winston, 1968.

––––––. "Lexical Entries for Verbs." *Foundations of Language* 4 (1968): 373–93.

Fiske, S. T., and P. W. Linville. "What Does the Schema Concept Buy Us?" *Personality and Social Psychology Bulletin* 6 (1980): 543–57.

Flammer, A., and W. Kintsch, ed. *Discourse Processing.* Amsterdam: North Holland, 1982.

Flower, Linda, and John Hayes. "A Cognitive Process Theory of Writing." *College Composition & Communiction* 32 (1981): 365–387.

Flower, Linda, and John Hayes, and Heidi Swarts. "Revising Functional Documents: The Scenario Principle." In *New Essays in Technical and Scientific Communication: Research, Theory, Practice,* ed. Paul Anderson, R. John Brockman, and Carolyn Miller, 41–58. Farmingdale: Baywood, 1983.

Fowler, Roger. "Cohesion, Progressive and Localizing Aspects of Text Structure." In *Grammars and Descriptions,* ed. Teun van Dijk and Janós Petòfi, 64–82. Berlin: Walter de Gruyter, 1977.

Freedle, Roy, ed. *Discourse Production and Comprehension.* New York: Ablex, 1977.

––––––. *New Directions in Discourse Processing.* Norwood: Ablex, 1979.

Freedle, Roy, and Gordon Hale. "Acquisition of New Comprehension Schemata for Expository Prose by Transfer of Narrative Structure." In *New Directions in Discourse Processing,* ed. R. Freedle, 121–35. Norwood: Ablex, 1979.

Fulbright, J. W. *The Pentagon Propaganda Machine.* New York: Liveright, 1970.

Garcia-Berrio, A., and T. Albaledejo Majordomo. "Compositional Structures: Macrostructures." In *Text and Discourse Constitution: Empirical Aspects, Theoretical Approaches,* ed. Janós Petòfi, 170–211. New York: Walter de Gruyter, 1988.

*Geysers.* U.S. Geological Survey. Government Printing 1986-491-402/01.

Gibson, Eleanor, and Harry Levin. *The Psychology of Reading.* Cambridge: MIT, 1975.

Giles, Howard, Donald Taylor, and Richard Bourhis. "Towards a Theory of Interpersonal Accommodation through Language." *Language in Society* 2 (1973): 177–92.

Goffman, Erving. *Forms of Talk.* Philadelphia: University of Pennsylvania Press, 1981.

————. *Frame Analysis: An Essay on the Organization of Experience.* Boston: Northeastern University Press, 1974.

Goodin, George, and Kyle Perkins. "Discourse Analysis and the Art of Coherence." *College English* 44 (1982): 57–64.

Grant, William. "Pre-Text—Re-Text—Post-Text: A Study in Revision Strategies." Unpublished.

Gray, Michael. "What Really Happened at Three Mile Island." In *Popular Writing in America: The Interaction of Style and Audience,* ed. Donald McQuade and Robert Atwan, 350–62. New York: Oxford, 1980. Originally published in *Rolling Stone,* May 17, 1979.

Greimas, Algirdas. "Elements of a Narrative Grammar." *Diacritics* 7 (1977).

————. "La structure des actants du recit: Essai d'approache generative." *Word* 23 (1967): 221–38.

Grice, Paul. "Logic and Conversation." In *Syntax and Semantics III,* ed. Peter Cole and Jerry Morgan, 41–58. New York: Academic, 1975.

Gumperz, J. "Sociocultural Knowledge in Conversation Inference." In *28th Annual Roundtable, Monograph Series on Languages and Linguistics,* ed. M. Saville-Troike. Georgetown: Georgetown, 1977.

Halle, M., J. Bresnan, and G. Miller. *Linguistic Theory and Psychological Reality.* Cambridge: MIT, 1978.

Halliday, M. A. K. *Language as a Social Semiotic.* London: Edward Arnold, 1978.

————. "Modes of Meaning and Modes of Expression: Types of Grammatical Structure, and Their Determination by Different Semantic Function." In *Function and Context in Linguistic Analysis,* ed. D. J. Allerton, Edward Corney, and David Holdcroft, 57–79. Cambridge: Cambridge University Press, 1979.

————. "Notes on Transitivity and Theme in English." *Journal of Linguistics* 3 (1967): 199–244.

Halliday, M. A. K., and Ruqaiya Hasan. *Cohesion in English.* London: Longman, 1976.

Harweg, Roland. "Sentence Sequences and Cotextual Connexity." In *Text and Discourse Constitution,* ed. János Petòfi, 26–53. New York: Walter de Gruyter, 1988.

Haviland, S., and H. H. Clark. "Comprehension and the Given-New Contract." In *Discourse Production and Comprehension*, ed. Roy Freedle, 1–40. New York: Ablex, 1977.

————. "What's New? Acquiring New Information as a Process in Comprehension." *Journal of Verbal Learning and Verbal Behavior* 13 (1974): 512–21.

Hayes, John, Linda Flower, Karen Schriver, James Stratman, and Linda Carey. "Cognitive Processes in Revision." In *Advances in Applied Psycholinguistics, Vol. 2: Reading, Writing and Language Learning*, ed. Sheldon Rosenberg, 176–240. New York: Cambridge, 1987.

Herrstrom, David. "Technical Writing as Mapping Description onto Diagram: The Graphic Paradigms of Explanation." *Journal of Technical Writing and Communication* 14 (1984): 223–39.

Hinds, J. "Paragraph Structure and Pronominalization." *Papers in Linguistics* 10 (1977): 91–108.

Hobbs, Jerry. "Coherence and Corefernce." *Cognitive Science* 3 (1979): 67–90.

Hockett, C. F. *A Course in Modern Linguistics*. New York: Macmillan, 1958.

————. "The Origin of Speech." *Scientific America* 203 (1960): 89–96.

Huckin, Thomas. "A Cognitive Approach to Readability." In *New Essays in Technical and Scientific Communication: Research, Theory, Practice*, ed. Paul Anderson, R. John Brockman, and Carolyn Miller, 90–108. Farmingdale: Baywood, 1983.

Hymes, Dell. *Foundations in Sociolinguistics: An Ethnographic Approach*. Philadelphia: Pennsylvania University Press, 1974.

————. "Ways of Speaking." *Explorations in the Ethnography of Speaking*. Cambridge: Cambridge, 1974.

Johnson, Ronald. "Retrieval Cues and Remembering Prose: A Review." In *Discourse Processing*, ed. A. Flammer and W. Kintsch, 219–37. Amsterdam: North Holland, 1982.

Johnson-Laird, Philip. "Mental Models in Cognitive Science." *Cognitive Science* 4 (1980): 71–115.

————. "Mental Models of Meaning." In *Elements of Discourse Understanding*, ed. A. K. Joshi, B. L. Webber, and I. A. Sag. Cambridge: Cambridge, 1981.

————. "Procedural Semantics." *Cognition* 5 (1977): 189–214.

Joshi, A. K., B. L. Webber, and I. A. Sag, ed. *Elements of Discourse Understanding*. Cambridge: Cambridge, 1981.

Katz, J. J., and J. A. Fodor. "The Structure of Semantic Theory." *Language* 39 (1963): 170–210.

Kintsch, Walter. *Memory and Cognition*. New York: Wiley, 1977.

Kintsch, Walter, E. Kozminsky, W. Streby, G. McKoon, and J. Keenen. "Comprehension and Recall of Texts as a Function of Content Variables." *Journal of Verbal Learning Behavior* 14 (1975): 196–214.

Kintsch, Walter, and Teun van Dijk. "Toward a Model of Text Comprehension and Production." *Psychological Review* 85 (1978): 363–94.

Kuipers, Benjamin. "A Frame for Frames: Representing Knowledge for Recognition." In *Representation and Understanding: Studies in Cognitive Science*. ed. Daniel Bobrow and Allan Collins, 151–183. New York: Academic, 1975.

Labov, William. *Sociolinguistic Patterns*. Philadelphia: Pennsylvania University Press, 1972.

———. "The Study of Language in Its Social Context." *Studium Generale* 23 (1970): 30–87.

Labov, William, and Joshua Waletzky. "Narrative Analysis: Oral Versions of Personal Experience." In *Essays on the Verbal and Visual Arts*, ed. June Helm, 12–44. Seattle: Washington University Press, 1967.

Lakoff, Robin. *Language and Woman's Place*. New York: Harper and Row, 1975.

Langendoen, D. Terence. *Essentials of English Grammar*. New York: Holt, Rinehart, and Winston, 1970.

Laurence, William. "The Atomic Bombing of Nagasaki Told by a Flight Member." In *Popular Writing in America: The Interaction of Style and Audience*, ed. Donald McQuade and Robert Atwan. 141–46. New York: Oxford, 1980. Originally published in *New York Times*, September 9, 1945.

Lederer, Richard. *Anguished English*. New York: Doubleday, 1987.

Levinson, S. C. "Speech Act Theory: The State of the Art." *Language Teaching and Linguistics: Abstracts* 13 (1980): 5–24.

Lévi-Strauss, Claude. *The Savage Mind*. Chicago: University of Chicago Press, 1966.

Lewis, Eugene. "Some Uses and Abuses of Economic Multipliers." *Wyoming Issues* 1 (1978): 7–11.

Li, Charles, ed. *Subject and Topic*. New York: Academic Press, 1976.

Linde, Charolette, and William Labov. "Spatial Networks as a Site for the Study of Language and Thought." *Language* 51 (1975): 924–39.

Lyons, John. *Noam Chomsky*. New York: Penguin, 1978.

———. *Semantics*. Cambridge: Cambridge University Press, 1977.

Marello, Carla. "Text, Coherence, and Lexicon." In *Text vs. Sentence: Basic Questions of Text Linguistics*, Part 2, ed. János Petöfi, 618–33. Hamburg: Helmut Buske Verlag, 1985.

Mathes, J. C., and Dwight Stevenson. "Audience Analysis: The Problem and a Solution." In *Designing Technical Reports*, ed. John Mathes. Indianapolis, Ind.: Bobbs-Merrill 1976.

Mayer, R. E., and J. G. Greeno. "Structural Differences between Learning Outcomes Produced by Different Instructional Methods." *Journal of Educational Psychology* 63 (1972): 165–73.

McGuinness, Carol. "Problem Representation: The Effects of Spatial Arrays." *Memory and Cognition* 14 (1986): 270–80.

Means, Mary, and James Voss. "Star Wars: A Developmental Study of Expert and Novice Knowledge Structures." *Journal of Memory and Language* 24 (1985): 746–57.

Melcuk, I. A., and A. Z. Zolkovsky. "Toward a Functioning 'Meaning Text' Model of Language." *Linguistics* 57 (1970): 10–47.

Metzing, Dieter, ed. *Frame Conceptions and Text Understanding.* New York: Walter de Gruyter, 1980.

Miller, George. "The Magical Number Seven, Plus or Minus Two: Some Limits on Our Capacity for Processing Information." *Psychological Review* 63 (1956): 87–97.

————. "Prose Comprehension and the Management of Working Memory." In *New Methods in Reading Comprehension Research,* ed. David Kieras and Marcel Just, 327–46. Hillsdale: L. Erlbaum, 1984.

Minsky, M. "A Framework for Representing Knowledge." In *Frame Conceptions and Text Understanding,* ed. Dieter Metzing, 1–25. New York: de Gruyter, 1980.

Nef, Fredric. "Case Grammar vs. Actantial Grammar: Some Remarks on Semantic Roles." In *Text vs. Sentence: Basic Questions of Text Linguistics,* Part 2, ed. János Petòfi, 634–53. Hamburg: Helmut Buske Verlag, 1985.

Nix, Donald, and Marian Schwarz. "Toward a Phenomenology of Reading Comprehension. In *New Directions in Discourse Processing,* ed. R. Freedle, 183–95. Norwood: Ablex, 1979.

Nold, Ellen, and Brent Davis. "The Discourse Matrix." *College Composition and Communication* 31 (1980): 141–52.

Norman, D. A., and D. G. Bobrow. "On Data-Limited and Resource-Limited Processes." *Cognitive Psychology* 7 (1975): 44–64.

Norman, D. A., D. E. Rumelhart, and the LNR Research Group. *Explorations in Cognition.* San Francisco: Freeman, 1975.

Norman, Donald. *Memory and Attention: An Introduction to Human Information Processing.* 2d ed. New York: Wiley, 1976.

Ong, Walter. "The Writer's Audience Is Always a Fiction." *Publications of the Modern Language Association* (90) 1975: 9–21.

Osgood, Charles. "Toward an Abstract Performance Grammar." In *Talking Minds: The Study of Language in Cognitive Science,* ed. Thomas Bever, John Carroll, and Lance Miller, 147–80. Cambridge: MIT, 1984.

Palmer, S. E. "Visual Perception and World Knowledge." In *Explorations in Cognition,* ed. Norman, Rumlehart, and the LNR groups, 279–308. San Francisco: Freeman, 1975.

Park, Douglas. "The Meaning of 'Audience.'" *College English* 44 (1982): 247–57.

Parker, Frank. *Linguistics for Non-Linguists.* Boston: College-Hill, 1986.

Parker, Frank, and Kathryn Riley. *Exercises in Linguistics.* Boston: Little, Brown, and Co., 1990.

Petòfi, Janós, ed. *Text and Discourse Constitution: Empirical Aspects, Theoretical Approaches.* New York: Walter de Gruyter, 1988.

————. *Text vs. Sentence: Basic Questions of Text Linguistics,* Part II. Hamburg: Helmut Buske Verlag, 1985.

Phillips, Martin. *Aspects of Text Structure: An Investigation of the Lexical Organisation of Texts.* Amsterdam: North-Holland, 1985.

Postal, Paul. "Underlying and Superficial Structure." *Harvard Educational Review* 34 (1964): 246–66.

Pratt, Elizabeth. *Toward a Speech Act Theory of Literary Discourse.* Bloomington: Indiana University Press, 1977.

Pratt, Mary, and Elizabeth Traugott. *Linguistics for Students of Literature.* New York: Harcourt, Brace, Jovanovich, 1980.

Prince, E. F. "Toward a Taxonomy of Given—New Information." In *Radical Pragmatics,* ed. Peter Cole. New York: Academic, 1981.

Pyles, Thomas. *The Origins and Development of the English Language.* 2d ed. New York: Harcourt Brace Jovanovich, 1971.

Quine, W. V. *Ontological Relativity and Other Essays.* New York: Columbia University Press, 1969.

Reichman, Rachel. "Conversational Coherence." *Cognitive Science* 2 (1978): 283–327.

Rihs-Middel, Margret. "Expectancy Structures in Prose Readings." In *Discourse Processing,* ed. A. Flammer and W. Kintsch, 75–86. Amsterdam: North Holland, 1982.

Rosenberg, St. T. "Frame-Based Processing." In *Frame Conceptions and Text Understanding,* ed. Dieter Metzing, 96–119. New York: Walter de Gruyter, 1980.

Rudolph, Elisabeth. "Connective Relations—Connective Expressions — Connective Structures." In *Text and Discourse,* ed. Janós Petòfi, 97–133. New York: Walter de Gruyter, 1988.

Rumelhart, David. "Notes on a Schema for Stories." In *Representation and Understanding: Studies in Cognitive Science,* ed. Daniel Bobrow and Allan Collins, 211–36. New York: Academic, 1975.

Sacks, Harvey, Emmanuel Schegloff, and Gail Jefferson. "A Simplest Systematics for the Organization of Turn-Taking for Conversation." *Language* 50 (1974): 696–735.

Sadock, Jerrold. *Towards a Linguistic Theory of Speech Acts.* New York: Academic, 1974.

Sapir, Edward. *Language: An Introduction to the Study of Speech.* New York: Harcourt Brace Jovanovich, 1921.

Sartre, Jean-Paul. *Being and Nothingness*, trans. and intro. Hazel Barnes. New York: Washington Square Press, 1966.

Saussure, Ferdinand de. *Course in General Linguistics*, trans. Wade Baskin, ed. Charles Bally, Albert Sechehaye, and Albert Riedlinger. New York: McGraw Hill, 1966.

Schank, Roger. "Rules and Topics in Conversation." *Cognitive Science* 1 (1977): 421–41.

————. "The Structure of Episodes in Memory." In *Representation and Understanding: Studies in Cognitive Science*, ed. Daniel Bobrow and Allan Collins, 237–72. New York: Academic, 1975.

Schank, Roger, and Robert Abelson. *Scripts, Plans, Goals and Understanding: An Inquiry into Human Knowledge Structures*. Hillsdale: Erlbaum, 1977.

Schank, Roger, and Lawrence Birnbaum. "Memory, Meaning, and Syntax." In *Talking Minds: The Study of Language in Cognitive Science*, ed. Thomas Bever, John Carroll, and Lance Miller. 209–52. Cambridge: MIT, 1984.

Schnotz, Wolfgang. "How Do Different Readers Learn with Different Text Organizations?" In *Discourse Processing and Comprehension*, ed. Roy Freedle, 87–97. New York: Ablex, 1977.

Searle, John. "The Classification of Illocutionary Acts." *Language in Society* 5 (1976): 1–24.

————. *Expression and Meaning: Studies in the Theory of Speech Acts*. Cambridge: Cambridge University Press, 1979.

————. "Indirect Speech Acts." In *Syntax and Semantics 3*, ed. Peter Cole and Jerry Morgan, 59–82. New York: Academic, 1975.

————. *Speech Acts: An Essay in the Philosophy of Language*. Cambridge: Cambridge University Press, 1969.

Simard, Lisa, Donald Taylor, and Howard Giles. "Attribution Processes and Interpersonal Accommodation in a Bilingual Setting." *Language and Speech* 19 (1976): 374–87.

Smith, Edward, Edward Shoben, and Lance Rips. "Structure and Process in Semantic Memory: A Featural Model for Semantic Discourse." *Psychological Review* 81 (1974): 214–41.

Smith, Frank. *Understanding Reading: A Psycholinguistic Analysis of Reading and Learning to Read*. New York: Holt, Rinehart, and Winston, 1978.

Spyridakis, Jan, and Timothy Standal. "Headings, Previews, Logical Connectives: Effects on Reading Comprehension." *Journal of Technical Writing and Communication* 16 (1986): 343–54.

————. "Signals in Expository Writing: Effects on Reading Comprehension." *Reading Research Quarterly* 22 (1987): 285–98.

Stockwell, Robert, Paul Schachter, and Barbara Hall Partee. *The Major Syntactic Structures of English*. New York: Holt, Rinehart, and Winston, 1973.

Tannen, Deborah. "What's in a Frame?" In *New Directions in Discourse Processing*, ed. Roy Freedle, 137–81. Norwood: Ablex, 1979.

Thomas, Lewis. *Lives of a Cell: Notes of a Biology Watcher.* New York: Viking, 1974.

Thompson, D. M., and E. Tulving. "Associative Encoding and Retrieval: Weak and Strong Cues." *Journal of Experimental Psychology* 86 (1979): 225–62.

Triesman, Anne. "Verbal Cues, Language and Meaning in Selective Attention." *American Journal of Psychology* 77 (1964): 215–16.

Vande Kopple, James. "Some Exploratory Discourse on Metadiscourse." *College Composition & Composition* 36 (1985): 82–93.

Van De Velde, Roger. "Inferences as (De)Compositional Principles." In *Text and Discourse Constitution*, ed. János Petòfi, 283–316. New York: Walter de Gruyter, 1988.

Vasiliu, Emanuel. "On Some Meanings of 'Coherence'." In *Text vs. Sentence: Basic Questions of Text Linguistics*, Part II, ed. János Petòfi, 450–66. Hamburg: Helmut Buske Verlag, 1985.

Walter, Arthur. "Articles from the 'California Divorce Project': A Case Study of the Concept of Audience." *College Composition and Communication* 36 (1985): 150–59.

Waugh, N. C., and Donald Norman. "Primary Memory." *Psychological Review* 72 (1965): 89–104.

Weisman, John. "Why American TV Is So Vulnerable to Foreign Propaganda." *TV Guide*, June 12, 1982: 6–16.

Widdowson, H. G. *Explorations in Applied Linguistics.* Oxford: Oxford, 1979.

Williams, Joseph. *Style: Ten Lessons in Clarity and Grace.* 3d ed. Glenview: Scott, Foresman, 1989.

Winograd, Terry. In "Frame Representation and the Declarative-Procedural Controversy." In *Representation and Understanding: Studies in Cognitive Science*, ed. Daniel Bobrow and Allan Collins, 185–210. New York: Academic, 1975.

Wittgenstein, Ludwig. *Philosophical Investigations.* Oxford: Basil Blackwood, 1953.

Woods, William. "What's in a Link: Foundations For Semantic Networks." In *Representation and Understanding: Studies in Cognitive Science*, ed. Daniel Bobrow and Allan Collins, 3–82. New York: Academic, 1975.

Yerkes, R. M., and J. D. Dodson. "The Relation of Strength of Stimulus to Rapidity of Habit-Formation." *Journal of Comparative Neurology of Psychology* 18 (1908): 459–82.

Yorkin, Peg. "Reviews from a Feminist Perspective." *Reports from the Feminist Majority* 2 (1990): 7.

# Index